بسم الله الرحمن الرحيم

الحمد لله رب العالمين
والصلاة والسلام على خاتم الأنبياء والمرسلين

وقل رب زدني علما

In the Name of Allah,
the Compassionate, the Merciful,
Praise be to Allah, Lord of the Universe,
and Peace and Prayers be upon
His Final Prophet and Messenger.

"... and say: My Lord!
Cause Me to Grow in Knowledge."

بِسْمِ ٱللَّهِ ٱلرَّحْمَٰنِ ٱلرَّحِيمِ

ٱقْرَأْ بِٱسْمِ رَبِّكَ ٱلَّذِى خَلَقَ ﴿١﴾ خَلَقَ ٱلْإِنسَٰنَ مِنْ عَلَقٍ ﴿٢﴾
ٱقْرَأْ وَرَبُّكَ ٱلْأَكْرَمُ ﴿٣﴾ ٱلَّذِى عَلَّمَ بِٱلْقَلَمِ ﴿٤﴾ عَلَّمَ ٱلْإِنسَٰنَ
مَا لَمْ يَعْلَمْ ﴿٥﴾

(العلق: ١ ـ ٥)

Read in the name of your Sustainer, Who has Created man out of a germ cell. Read – for your Sustainer is the Most bountiful One. Who has taught (man) the use of the pen. Taught Man what he did not know.

(Qur'an 96:1-5)

وَٱللَّهُ أَخْرَجَكُم مِّنۢ بُطُونِ أُمَّهَٰتِكُمْ لَا تَعْلَمُونَ شَيْـًٔا
وَجَعَلَ لَكُمُ ٱلسَّمْعَ وَٱلْأَبْصَٰرَ وَٱلْأَفْـِٔدَةَ
لَعَلَّكُمْ تَشْكُرُونَ ﴿٧٨﴾

(النحل: ٧٨)

And Allah has brought you forth from your mother's womb knowing nothing – but He has endowed you with hearing, and sight, and minds, so that you might have cause to be grateful.

(Qur'an 16:78)

Towards an Islamic Theory of International Relations:

New Directions for Methodology and Thought

First Edition
(1407 / 1987)

Second Revised Edition
(1414 / 1993)

Views and opinions expressed by the author are not necessarily those of the Institute

The International Institute of Islamic Thought

Herndon -- Virginia -- The United States of America

1401AH—1981AC

Towards an Islamic Theory of International Relations:

New Directions for Methodology and Thought

ʻAbdulḤamīd A. AbūSulaymān

The International Institute of Islamic Thought
Herndon, Virginia USA
1414/1993

1/8/14

Islamization of Knowledge Series (1)

Library of Congress Cataloging-in-Publication Data

AbūSulaymān, ʻAbdulḤamīd A. 1936 / (1355)-
Towards an Islamic Theory of International Relations: New Directions for Methodolgy and Thought / AbūSulaymān, ʻAbdulḤamīd.
p. 240 cm. 22.5X15 (Islamization of Knowledge series : no. 1)
Reprint. Originally published: 1987, as *The Islamic Theory of International Relations: New Directions for Islamic Methodology and Thought*. Originally presented as the author's thesis (doctoral), University of Pennsylvania.
Includes bibliographical references and index.
ISBN 0-912463-71-6 (pbk.).
ISBN 0-912463-52-X
1. Islam and world politics. I. International Institute of Islamic Thought. II. Title. III. Series.
BP173.5.A28 1990
297'.19787--dc20

90-5171
CIP

IIIT In-House DTP
by Y. T. DeLorenzo
Printed in the United States of America
by International Graphics
4411 41st Street
Brentwood, MD 20722 USA
Tel. (301) 779-7774 Fax (301) 779-0570

Dedication

To the memory of my parents:

May Allah grant them His mercy for the loving wisdom with which they nourished me.

Also to my brother Jamīl:

With deep appreciation for his love and encouragement..

And to my Muslim colleagues, al Shuhadā', Dr. Eltigani AbuGideiri and Dr. Ismā'īl R. al Fārūqī; may Allah grant them His mercy; and to the ones who still work for the supreme cause of Islam, khilāfah, Islamization of contemporary knowledge, reform of Muslim thought, the revival of the Muslim Ummah, and the peace, progress, fulfillment, and happiness of all humankind. May Allah grant strength, success, and the reward promised, in this life and in eternity, to all sincere and efficient workers.

CONTENTS

Chapter 3
REFORM OF METHODOLOGY
(63 - 96)

Chapter 4
FROM LEGALISTIC TO POLITICAL THOUGHT
(97 - 161)

ADDENDA

(163 - 192)

PREFACE TO THE SECOND EDITION

The second edition of this book appears at a time when the first edition has long since been out of print and when the changed international situation requires a reexamination of the sections dealing with the picture of contemporary relations between nations and, in particular, the policies adopted by states in the Muslim world in response to those changes.

Owing, however, to the magnitude and priorities of my work, I was not able to attend to the book earlier. In fact, time has been so short that, for this edition, I have had to content myself with writing a new preface and making a few additions to the fourth chapter under the subheading, Major Muslim Policies Examined. This was because the nature of that section is such that it must take into account the policies formulated in the Muslim world in response to changes that occur internationally, and thus analyze the extent to which those policies serve the interests of the Ummah of Islam and its objectives.

Recent international developments and the condition of nations in the Muslim world today emphasize the conclusions I reached over the long course of my life and experience, conclusions which I recently published in a book entitled, *Crisis in the Muslim Mind.* These begin with the perception that change must come from within, on the basis of the beliefs and values of the Ummah. Reform must begin with intellectual reform, especially with the development of disciplined and systematic methodology for thought based on rational principles and approaches that incorporate Islamic objectives.

If Muslim thought can be reformed, Muslims will be able to penetrate to the root causes of the Ummah's decline. Only if this is accomplished will Muslims be able to extract themselves from the problems which beset them, and thus become capable of new undertakings that put its spiritual, intellectual, and material resources to work for it in a way that effectively acheives its Islamic goals, while presenting for the rest of humankind an example of how Islam works for its own interests and those of civilization as a whole.

The recent experience of Muslims in Afghanistan provides an excellent example of the need for internal reform. For although the mujahidin were victorious with the help of the USA against the soviet aggressor, the quality and nature of the state in Afghanistan after the war clearly demonstrate the need for major reform, beginning with intellectual reform. Unless the Muslim mind is reformed, all social organization and all economic, military, and political successes will be shortlived and ineffectual.

Among the important results of my research, and one which continues to be affirmed by events, is the need for Muslim states to develop, at various levels and forums, policies of cooperation and mutual assistance. In the current international situation in which regional alliances based on political and economic interests are on the increase, states which choose not to ally themselves with others are disadvantaged and open themselves to the depredations of nations and peoples stronger than themselves.

The dangers faced by the Muslim world following the collapse of the Soviet Union and its secular, materialist, and totalitarian form of Marxism remain as before. In fact, the evidence indicates that those dangers are growing more menacing. The new set of international circumstances, those based on nationalistic and economic struggle (as opposed to the former balance of power maintained by the two superpowers), serve only to create an atmosphere of confrontation and contention between nations. In such an atmosphere, emotions and negative concepts are allowed to thrive and lead inevitably to aggression and mindless destruction.

It is important to note here that the economic ills and social problems experienced in the former Soviet Union and its satellites are as equally widespread in Europe and the United States. There can be little doubt, therefore, that this situation has its roots in the secular materialist worldview shared by all of Western civilization.

In view of these circumstances, it becomes all the more essential for the Ummah and the states which comprise it to revitalize their intellectual well-being and, by means of it, activate the psychological and religious vigor that will enable them to reclaim their political and economic strength. If this is accomplished, a new generation of Muslims will emerge, one that understands and respects the concept of the Ummah and its unity, solidarity, and cultural, economic, and political self-sufficiency.

The existence of international and regional alliances for political and economic purposes makes it essential that states in the Muslim world develop and adopt innovative and effective policies for appropriate cooperation with regard to their long and short term needs in the spheres of economics and security. Only if this is accomplished will these states be able to protect their interests and themselves from falling prey to the sort of bilateral relations in which despotic colonial ambitions are cloaked in endearing rhetoric and diplomacy. A number of Western leaders and thinkers have already given voice to their suspicious and even aggressive intentions regarding Islam and the Muslim world. Clearly, such statements evince the Western desire to maintain influence and hegemony over the region. Another function they serve is to probe for new arenas in which to pull their ranks together (as if against a common foe) and thereby be afforded the opportunity to ignore the issues which threaten their own unity.

The evidence confronting the leaders of the Ummah is such that it cannot be ignored. The history of the mongols, the crusaders, Granada, and Jerusalem is in danger of repeating itself. Under such circumstances, there can be no escape from reform, no existence except for the capable, and no respect, no dealing, and no cooperation except with equals and partners.

The philosophy of peace, beginning with the individual soul and ending with the whole world, will never be realized or take part in the reform of civilization unless it comes about by means of a living Islamic model representing the ambitions of the various peoples of the Ummah and its thinkers.

Recent events in the Muslim world, like the West's support for corrupt political regimes, or for military dictators, or its refusal to recognize the right of Muslim populaces to elect their own leadership, especially when that leadership tends to be Islamic in nature, indicate that the West has failed to understand Islam and that its positions are colored by considerations stemming from the Middle Ages. It is therefore essential that Muslim thinkers realize the nature of the world situation today, the extent of their need to learn the ways of cooperation and coexistence between peoples, and then suggest what Islam has to offer for the betterment of humankind and the development of civilization.

Social moderation is Islam's objective in the sphere of economics and the market economy is its means. In a like manner, Islam is committed to the rights of the individual and the group, insofar as beliefs and ways of life are concerned, so long as there is no detriment to society in general, or to the rights of other individuals, groups, peoples, or nations. Islam calls to justice and shuns all forms of excess and physical and moral corruption. Modern Western civilization, however, is not concerned with moderation or justice. Instead, it has opened its doors to excess and desecration, with the result that it is forced to reap a bitter harvest in which the family and society are threatened by the spread of crime, mental illness, and sexually transmitted diseases.

Muslim thinkers must also realize that it is their responsibility to treat the malaise of their own community through a correct understanding of Islam as the universal message of reform and peace. Moreover, the reform of the Muslim intellect and, consequently, of the Ummah itself must not stop at any physical borders, but must extend to every corner of the earth and contemporary civilization. In today's global village and market, isolationism is no longer a viable choice. Rather, there must be a common degree of principles, values, and considerations that allow world society to function and maintain human existence.

Generally speaking, reform in the Muslim world, and particularly intellectual reform, has been hindered by the static nature of the Muslim leadership and their fears and ignorance. At the same time, the spirit of the crusades and dreams of colonial greatness will never serve the interests of contemporary civilization. All of these factors may be taken as major impediments to the reform of contemporary world civilization, and factors in perpetuating the aggression and armed conflict which now plague the world.

Today the world finds itself at a new crossroads, leading either toward reform and moderation or toward the escalation of strife and destruction. Much will be determined by the intellectuals and thinkers of Islam as they pursue the course of reform. Likewise, the rapidity with which reform may proceed will be determined by the social and political leadership of the Ummah and their ability to pursue policies of cooperation and reform in the life of the Ummah and, in particular, in its educational and scientific institutions.

Unfortunately, however, certain Muslim states have acted shortsightedly in their futile and misguided attempts to "liberate" Muslims in neighboring states. Through their actions and policies they have undermined the confidence of others and destroyed the possibility of cooperation between Muslim states. Clearly, Muslims must learn tolerance and respect for one another if they are to achieve solidarity. In all of this, the reform of the Muslim mind and intellect must take precedence.

Many of the issues raised by this work when it was first published have become common knowledge to the intellectuals of the Ummah. Even so, there are several issues with which only very few readers will be familiar. The author welcomes criticism and discussion on the points raised in the book, for it is only by means of objective discussion that ideas may develop and be clarified. The objectives of the book and its author may be summarized as encouraging a new beginning to the reform of Muslim thought and society after the dialogue and interaction between Muslim leaders and intellectuals came to a halt several centuries ago and the Muslim mind fell victim to stagnation and trepidation.

In closing, I should like to acknowledge a debt of gratitude to all those who worked to produce this revised edition of *Towards an Islamic Theory of International Relations*. The task of final editing was undertaken by Y. T. DeLorenzo who also prepared the index. Stylistic editing of the revised work was performed by Jay Willoughby. Yahya Monastra carefully edited the footnotes and bibliography, and the London office of IIIT painstakingly proofread the book. The entire project was coordinated by Ali Ramadan, director of IIIT publications.

It is only Allah who grants *tawfīq* and guides to the right way...

Dr. ʻAbdulḤamīd A. AbūSulaymān
Kuala Lumpur, Malaysia
Rabīʻ al Ākhir 1414 / October 1993

PREFACE TO THE FIRST EDITION

This book serves two major purposes. First, it presents the Islamic point of view, introduces basic resources of Islamic thought, and develops among intellectuals, both Muslim and non-Muslim, secular and nonsecular, the Islamic theory of international relations. The second purpose is to examine the reasons why Islamic thought has apparently failed to play an active and constructive role in the contemporary world of thought and ideas, as well as to offer new alternatives to Western thought in the field of international relations, and thus address the growing need for peace, security, cooperation, and participation.

The origins of this book go back to my experience in preparing an earlier book (in Arabic) entitled *The Theory of Islam in Economics: Philosophy and Contemporary Means* (Cairo: 1960). For a good summary of that book, see *Contemporary Aspects of Economic Thinking in Islam: The Proceedings of the Third East Coast Conference of the Muslim Students' Association of the United States and Canada, April, 1968* (Plainfield, IN: American Trust Publications, 1976).

That experience taught me that stagnation and the narrow application of classical Muslim methodology were behind the rigidity and exclusiveness of Islamic thought. This venture in the field of international relations provides an opportunity to outline and address the approach of the book on the Islamic philosophy of economics. The methodology applied in that book started with a comprehensive assembly of all Islamic textual materials (*nuṣūṣ*) in the Qur'an and Sunnah related to the field of economics. The next step was to identify, explicitly construct, and then explain the internal line of logic in these materials. This required linguistic study, analysis of the historical circumstances, means, capabilities, environment, and systematic use of my technical knowledge as a graduate in the field of political science and economics. Applying the line of thought and logic to the texts of the Qur'an and Sunnah concerning Islamic objectives and goals in the field of economics helped me to develop a coherent and systematic approach and method.

This method enabled me to see the relevance and significance of the different actions, policies, and stages of development in this historical experience of early Islam and thereby avoid any temptation to ignore, twist, abrogate, or jump to conclusions regarding a sacred purpose beyond human understanding or comprehension (*aḥkām tawqīfiyah*). The distinction between the goals and purposes of the Shari'ah and the policy considerations of the particular time and place where they were articulated by scholars was very useful in opening the door for policy reconsiderations needed in order to suggest new alternatives to fit contemporary needs and means.

This book tries to offer fresh insights into the Islamic understanding and approach to the pursuit of peace, security, cooperation, and participation in relations among peoples and nations. Also, it serves as a vehicle to study and analyze the classical Islamic methodology and the traditional way of applying it in the field of Islamic thought.

Specifically, this book takes a new look at many problematic issues in contemporary Islamic thought, such as apostasy (*riddah*), freedom of belief, and poll tax (*jizyah*). It also thoroughly examines Islamic methodology (*uṣūl*), its role, and the role of the ulama as distinct from the secular scholars and intellectuals, in the persistent stagnation of Muslim thought and of the Ummah.

This book contends that the Islamic theory and philosophy of relations among nations is the only adequate philosophy of peace in the contemporary world. It is the only philosophy, concept, and approach that emphasizes the common origin, interest, and destiny of man as the only firm base for understanding man's nature, interpersonal relations, and group interactions. Man's nature, interests, and relations in Islam look like overlapping circles. Other world ideologies and philosophies focus on conflict management and consequently on war. The Western philosophies of nationalism and class conflict emphasize the negative factor of conflicting perceptions, interests, and destinies. This attitude of conflict always leads to war and destruction.

History shows that lasting peace can come only from an attitude of mutual understanding and appreciation based on a firm belief in our common nature, common interests, and common destiny.

The long road of global functionalism and world organization the world community has already travelled along is a great achievement and should be maintained. This achievement can be further developed only in the frame and shade of the constructive philosophy and attitude of harmony and peace offered by Islam and the sacred commitment of Muslims to it.

This book, by revealing and explaining objectively the Islamic philosophy and understanding of relations among human communities, nations, and states offers fresh hope for human civilization.

Muslim intellectuals, scholars, and leaders, it is hoped, can better appreciate from this book what Islam means to them and how they can best work to secure the future of human civilization. Muslim scholars may also benefit from this analytical study of the Islamic methodology of thought so that they can introduce into their studies a systematic and scientific approach to human nature, human relations, and the human environment in line with Islamic goals, principles, values, and directions. This should produce not merely insights, but whole new disciplines of Islamic social, human, natural, and technical science, (*khilāfah* sciences).

In this book, it may seem that I unduly emphasize the shortcomings of the Muslim Ummah and of its past life and thought. This emphasis on the practice of Muslims is needed in order to probe deeply into the root causes of the Ummah's decline in its cultural, economic, political, technological, and military spheres.

As a Muslim and a social scientist, I am well aware and appreciative of the Islamic goals and ideology, as well as of the historical achievements of the Muslims. It is precisely because of this appreciation that I try to apply an open and critical mind without inhibition to the task of restoring the health and proper role of the Muslim Ummah in the contemporary world.

I also clearly see the need of the contemporary world for Islamic values and concepts and for Islam as a faith. Thus I have attempted to identify in this book those basic values and concepts which can provide an essential framework for relations among nations in the contemporary world.

Non-Muslim intellectuals are urged to look in this comprehensive study for a more thorough understanding of the reasons behind the conditions of the contemporary Muslims, including the Muslims' distortion of their own religion, so they can appreciate the Islamic point of view in the contemporary world, set aside their historical hatred and prejudices against Islam and Muslims, and cooperate as partners in building a common destiny in accordance with these principles and values.

It is important for Muslims and non-Muslims to appreciate the responsibility of Muslims, according to their ideology and religion, in establishing, guarding, and maintaining a world order of peace and cooperation. The Islamic world order envisions a world where all individuals and peoples are free to live according to their deepest beliefs and to maintain their freedom to cooperate on the basis of understanding and respect.

This kind of outlook, attitude, and philosophy can bring peoples together and develop common human parameters of purpose, value, interest, and understanding that are broad enough to establish workable political structures and the rule of law among communities at all levels, from the neighborhood to the wider community of all mankind. This is the only valid and practical way which can lead to a workable world order of peace, security, cooperation, and partnership.

Muslims must start with themselves in order to restore their vision, their psychological and civilizational health and strength, and reestablish brotherhood and solidarity. They should revive the best of their thoughts and methodology and the institutions based thereon. They must be true and useful to themselves before they can be respected and taken seriously by others and thereby contribute positively toward building a better and more peaceful world.

This work, originally written more than fourteen years ago to offer a healthy and dynamic vision to the new Muslim generation, is meant to open the discussion on how to revive Islamic thought and methodology. The work is concerned not so much with what is correct, but with what went wrong and how to correct it. The condition of the Ummah is so troubled that we can lose little and gain much if we open our minds and start thinking, analyzing, and discussing what is wrong with our life, our thoughts, and our way of approaching life.

What is offered here are not *fatāwà* or decrees, but rather analysis and opinions offered to others for their own analysis and discussion in order to correct any false ideas and produce more new dynamic ideas and approaches. This process of self-analysis makes the goals of a healthy Ummah and healthy Islamic thought both possible and plausible.

It is a great honor for this book to carry as an introduction the last words written by Professor Ismā'īl al Fārūqī. In these pages we read a typical example of his beautiful sincerity and love for Islam, the Ummah, and humanity. The ideas in this introduction and of his many Islamic works and writings will be, *in shā'a Allāh, raḥmah* and a blessing for his soul in the hereafter and will give lasting benefits to Muslims and to all sincere people in this world.

Finally, as the author of this work, I would like to emphasize and make clear that I welcome all analysis and criticism that can contribute to the common goal of reviving Islamic values, principles, and objectives in Muslim life, methodology, thought, and culture.

I ask Allah to give me the two rewards in the now and the hereafter by guiding me to say what is right and true. I ask Allah to guide more Muslim brothers and sisters to join me in the search for what is right and true, to help us all promote the reign of truth, and to make it possible for man to understand, follow, and benefit from the message of Islam.

Ramaḍān 1407/ May 1987 'AbdulḤamīd A. AbūSulaymān
Washington, D.C.

INTRODUCTION

Dr. Ismā'īl Rājī al Fārūqī

This book, which the International Institute of Islamic Thought is presenting to the reader, was originally submitted to the University of Pennsylvania as a doctoral dissertation in international relations. Its academic merit is certainly great, but its value far transcends that merit, for its subject matter is Islamic international relations. From these, as they developed in early Muslim history, the author has endeavored to cull the general principles which governed the practices of the early Islamic world. In fact, this dissertation has rendered a service far greater than winning a doctorate for its author: it has exposed truths of Islam which are relevant to one of the most important fields of study in this century - namely, world order.

Nothing could be more urgently needed today than the enlightenment of humankind concerning the threat of annihilation that the present world order poses for it. The hegemony of the West over the world in the last two centuries is certainly responsible for the terror under which humankind lives today, and the world's present predicament is the result of the tortuous history of the ideal of the universal community in the West. To understand and solve this predicament, we must know the history of that ideal.

The Universal Community Ideal until the End of the Nineteenth Century

In contrast to Judaic Christianity, which regarded itself as a reform movement within Judaism and was meant for "the lost tribes of Israel," Western Christianity proclaimed the universal community ideal as a substitute for the *imperium romanum*. For centuries thereafter the Church continued to proclaim this ideal. Its success was extremely limited, and no sooner had it succeeded in establishing a state with the potential to become universal than the state divided into two or more states. The challenge to the worldly dominion of the Church was constant, arising both from within and outside the Christian state.

Without having to recount the long list of grievances the Christians of Europe suffered at the hands of the Church, there can be no doubt that the Reformation was right in dismantling the Church's worldly authority. Her domination of political and economic affairs, however, was not to go down alone. Along with it, the Reformation destroyed the Church's magisterium, liberating the mind to plumb the depths of nature and unravel the secrets of the stars. Equally significant was Europe's repudiation of the Christian faith as the basis of identity and the elevation of reason as the definer of selfhood, criterion of judgment, and foundation for citizenship.

This trend grew rapidly following the Reformation and brought forth the Enlightenment which raised again the ideal of the universal community, this time on the grounds of reason rather than faith. The European Enlightenment, however, did not have the courage of its own convictions. On the one hand, its advocates compromised their rationalism in order to accommodate faith, thus providing a cracked foundation on which no universal superstructure could be secured. On the other hand, the advocates of the Enlightenment gave the lie to their own profession when they naively spoke of humanity and the universe but actually meant only Europe and its peoples. Indeed, the Enlightenment met with devastating opposition; Christianity regarded it as a threat on account of its claimed rationalism, and the princes of Europe resisted it because it threatened the gains they had made as substitutes for Church authority. The former favored romanticism, the latter nationalism.

Thus, the universal community ideal of the Enlightenment was doomed from the beginning. The "reformed" churches of Europe joined hands with the European dynasties to combat rationalism and its consequent universalism. They promoted romanticism, a movement which secured Christianity by basing truth and value upon feeling rather than reason. And they secured the princes' seats of power by founding group loyalty on a nationalism or ethnocentrism which defined the public good in terms of the group's egotistic self-interest and of loyalty to prince or "nation." Schleiermacher was responsible for the former, Fustel de Coulanges for the latter, and both wrote the best defenses and expositions of two aspects of one and the same disease, namely, romanticism, a variety of particularism blown up into a metaphysic and an axiology. Under their hammering pens, the universal community ideal was shattered.

The debacle of the Enlightenment produced two more results. Reason, as the prime factor of science, became the sole and absolute master of nature and keeper of her truths. Its major prompting came from competition among the nations to unlock more of nature's secrets and place her processes entirely under national control, at the service of national interest and, above all, defense. The realms of value, ethics, and aesthetics were abandoned as provinces in which truth may be discovered, or in which reason may have anything to say. As domains of feeling and personal experience, those realms were "free and open fields" for anyone to ride through. The relativism and subjectivism to which Christianity had recourse in order to save itself from the onslaught of Enlightenment-rationalism soon showed their effect upon Christianity itself.

The Universal Community Ideal until the Mid-Twentieth Century

The repudiation of Christianity's main tenets as well as of the universal community ideal was in the making. On the collective level, Europe gave religion itself a bad name in the world, and enabled Friedrich Engels and Karl Marx to call it "the opium of the people." On the personal level, Friedrich Nietzsche and Sigmund Freud analyzed the religious ethic and psychology to death, predicting "the end of" religion as "illusion" and bringing about the "transvaluation of its values."

All this happened in Europe where the only dominant religion was Christianity. Like their Enlightenment predecessors, these European critics spoke of religion when they meant Christianity. Communism combined the forces raging in the soul of Europe and added to them its opposition to the absurd order of competition and war among the nations of Europe. It condemned romanticism as the base of an unholy alliance between religion and nationalism, both resting, as they did, on feeling, personal experience, and cultural relativism.

Communism raised again the ideal of the universal community. But this time, instead of feeling and personal experience, matter and the material interpretation of history were to be the foundation. Until World War II, Communism combated both Christianity and nationalism and promoted the universal community ideal as the goal of a world dominated by matter and the proletariat. During and following World War II, the ideal was abandoned in favor of "Mother Russia" and thereafter, in favor of the consumer society. Picked up for an instant by the Chinese revolution at the conclusion of World War II, the ideal collapsed, even before the death of its author, Mao Zedong, in reaction to its violation by the U.S.S.R. Had the U.S.S.R. remained true to the universalist ideal, and had it helped China to overcome its ethnocentrism, the ideal of the universal community might have had a chance to survive. Unfortunately, in the West as well as in the Communist world, today that ideal lies dead.

Between the two world wars, Great Britain and France, the powers in control of the League of Nations, tried in vain to maintain a semblance of world order through the League. But their manipulation of it was crassly offensive since they used it to cover up their own colonial policies in Asia and Africa and their competition with one another. Influenced by Enlightenment idealism and in response to American isolationist opposition to ratification, President Woodrow Wilson pulled the United States out of the League in disgust at Europe's manipulation of its decision-making process. The U.S.S.R was excluded beforehand by virtue of both its opposition and its deliberate isolationism.

After World War II, the ideal of the universal community was raised again, for the fourth time, through the United Nations Organization which, it was hoped, would out-perform its predecessor. But the same weaknesses affected both world organizations. The constitutive principle of membership in the United Nations was again declared to the nation-state as sovereign and able to pursue its own self-interest. In consequence, implementation of resolutions by the member states had to be voluntary and no nation was to be forced to comply. Of course, the big powers always found a way to twist the arms of the smaller nations and obtain compliance. But among themselves, consent was absolutely necessary. In the League of Nations, conflicts were referred to the International High Court of Justice for resolution. After World War II, the International Court of Justice continued to exist, but only as a showpiece and propaganda platform.

As to the United Nations, its authority and jurisdiction were divided between the General Assembly and Security Council. The latter, consisting of five superpowers as permanent members possessing the right of veto, and a number of General Assembly members chosen on rotation, controls the executive machinery and can render the decisions of the General Assembly invalid. Furthermore, the Security Council hardly acts as an integrated body, since each of its five permanent members can and does take recourse to its veto power against the other four whenever decisions run counter to its national self-interest.

Obviously, both world organizations were built on a self-contradictory foundation. The qualification for membership is nationhood, that is, national sovereignty over territory and people, and nationalism, the principle that the national interest is the ultimate good, the ultimate criterion and justification. For the nationalist state to serve the universal community is impossible, since its very constitution dictates that it sacrifice everything in pursuit of its own self-interest.

Nationalism precludes surrender of national sovereignty, the first prerequisite of an effective universal community that seeks to actualize justice among the member states. National interest as the ultimate criterion compels the nation-state to pursue that interest at all costs and at the expense of morality and justice. Hence, to protect their own self-interest against one another and the world, the superpowers vested themselves with the right to veto any resolution in the Security Council. To frustrate any resolution of the General Assembly, the superpowers made its execution dependent upon the executive machinery which they controlled through the Council. The United Nations created other organs either for special projects or problems or for dealing with a permanent need of the world's nations. Some of these the superpowers control directly, others indirectly through their contributions to the budget. In either case, only what the superpowers wish gets done. Where resolutions run against their wishes, they withdraw or threaten to do so, bringing the executive machinery to a halt. Where they do not agree with one another, they use the veto to stop the passing of any resolution. On countless occasions, Israel has defied the will of the General Assembly, which represents the overwhelming majority of humankind. Not only devoid of will, the United Nations is also devoid of a standing army with which to stop aggression among nations. Often, because the superpowers themselves or their satellites are the perpetrators of aggression, the United Nations stands impotently on the sidelines, allowing its General Assembly to vote against the aggressor while the latter proceeds with its aggression undeterred.

By definition, the United Nations is not a world government. It was designed to play only the negative role of stopping aggression among members. But even for this minor role, it proved itself incapable. It continues to exist, like its predecessor, as a theater for the world's orators. When the national interests of the superpowers are involved, the United Nations has been either a rubber stamp or an impotent observer. For a brief time following World War II, the superpowers spread the idea and hope that there would henceforth be no war and that the United Nations would bring about a federal union of the world's nations for peace and justice. Today only the naive simpleton still entertains this hope.

Competition among the European powers to control the political, economic, military, and educational machineries of their former colonies continues just as fiercely as before, though with different forms and techniques. The struggle between the former colonies and their old colonizers has been further exacerbated since World War II by the entrance of the two superpowers, the United States and the USSR. These sought to replace the colonial empires of Europe with their own and to extend their dominions to cover the globe.

The Ideal of the Universal Community and America

Born as a satellite of the European Enlightenment, as it were, revolutionary America presented the universal ideal as an alternative to Europe's predicament. Since its independence in 1776, it has remained sufficiently isolated from Europe and the world to be able to play the role of the world's haven from religious and nationalist particularism and to welcome under the aegis of a "new world" all those who emigrated to her shores. This lent credence to the claim that it is America's "manifest destiny" to supplant the old world with its own new universal community. The enthusiasm this idealism has generated lasted but a few decades, and universalist language began to give way to nationalism *à l'Européen*. Competition with Britain and Spain had aroused America to assert its nationalist will through the Monroe doctrine of "America for the Americans." Her victory in the Spanish American War enabled her to press nationalism yet further, this time by redefining herself in Anglo-Saxon terms over and against the Latin American states and their cultural progenitor, Spain. After a brief period of self-isolation following World War I and the upset of European colonialism after World War II, America emerged as the full heir to Europe's ethnocentrist self-esteem and colonialist view of the rest of the world.

The Failure of the West

This, in brief, is the story of the failure of the West, including Eastern Europe, to provide a world order of peace and justice for the world's population. The failure is due to the fact that neither of them knows a principle which makes the ideal of the universal community operative. The mind and culture of the West have never risen beyond "the nation" as a form of social organization. Surely, Christianity cherished that ideal and taught it through the ages, but it contradicted it with its separation of Church and state and its eschatological hope for a kingdom that is other than this world. The religiously oriented advocated the universal community ideal, if at all, out of contempt for the world and history, which they held to be forever fallen, hopeless, and the domain of Satan. As a substitute, they sought the universal community in the Church as the Mystical Body of Christ. Naturally, they could not entertain the ideal as an organization with the law, law-courts, and an army. On the other hand, the secularly oriented in the East or the West gave only lip service to the ideal, and used it, as the political history of this century amply shows, to further the "national interests" of their own peoples.

Far greater in implication for world history and far more dangerous for the peace and security of humankind is what the superpowers have done in this century. The undisputed hegemony of Western culture in the last two hundred years led to the division of the world between two giants capable of destroying each other and the whole world many times over. It is told that the firepower at their command equals more than five hundred pounds of high explosives for every man, woman, and child on earth. Their differences are infinite and irreconcilable. Each wants to subdue the other, dominate the world, and exploit the resources of the earth and the energies of its people. If any peace or accommodation is possible, it is always for their own aggrandizement at the cost of the rest of the world, which is the victim. By definition, therefore, any arrangement is temporary until one or the other giant gets ready to devour another chunk of the world. Though called "the cold war," the last forty years of peace were due to the "balance of terror" the superpowers themselves had established between themselves, i.e., their nearly equal capability to destroy each other totally, not to any will for peace or justice. Humankind trembles whenever one of them complains or threatens, never sure whether the moment has come for either giant to start the tragic end of mankind. In the last three decades, the world may have stood on the brink of extinction several times because of their disagreements on Berlin, Palestine, Hungary, Cyprus, Vietnam, Cuba, and Korea. The two giants press their preparations for war constantly, making no point on earth secure.

The two giants, and to a lesser extent their European allies, spend an inordinate proportion of their national incomes on research, development, manufacture, and deployment of the tools of war. Is it to subsidize this expenditure, and partly to test the efficacy of their weapons against one another, that the two blocs promote hostility among the peoples of the Third World? These peoples were organized by the colonial powers into nation-states with boundaries designed to leave them in perpetual conflict with their neighbors. Both power blocs continuously encourage hostilities among the Third World nations, fan old conflicts or create new ones, and prod the nations of the Third World to open hostility against one another. They subsidize all sorts of subversive movements within each nation-state, precisely in order to instill in the ruling classes of the Third World the fear of their own people and of their neighbors, all with the intent of making them more dependent for their security upon the superpowers. Is it unreasonable to see in this a Western drive to compel these poor nations to buy Western weapons, to use and have to replace them, to destroy their development projects through stalemated wars so they can build them again - all with materials, equipment, and expertise supplied by either of the two blocs? If the victimized nation is strong, this Machiavellian policy aims at draining it of its resources and diverting such resources from being used for a really constructive purpose, thus perpetuating its dependent status. If, on the other hand, the nation is poor, they lend it money in order that it will buy their weapons and consumers' products and thus be forced to mortgage its future.

An impoverished Third World, rent with internecine conflicts and armed hostilities, producing raw materials which the two power blocs buy at prices they dictate themselves, using products of European and American industry and agriculture, and dependent for their staple foods and other essentials (even their daily bread) upon the bounty of either bloc - that is the order the superpowers and their allies have designed for the Third World. The principles of secularism dominate, and their policies are utterly devoid of moral consideration. The separation of the realms of Caesar and Christ, as Reinhold Niebuhr had affirmed, liberates national policy from the ethic of Christ and permits the nation-state to flout every moral precept.

This is why it makes perfect sense for the West to pay its citizens from the national treasury in order to produce below their capacities so as not to cause prices to fall. Their moral logic permits them to buy, stockpile and, when the warehouses are filled to capacity, to destroy the foodstuffs they had bought so as to maintain their price and trade patterns. The core of immorality and inhumanity in this Western practice is that all this prevention of production and destruction and stockpiling of foodstuffs takes place while the majority of mankind goes undernourished, while hundreds of millions suffer from hunger, and scores of millions perish from hunger and famine every year.

For humanity to live under the shadows of terror and annihilation, and for the two power blocs to prosper on the production, destruction, and resupply of the tools of war constitutes a terrible sin against humanity. It is truly immoral to be unconcerned about the fact that the war industry (with sales topping one trillion dollars in the current year) is the most crucial economic activity, and to give rein to a vested interest in developing interhuman hatred and hostility in order to maintain one's power or egotistical advantage. But that is precisely the result of the West's hegemony over the world during the last two centuries. The world is neither safe, nor peaceful, nor contented. It is a time bomb whose hour to explode can strike at any moment. A very few million in the two power blocs sit at the summit of power and affluence while the majority of their compatriots are poor, devoid of spirit or idealism, some of them pining for a lottery miracle to bring them some of the power or affluence of the fortunate few. The rest of humanity is undernourished, hungry, or dying. That is not only a capital failure; it is indeed a tragic disaster.

Poverty of Thought in the Field of World Order

The Western tradition of thought in the field of international law or world order is extremely poor. With the little inspiration that tradition has provided, it is no wonder the West's record in world-order affairs is little more than convention and force. Was this poverty of ideas the cause or the mirror of the practice? In the realm of practice, the West has never known or applied international law except on the basis of convention. Differences between one state and another were solved by negotiation or with reference to previous agreement. In most cases, the appeal was to some treaty or convention between the parties from which the conflict in question was regarded as a departure. In the total absence of such agreement, treaty, or convention, the conflict was deemed soluble only by force, or *ad baculum*.

The doctrine of natural law, known and discussed in the Middle Ages especially after the rise of scholasticism, remained an academic/theological matter and was never applied to the field of international relations. It was not until the seventeenth century that any Western thinker first sought to link international relations to law. The religious wars and the scramble for colonies in the New World, Asia, and Africa, with all the conflicts it brought in its trail among the states of Europe, inspired Grotius to appeal to the law of nature as a ground for inter-European agreement and harmony. The Enlightenment repeated the appeal for a while, but its voice was soon silenced by the advent of romanticism. The actual processes of international activity remained far removed from theory and were never affected. As to relations with non-Europeans, there was neither treaty nor convention to invoke. Furthermore, the Asians and Africans were infidels already condemned by God. Only the argument of force would hence apply to them. Nothing therefore could stop the Europeans from using the harshest measures of force and brutality in defeating and subjugating them individually and collectively.

We have seen the circumstances under which the League of Nations and the United Nations were formed. We have noted their failure. Surprisingly, that failure did not stimulate the Western mind, either after World War I or after World War II, to think of alternatives. That mind, whether American, Western or East European, has remained unmoved and incapable of thinking through the failure or of reaching a solution to the predicament.

The Present Need for a New World Order

There is a great need in the world today for an international order that would establish a just and permanent peace without tyranny, one which recognizes the differences and distinctions - religious, cultural, social, and economic - of the peoples of the world as legitimate, and that would found its law upon their common need to order their lives as they wish in justice and freedom. Such a world order would establish a federal or confederal world government with the executive and police machinery necessary for implementation. It would be backed by international law and a system of courts that would place international justice within reach of all - governments, institutions, communities, and individuals. Without such an order, the world will never find peace. Justice and reassurance will never come if the nation-state does not give up its "national sovereignty" in favor of the government of a federated world.

World government - whatever its form - has become in this age an absolute and inevitable necessity. With nuclear weapons proliferating, the world population exploding, the superpowers' greed for the world's wealth growing as rapidly as their nuclear arsenals, and - most importantly - the majority of humanity seething with hatred and discontent and growing ever more radical and restive, this world order of ours, brought about by the West and propped up by it for the last two centuries, cannot last. Either it will come down in a holocaust or it has to change peacefully and rationally in fulfillment of the aspirations of humanity.

Either the inhabitants of the planet Earth act as sheep and jump over the cliff to their death for no reason but to follow their leader, to use Arnold Toynbee's metaphor, or as rational beings they give up their nationalist madness and establish the new world order. To design and articulate the new world order, to elaborate its implementation - that is humanity's first duty. But humanity has no legacy of thought concerning world order except that of Islam.

Only very recently, the United Nations tried to institute such a law to govern the relations of its members. Its efforts resulted in the Universal Bill of Human Rights, a document which contains much good - genuinely universal and truly basic human rights - but which falls far short of the ideal. Some of the values it has incorporated were purely Western values, and they were accepted by puppet nation-states which did not represent the people or their moralities. The Charter of Human Rights was defeated by its own enthusiastic promulgators, who used it as a means of propaganda war against their competitors or enemies. It never produced a court system under which the individual sufferers could voice their grievances and obtain justice against the violators of those rights. Thus the charter remains, to this day, mere ink on paper whenever the violation of human rights agrees with the national interest of a superpower or one of its satellites. The charter appears to be merely a tool of propaganda.

The World Order of Islam

The fact remains that in the field of international ethics, as well as of law and jurisprudence, the world is dependent on the Islamic heritage. All the more justification therefore for publishing this book and presenting it for public debate. Our hope is to stimulate people everywhere, Muslim and non-Muslim, to ponder over the principles of the international order presented and to begin to lay the foundations in the mind and will for its implementation.

Rather than summarize or evaluate the contribution of Islam as presented in this work - such being the conclusion of the expected debate - it is the intention to present in this introduction, in addition to the foregoing and by way of introduction to the subject, a skeleton outline of the Islamic thesis as a whole.

Islam's Commitment

Islam and its adherents regard themselves as committed to the task of bringing about a new world order. They regard this commitment as the only viable response to the present predicament: first, because this is how we can render obedience to God, Who has commanded all humans to enter the realm of peace and to organize their affairs and order their lives in justice and responsible brotherhood; and second, because this is the only way to save humanity from endless competition and meaningless suffering in the present and from imminent destruction in the future. Thus, Muslim commitment to a world order of peace, justice, and brotherhood is both religious and utilitarian. Islam holds that desiring this world order, working for it, and sacrificing to bring it about are constituents of heroism and virtue, of piety and saintliness. To lay down one's life in the process of its actualization is martyrdom (*shahādah*), earning for its subject eternal paradise. No nobler or stronger motivation is possible.

Pax Islamica

The world order that Islam seeks is one from which war is banished once and for all. Islam's commitment to peace is absolute, universal, and comprehensive. For any people to enter the new order, it is necessary for them to disband their army, destroy their weapons, or surrender them to the world government, except those necessary for the maintenance of public order or for the enforcement of the verdicts of the courts of law. The covenant of peace, under which no dispute or claim may be settled except through adjudication, arbitration, or negotiation, must be offered to all peoples. Every people is entitled, as well as obliged, to join it. To reject adjudication under international law or the invitation to enter the covenant of peace is indeed to opt for war or isolationism, neither of which is rationally or morally tenable. Islam demands that all nations and peoples enter the realm of peace and it commands it adherents to do so with enthusiasm. It justifies coercive action by the whole (i.e. by those who have entered the realm of peace) against the recalcitrant nation. If a nation repudiates the peace accepted by everyone else on the same universal terms, Islam understands this to be a declaration of war.

Bases for Membership

Islam's international law regards the *millah,* or religious society, as the basic identity framework, and the Islamic world order has historically been composed of the Muslim, Christian, Jewish, Zoroastrian, Sabaean, Hindu and Buddhist religious communities. The reasoning of Islam is founded on the repudiation of tribalism and nationalism, for it regards ethnocentrism, whether based on racial, territorial, linguistic or cultural particularism, as evil and unbecoming of humans created equally by God and endowed by Him with His spirit. Ethnic characterization is demeaning of humans; every human would rather be identified by thoughts and ideals, or by voluntary deeds and accomplishments, rather than by the circumstances of birth and biological or social formation, which are never of the person's own choosing. The Jews were the first non-Muslim group recognized by the Islamic constitution of Madīnah in 1 AH/622 AC, and they were followed by the Christians, Sabeans, Hindus, and Buddhists who opted for self-identification by religious affiliation. Islamic jurisprudence equally recognizes those peoples who opt for nonreligious identification provided they have a legacy of laws (even if secular) by which they wish to order their lives. The only group which may be barred from membership is that group whose law is antiworld order and antipeace. Whatever the religious, ethical, and sociopolitical content of their dominant ideology, their title to join the world order rests on their humanity and will to peace alone. Islamic jurisprudence thus enables one to affirm today that any group claiming itself to be a religious society on whatever grounds is entitled to membership.

Liberty

Islam holds, and the world order envisaged by it affirms, that unless born in captivity to captive parents, human beings are all born free and remain so as long as they live. Capture of fighters in the field of battle is the only recognized source of captivity. Such captives, however, can be legally ransomed by anyone concerned for them and are capable of contracting for their own liberation or manumission by their captors for a reasonable remuneration. In the eyes of Islamic law, it is illegal for the captor to reject the captives' offer to ransom themselves by their own productive work.

Equally, by virtue of their humanity, people may not be seized, detained, or incarcerated without due legal process. And no law is regarded by Islam as legitimate which empowers any government to seize, detain, or incarcerate any person without legal charge before a court of law. All people enjoy the full liberty to educate their children as they please and to order their lives according to the dictates of their consciences as formulated, institutionalized, and interpreted by the tradition of the *millah* with which they are affiliated. Nobody may be coerced into membership of any *millah,* including the Muslim, and anyone may move from one *millah* to another if he so chooses. As long as his movement is his own free and solemn decision, it must be honored by all concerned.

Openness

The world order Islam seeks to build regards the planet Earth as a manor of God in which His human creatures are free to seek His bounty. This means that humans may not be restricted in their movements. They should be free to settle wherever they choose. As long as they are willing to abide by the laws governing the territory and its people, they must be free to enter, to reside, and to leave as well. The movement of persons and their goods must remain unhampered by exit and entry permits, residence or work permits, protectionist custom duties, tariffs, and the like. All these measures, which are hardly older than a century, as well as the government institutions which administer them, must be abolished. An individual's choice of profession or work is an inviolable right in God's cosmic order, and so is one's title to one's earthly possessions, and one's freedom to move such possessions wherever one desires. A person's liberty may not be hampered except in cases where its exercise constitutes a trespass or aggression upon another person's property. In a truly Islamic world order, the economy and administration of any country would be in tune with the situation of the globe as well.

Egalitarianism

All humans are born equal and remain so in the eye of the law. They are entitled to equal opportunity in education and employment, in work and compensation. Distinction must be made purely on the basis of intelligence and knowledge, work and productivity, by excellence, virtue, or righteousness. Certainly, a person's wealth may pass to the heirs through death, gift, or will, and this may significantly increase their opportunities in life over and above those of others. That is no threat to egalitarianism, though it may result in the stratification of society. But no social stratum or class may be a closed club. An Islamic world order would know of no group, class, or association which is not open to anyone who qualifies and wishes to join it, and no qualification requisite would be legitimate that is not realizable by voluntary decision and/or personal effort. Islam regards any kind of apartheid built on race or biology, language or culture, geography or age, as an offense against humanity as well as its Creator and treats it as a punishable crime.

Universalism

In the world order of Islam all humans would be members of one brotherhood. Ethnic particularity, whether biological, social, or cultural, would provide no basis for distinction or discrimination. On the contrary, it has fuelled war and hostility among the tribes, nations, and states of the world for millennia. The laws of citizenship, immigration, and naturalization enacted by the nation-states to safeguard and perpetuate their ethnocentric identity or their advantaged socio-economic and political position would be abolished. Nothing would prevent the communities of the world from intermixing with one another, and they would indeed be encouraged to do so.

No doubt, true universalism would cause great social changes in the fabric of humanity and, under it, many communities might be submerged along with their ethnocentrisms. But this is necessary if the human community is to be purged of its particularism and humans are to be regarded as truly human and judged on the basis of their personal excellence as humans. The emerging universal community or human brotherhood is a far nobler and stronger social ideal, and it would constitute a significant advance for its members over their previous status in the ethnic or national community. It would enable them to remain in local or intermediate communities open to all, and at the same time to rise to the universal humanistic ideal.

Justice

No minority in the world would remain a minority compelled to live under the laws of the surrounding majority and thus to suffer its own character to be gradually eroded or changed. The world order of Islam would recognize the minority as a *millah,* constitutionally empowered to order the lives of its members by its own laws. If another human group were of the same *millah,* both would be free to merge by emigration and thus constitute a larger whole. The Islamic law of nations is pluralistic, providing legitimacy and protection to the laws of all human groups. Under it, no minority would be a "minority," since it would enjoy as much legitimacy in the eye of international law as any larger or majority community. This legitimacy notwithstanding, if the minority group loses a member to a majority, it would be by the voluntary and free choice of that member, a decision which the world order must respect and honor.

If a *millah* should encroach upon another, the victim could bring its complaint to court. The law being public, any court of law would be empowered to consider the litigation and give a verdict. The law courts would also be empowered to look into any complaint brought about by any individual against his *millah* or against the world order itself. Justice being free, its process unencumbered, and its verdict swift of execution, every citizen of the world order of Islam would stand reassured that his or her rights are sacrosanct. Above all, every citizen would be reassured that justice is possible, that it is indeed obtainable. This ready availability of justice is not expected to increase litigation nor make it unmanageable, for in Islamic law, contempt of court, perjury, and false witness would receive the severe punishment of loss of legal status, in addition to retributory or compensatory fines; and where the latter are not possible due to poverty or bankruptcy, they would be translated into corporal punishment. Finally, the public implementation of corporal punishment would act as didactic and preventive pedagogy for the people. To the victim of injustice, however, there is nothing greater than the reassurance that, despite his or her weakness, justice is there for the asking.

The Freedom to Convince and to Be Convinced

Finally, the world order of Islam would confer upon every person by virtue of birth and humanity, the ultimate right and honor, namely, the capacity to think and make up one's mind as to which *millah* one wishes to belong and hence, by which law one desires to order one's life and that of one's dependents. It regards the individual as endowed by God at birth with the capacity to judge between alternatives presented to the mind, and as responsible in the exercise of his faculties and choice. Islam countenances no tutelage whatever in this matter. On the contrary, it regards censorship and spiritual guardianship in matters of religion and law as an affront to the person and to humanity and compromise of the divine design for creation. Islamic international law would tear down all "curtains" erected by the nation-states to "shield" their citizens against counterclaims to the truth, confident that the truth will ultimately prevail. For the truth theoretically is God's knowledge, and the truth practically and axiologically is His will.

Philadelphia, PA February 1986

CHAPTER 1

BACKGROUND

Internally weak, relatively backward, frustrated, conflict-ridden, suffering from internal tensions, and often controlled and abused by foreign powers, the Muslim world is in a state of crisis. For Muslims, all of modern history is a tragedy. At an earlier time, during the sweeping revolution of Islam, Muslims were the custodians of civilization and both the center and masters of the civilized world. But at present, the Muslim polity is neither master nor partner, and both Muslims and Islam are often regarded in world politics as little more than problematic.[1]

How did such a state of affairs come about, and in what ways can the Muslim peoples alter this condition?

In Muslim countries it is customary to blame external powers and imperialism for all manner of ills. Although this habit may point up many of the grievances and obstacles Muslims face, it cannot explain the internal cause of the ills. These ills put in motion a process of decay that dissipated the internal power of the Muslim world. The resultant weakness brought external powers into the picture, complicating the difficulties. The problem of the external factors, along with the complications they caused for the Muslim world, cannot be dealt with before the internal factors are fully understood.

---

[1] The Muslim world here refers to all people who call themselves Muslims and associate themselves with the Islamic religion and heritage, wherever they may happen to reside.

Preliminary and Basic Definitions

Any elaboration on this subject will first require a discussion of basic historical background and definitions.

Islam as a religion and complete way of life made its appearance in the early seventh century AC with Muhammad, the last Prophet of Islam (570-632 AC), who belonged to the well-known Arab tribe of Quraysh. The Quraysh, descendants of Ismā'īl, son of Ibrāhīm, were the custodians of the holy city of Makkah in the western part of the Arabian peninsula. At the mature age of forty, Muhammad received a *waḥy* (revelation) from Allah that he had been appointed Prophet and Messenger of Allah. This *waḥy*, as recorded in the Qur'an, constitutes the first source of the Shari'ah (the revealed will of Allah through the Prophet regarding the conduct of all human life on earth).[2] The Sunnah (way) of the Prophet, that is, the collection of his reported sayings, actions, and approvals or disapprovals, is regarded as the second source of the Shari'ah.

Muslim jurisprudence (fiqh) developed a methodology of its own to interpret and make deductions in line with the Shari'ah, for example *qiyās* (analogy) and *ijmā'* (consensus). The source material coupled with the methodology is called *uṣūl* (sources and methods of Muslim jurisprudence). Some of the *uṣūl* are Sunnah, *ijmā'*, and *qiyās*. The various schools of Muslim jurisprudence differ on the number of *uṣūl* to be used or emphasized, although all of them include the Qur'an and the Sunnah. In chapter 3 we will deal with *uṣūl* in detail when the methodology of Muslim thought is discussed.

By the end of the tenth century AC, Muslims had reduced the number of recognized schools of jurisprudence to four. These are called the four sunni schools of jurisprudence. Since then Muslim thought, with few exceptions, has become rigid, and

---

[2] In references to the Qur'an, either one of the following two translations will be used unless otherwise stated: Abdullah Yusuf Ali, *The Holy Qur'an: Text, Translation and Commentary* (Washington, DC: American International Printing Company, 1945), and Muhammad Marmaduke Pickthall, *The Meaning of the Glorious Kor'an* (New York: New American Library [n.d.]). See W. Montgomery Watt, *Muhammad: Prophet and Statesman* (London: Oxford University Press, 1961), pp. 242-243.

imitation (*taqlīd*) has been the dominant approach.[3] In the nineteenth century, modernists introduced the concept of "piecing together" (*talfīq*) Muslim jurisprudence and legislation as the dominant force of the so-called modern ijtihad.[4] As N.J. Coulson put it:

> The so-called modern ijtihad amounts to little more than forcing from the divine texts that particular interpretation which agrees with preconceived standards subjectively determined.... In sum, it appears that modern (Muslim) jurisprudence has not yet evolved any systematic approach.... Lacking any consistency of principle of methodology, it has tackled the process of reform as a whole in a spirit of juristic opportunism. Furthermore, many of the substantive reforms must appear, on long term view, as temporary expedients and piecemeal accommodations.

The "medieval" juristic thought pertaining to the area of international relations constitutes what will be referred to here as the classical theory of thought.[5]

Traditionalism and Westernization

While Muslim thought, technology, and social systems became stagnant with *taqlīd* as the established way of life, Europe began to develop new ideas and methods. By the seventeenth century, Europe had surpassed the Muslim world both in the fields of warfare and political organization. As a result, Muslims were forced into a defensive posture.

As a result of closer and more frequent contacts with Europe, Muslim authorities became aware of the need to learn and adopt European technology, especially in the military and related professions. They established military and professional schools, hired European instructors, and sent students to European schools to acquire the new skills and technical knowledge. This step created a serious problem in the Muslim social structure, for

---

[3] See Appendix, note 1.

[4] Ijtihad is the use of human reason in the elaboration of the law.

[5] N.J. Coulson, *A History of Islamic Law* (Edinburgh: Edinburgh University Press, 1964), pp. 75, 80-81, 152-154, 196-199, 211-217, 220-223. See also M. Khadduri, "From Religion to National Law," in *Modernization of the Arab World*, ed. J. Thompson and R. Reischauer (New York: Van Nostrand, 1966), p. 41.

it pitted the religious sector of society against the secular, a concept fundamentally alien to Islam. This situation developed because the ulama, the Muslim theologians and learned men, were for centuries deeply involved in *taqlīd* and arid legalism, thereby providing little leadership. Their education lacked the concept of systematic empirical observation and left them alienated from those specializing in the newly evolving social sciences with their emphasis on application and methods. They were unaware of the repercussions of the new knowledge and methods on the composition, interaction, and organization of society, nor were they able to envision the potential of this new knowledge harnessed to the values, goals, and the overall paradigm of Islam.

The rising power of the newly emerging Muslim classes of professionals and bureaucrats, who lacked the specialized Islamic knowledge, commitment, and ideological awareness of the ulama, and of the non-Muslim minorities with their leading professional role, as well as the increasing influence of European powers, led to the polarization of education and knowledge into religious and secular areas and drove the ulama into virtual isolation.

Religious education became the symbol and protector of a rigid set of historical religious traditions built originally on Islamic ideology. Alien to Muslim thought, secular education increasingly absorbed European ideas and attitudes. This process did little to contribute to a revitalization of Muslim thought and education. Systematic empirical observation never became a tool of Muslim religious education, which remained moribund.

This dichotomy had a crippling effect on motivation and determination in either direction, Islamic or secular, resulting in the isolation of the ulama from public life, the separation of the bureaucracy and government from the people, the polarization of the traditionalists who drew blindly on the past and of the secularists who relied totally on Western sources for inspiration and ideas. *Taqlīd* and *talfiq* as practiced by either segment of contemporary Muslim intellectuals have done more harm than good to the cause of creating a new Muslim psychology and outlook based on a revival of Islam. Unification of "sacred" and "secular" in Islam makes it necessary for the devout Muslim's conscience in the modern world to arrive at an agreement between the Islamic outlook and the material aspects of life. Thus, it behooves Muslims to clear up the space-time issue pertaining to their understanding and application of Islam. The resolution of this dilemma would bring about the original, dynamic, and realistic policies that are so badly needed. To make this task possible, we must explain and elaborate on the mechanisms developed and used in the classical Muslim social system, especially in the field of external relations, where political as well as legal factors were clearly present and where both war and peace with non-Muslim parties were involved.

Siyar : A Source of Law

Some writers, when analyzing and discussing Islamic works in the field of relations among nations, wrongly emphasize the idea that fiqh is law in itself and not a secondary source of Islamic law. It is very important, in the modern context, to recognize this aspect of fiqh. Moreover, it is essential to concentrate on the study of Muslim governmental systems in the Middle Ages if efforts by Muslims to reorganize and systematize the modern process of lawmaking are to bear fruit.[6]

The difference in meaning among fiqh, *uṣūl al fiqh,* and the Shari'ah must be clarified. The Islamic Shari'ah is the divine will revealed to the Prophet pertaining to the conduct of human life in this world. *Uṣūl al fiqh* is the science of deducing and extrapolating rules and injunctions from their sources in the data of revelation. Fiqh is the body of rules and injunctions deduced from the Qur'an and the Sunnah which contain the divine will as revealed to the Prophet.[7]

Law in the Islamic sense is a set of value-oriented guidelines directed toward the divine purposes of Allah. Islamic law is

---

[6] See Muhammad Hamidullah, *The Muslim Conduct of State* , 5th rev. ed. (Lahore, Pakistan: Sh. Muhammad Ashraf, 1963), pp.vii-viii and 3-10; Majid Khadduri, *War and Peace in the Law of Islam* (Baltimore: Johns Hopkins University Press, 1952), pp. 251-295, and Majid Khadduri's introduction to the classical work of *siyar*, *The Islamic Law of Nations* by Muhammad al Shaybānī, (Baltimore: Johns Hopkins University Press, 1966), pp. 63-68.

[7] See Appendix, note 2.

therefore primarily normative rather than prescriptive and is designed for moral education as well as for legal enforcement.

Law in the Western sense is a different concept. It is the body of rules and directions accepted and approved for enforcement by nations. This approval is achieved in many ways. These could be by treatise, legislation, or custom, or by moral or religious commitment, or by any combination thereof.

In order to single out the areas of strength and weakness and the causes for confusion and stagnation, conceptual clarity will be needed in studying and comparing with modern Western law the injunctions of the Shari'ah (either taken as a whole, or only those parts which concern the field of international relations).

In this way, it will be possible to trace one of the basic problems of the Muslim people in modern times, namely, incompatibility of thought methodology. The problem is not which rule the Muslims should select, approve, or reject, but rather what is wrong with Muslim thought and why the Shari'ah is no longer providing man with rules and regulations that can enable him to exert more effective control over his environment and destiny. In chapter 3, we will elaborate on this problem to show how defects of the traditional Muslim methodology, brought about by social changes, lie at the bottom of the dilemma of modern Muslim thought. This will enable us to deal with the future participation of Muslims in the modern world.

What has been attempted here is simply to shed some light on the nature of the problem and to clarify some confusion caused by faulty comparisons and conceptions. We are attempting to show that the real role assigned to fiqh and *siyar* in the mechanism of the classical social system was to provide a basic source of law for Muslim society. While making comparison with the modern Western lawmaking process, we have to be aware of the different processes involved and of the adjustments necessary to promulgate laws in a modern Muslim society.[8]

Before we examine the issue, we would like to quote al Sarakhsī's definition of the term *siyar*, since this will make clear the kinds of topics with which the Muslim jurisprudence used to

---

[8] Ibid.

deal. It will also make it easier to explain why *siyar* and fiqh as a whole did not function in the full sense of the term "law," but rather as just one major source of the Muslim law. Al Sarakhsī defined *siyar* in the jurisprudential sense as follows:

> Siyar... describes the conduct of the believers (Muslims) in their relations with the unbelievers of enemy territory as well as with people with whom the believers have made treaties, who may have been temporarily (*musta'man* - the subject of a state which was at war with a Muslim state and granted safe conduct to enter Muslim territory) or permanently *dhimmī* - (the non-Muslim subject of a Muslim state) in Muslim land; with apostates, murtaddūn... and with rebels... [9]

Siyar also includes the rules of civilized intercourse with peoples and states living in friendship with Muslims, which are contrasted in the Qur'an with those in hostility.

When we say that fiqh is a source Muslim law, this should not be confused with sources of fiqh itself, that is, the Qur'an and the Sunnah, which together constitute the Shari'ah. Fiqh represents the sum of jurisprudential interpretations, deductions, and opinions of the Muslim scholars, the ulama, and especially of those of the highest rank, the *mujtahidūn*, who showed marked competence and independence of thought.[10]

Fiqh achieved this position during the Ummawī dynasty following the first forty years of the history of the Islamic state. With the expansion of the Muslim community and state, and with the bloody struggle of the various parties for the control of the state, the elite which concerned itself with the welfare of the religious, social, and intellectual affairs of the Muslim peoples resumed its guardianship through the field of Muslim legal studies and the other fields of studies of *dīn* (Islamic way of life).

The early period of Islam, notably that of the Prophet and the first four caliphs (*al khulafā' al rāshidūn*) as well as the Companions of the Prophet, was considered an ideal period; and

---

[9] M. Khaddūrī's introduction to al Shaybānī, *The Islamic Law of Nations*, p. 40, quoting Shams al Dīn Muhammad ibn Ahmad ibn Sahl al Sarakhsī, *Kitāb al Mabsūt* (The Detailed Work of Jurisprudence) (Cairo: 1960), p. 2.

[10] See Appendix, note 3.

at that time many legal precedents were set. Starting with the Ummawīs, however, the acts and procedures of the government took into consideration other factors besides the opinion of the jurists. The peoples of the various lands conquered by Islam, under the influence of their pre-Islamic customs, acted differently in many ways, thus departing from the standards set by both government and the jurists.

The fiqh of the Sunni (followers of the Sunnah) Muslims or *al jamhūr* (the majority), as we know it today, is contained in the four legal schools: the Ḥanafī, the Mālikī, the Shāfiʻī, and the Ḥanbalī. These schools are generally accepted as a single group possessing similar Islamic attitudes. Nevertheless, although these schools may be unified on the basic principles of Islam (for instance, that the pillars of Islam are five, not four or six) and may also be unified on basic philosophical and theological issues, they do not take a unified position on all legal opinions.

Some examples from the area of international relations (*siyar*) will demonstrate how far-fetched is the notion that works of the classical jihad and *siyar* constitute, even today, an Islamic law among nations and offer a sort of unified classical legal code.[11] These examples show how the different schools could differ on basic issues concerning life and death. Where one school would express approval of the death sentence or even demand it in a particular case, another would not hesitate to claim the right to life and safety for the same accused individual. On other issues, it would not be unusual to see almost all possible attitudes expressed by the four schools. We have to keep in mind, however, that these sharp differences between schools did not necessarily result from different theoretical abstractions. As we shall see in chapter 3, these schools partially agreed and partially differed on the issue of what constitutes the basic sources from which stem the methods used to derive legal opinions. All of the schools are agreed on the Qur'an and the Sunnah in all respects. They also

[11] In this connection, M. Khadduri, *War and Peace*, and M. Hamidullah, *The Muslim Conduct of State*, are good examples. See also A. Khallaf, *Khulāṣat Tārīkh al Tashrīʻ al Islāmī* (Kuwait: Dār al Qalam, 1971), pp. 23-49 and 65-82, and S. Ramadan, *Three Major Problems Confronting the World of Islam* (Tacoma Park, MD: Crescent Publications, n.d.), pp. 1-6.

agree on *ijmā'* (consensus) as a source and method but differ on the scope of its application.

The issue revolved around the question of consensus by whom? Is it the consensus of the "Companions of the Prophet" only, or all of the Madīnans, or all those who "bind and loose" (in this context, elites and leaders of public opinion), or all the ulama, or the entire Ummah?[12] The disagreement was even sharper when it came to the method known as *istiḥsān* (juristic preference) as developed by the Ḥanafī school of jurisprudence. The Shāfi'ī school refused absolutely to include it among the *uṣūl*.

These differences were sharpened due the underlying nature of *uṣūl*. The sources and methods do not involve a systematic and comprehensive theorization. They merely constitute individual employment of the deductive method through the Qur'an and the Sunnah in order to handle specific issues and practices. This is the case because there already was a concrete social system, laid down by the Prophet, within which the jurists were satisfied to work.

More specifically, the following examples of Sunni Muslim jurisprudential opinion illustrate how far opinions could differ.

1. Is jihad an obligation to wage an offensive war or an obligation to defend Islam?

Al Thawrī and Abū Ḥanīfah take a similar position in dealing with this question, while al Sarakhsī, the Ḥanafī jurist, takes an opposite position in conformity with the Shāfi'ī school.[13]

Al Thawrī says:

> Fighting against the associators (nonbelievers, i.e., those who associate others with God's divinity) is not an obligation unless they start the fight; then it is an obligation to fight back (against them)...

---

[12] Muhammad Abū Zahrah, *Mālik: Ḥayātuh wa 'Aṣruh wa Ārā'uh wa Fiqhuh* (Mālik: His Life, His Age, His Opinions, and His Jurisprudence) (Cairo: Dār al Fikr al 'Arabī, 1963), pp. 322-335, 352-360.

[13] Al Shāfi'ī, *Al Umm* (Cairo: Dār al Sha'b, 1903), vol. IV, pp. 84-85 and 90, and al Shaybānī, *Sharḥ al Siyar* (Cairo: Ma'had al Mukhtūtāt bi Jāmi'at al Duwal al 'Arabīyah, 1958), vol. I, p. 188.

Al Sarakhsī says:

> To sum up, injunctions about jihad and fighting (to Muslims) were revealed in stages... (the final stage being) the absolute command to fight (non-believers). This signifies an obligation, but an obligation that is meant to exalt the religion (of Islam) and to subdue the associators.

Al Shāfi'ī says:

> Allah made jihad an obligation after it had been a matter of choice.

Consequently, jihad is an obligation which every capable man (*kuf'*) must practice until two things are achieved: one, there are sufficient forces to face the enemies of Islam and, two, there are enough Muslim forces to carry on the jihad until all polytheists turn to Islam and all the People of the Book give the *jizyah* (the tax equivalent non-Muslim subjects pay to the Muslim state).[14] If enough Muslim forces fulfill this obligation, then the sin of those Muslims who do not join in jihad will not be counted.[15]

2. Are the non-Muslim enemy's subjects (*ḥarbī*) subject to Muslim legal punishment (*ḥudūd*) for a crime once they have been granted safe conduct or protection (*amān*) to enter Muslim territory?

One recognized authority, al Awzā'ī, says that they are not subject to Muslim legal punishment.

In answering a question about adultery or theft committed by an enemy who has been granted safe conduct, Abū Ḥanīfah says:

> He is not subject to the prescribed punishment (*ḥadd),* but he is responsible for returning what he has stolen.

Thus, he escapes punishment altogether for adultery.

Al Shāfi'ī says:

> When enemy subjects enter the Muslims' land and commit crimes, they are subject to Muslim legal punishment. Their treatment is of two kinds: one which does not entail human rights will be pardoned, ...[the other] which entails human rights will be subject to (punishment). [16]

---

[14] The word *jizyah* is derived from the Arabic verb *jazā'* meaning to fulfill or pay back.

[15] Al Shāfi'ī, *Al Umm*, vol, IV, p. 90.

[16] Ibid., vol. VII, pp. 325-326.

3. What is the punishment of a Muslim who intentionally kills a non-Muslim subject: The blood money of a Jew or a Christian or a Magian is the same as that of a Muslim. If a Muslim kills any one of those, is he then subject to execution (*qawd*)?

Al Shāfi'ī says:

> A believer will not be executed for killing a non-believer. The blood money of a Jew or a Christian is one third of that of a Muslim, whereas the blood money of a Magian is 800 dirhams.[17]

4. The fourth example concerns the question of sparing the life of non-Muslims and accepting the *jizyah* instead.

At least three positions have been taken by the different schools of Sunni jurisprudence. The Shāfi'ī and Ḥanbalī schools claim that the *jizyah* is acceptable only from the People of the Book and the Magians. It is not acceptable from any of the polytheists. The Ḥanafī and Mālikī schools state that *jizyah* is acceptable from all non-Muslims except the Arab polytheists. Another opinion, however, is attributed to Mālik who shares the position of al Awzā'ī and al Thawrī who maintain that *jizyah* is acceptable from all.[18] By way of contrast, the last position offers amnesty to polytheists, thus sparing their lives, while the first position denies them this privilege.

5. Should human lives be spared by widening or narrowing the categories of people whose lives are not subject to killing in war?

Mālik and Abū Ḥanīfah say that:

> People who are blind, mad, or very old [should not be killed]. People who belong to monasteries (*ahl al ṣawāmi'*) should be left with only enough of their possessions as are sufficient for them to live on.[19]

---

[17] Ibid., vol. VII, pp. 290-291.

[18] Ibn Qudāmah, *Al Mughnī* (Cairo: Maktabat al 'Āṣimah, n.d.), vol. IX, pp. 194-195, and 319-324, and Wahbah al Zuḥaylī, *Athār al Ḥarb fī al Fiqh al Islāmī: Dirāsah Muqāranah* (The Effects of War in Islamic Jurisprudence: A Comparative Study) 2nd ed. (Damascus: Al Maktabah al Ḥadīthah, 1965), pp. 712-715.

[19] Ibn Rushd, *Bidāyat al Mujtahid* (Cairo: Maktabah al Khānjī, n.d.), vol. I, pp. 310-311.

Al Thawrī and al Awzā'ī narrow the category down to "only very old people should not be killed."[20]

Al Shāfi'ī, in the most authentic of the positions attributed to him, says: "all these categories [of people] may be killed."[21]

On this subject, Ibn Rushd (Averroes) writes:

> The reason for their differences is the [apparent] contradiction between some of the *āthār* (traditions) and the general meanings of [both] the book [Qur'an] and the sayings of the Prophet.
>
> The reason for their differences is their having taken different positions with regard to the reason for the killing. Those who think the reason for killing is the state of non-belief did not make any exception. Those who think the reason for killing non-believers is their ability to fight did make exception for those who are unable to fight, or who do not engage in hostilities, such as plowmen and servants. This rule is justified on the basis of the Prophet's prohibition against killing women, even though they were non-believers.[22]

A contemporary Islamic writer expresses the issue involved in such arguments when he points out that jurists contradict themselves when they sanction compulsion-in-religion (in the case of apostates) and at the same time hold the position that free choice is a condition for assuming any responsibility.[23]

Another Muslim writer notes that if one were to compare all the works on fiqh one would find that the conclusions arrived at by one jurist will sometimes directly contradict those arrived at by another. Such differences may even reach the point where a life could be forfeit, according to one jurist, and saved, according to the ruling of another; where property is rightfully possessed according to one jurist and denied by another; and where a relationship agreeable to one is prohibited by another.[24]

---

20 Ibid.

21 Ibid.

22 Ibid.

23 'Abd al Muta'āl al Ṣa'īdī, *Al Ḥurrīyah al Dīnīyah fī al Islām* (Religious Freedom in Islam) 2nd ed. (Cairo: Dār al Fikr al 'Arabī, n.d.), p. 46.

24 Muhammad Fathī 'Uthmān, *Dawlat al Fikrah allatī Aqāmahā Rasūl al Islām 'Aqib al Hijrah: Tajribah Mubakkirah li al Dawlah al Idiyūlūjīyah fī al Tārīkh* (The Ideological State Which the Messenger of Islam Established after the Immigration: An Early Attempt for an Ideological State in History) (Kuwait: Al Dār

The same thing had been observed long before by Ibn al Muqaffa'. He suggested to the *khalīfah,* al Manṣūr, that all these jurisprudential opinions be put together in a book with their supporting evidence and arguments. Then the *khalīfah* could decide which one to authorize, so that all judgments thereafter would be uniform and correct.[25]

It has been said that al Manṣūr tried to persuade Mālik to authorize his opinions in legal matters as laws for the state. Although Mālik wrote a book on the Sunnah and jurisprudence, *al Muwaṭṭa'* (The Accessible), he objected to any such authorization.[26]

Throughout Muslim history, ulama have served as Shari'ah court judges and provided *fatāwà* (legal and/or religious pronouncements). At times, this legislative function was partly undertaken by the Ottoman sultans, who used to issue orders and administrative regulations and would either appoint themselves or someone else to deal with matters of political and administrative interests.[27]

The parts of fiqh manuals dealing with the question of international relations - chapters on jihad and related matters such as *jizyah* and *siyar* - deal with issues that are highly political and can not be looked upon as simply enforcement or the carrying out of opinions of the ulama who had become increasingly removed from the center of power and decision making.[28]

---

al Kuwaytīyah, 1968), p.83.

[25] Subḥī Maḥmaṣānī, *Al Awḍā' al Tashrī'īyah fī al Duwal al 'Arabīyah: Māḍīhā wa Ḥāḍiruhā* (Legal Systems in the Arab States: Past and Present) 3rd rev. ed. (Beirut: Dār al 'Ilm li al Malāyīn, 1965), pp. 158-159.

[26] 'Uthmān, Op. Cit..

[27] See H. A. R. Gibb, *Studies on the Civilization of Islam,* ed. Stanford J. Shaw and William R. Polk (Boston: Beacon Press, 1962), pp.7-14, 148-149. H. A. R. Gibb, "Religion and Politics in Christianity and Islam," in J. Procter, *Islam and International Relations* (New York: Frederick A. Praeger, 1965), pp. 10-12. S. Maḥmaṣānī, *Al Awḍā' al Tashrī'īyah,* pp. 174-175. Thomas Naff, "The Setting and Rationale of Ottoman Diplomacy in the Reign of Selim III (1789-1807)," pp.3-4, unpublished paper made available to me by the author.

[28] See Ibn al Qayyim, *Aḥkām Ahl al Dhimmah,* ed. Ṣubḥī al Ṣāliḥ (Damascus: Maṭba'at Jāmi'at Dimashq, 1971), vol. IX, pp. 178 and 319. Al Shāfi'ī, *Al Umm,* vol. IV, pp. 82, 155, 170; and T. Naff, "The Setting of Ottoman Diplomacy," p.17.

Putting the pieces together, we may say that fiqh, as a whole, was an integral part of classical Muslim thought during the height of Islamic civilization known as the High Caliphate, generally considered to extend from 750 to 1100 AC. Fiqh was the most unifying and articulate element of the traditional way of life, serving to develop and regulate a highly successful society and civilization in terms of economic, political, social, moral, and legal needs. Fiqh and *siyar* were part of the methods and attitudes of the policy-making process, and it is as such that they should be considered major sources of Islamic law, but not the law itself.

Identifying fiqh as such will help to explain why contemporary Muslims feel the urge to reexamine the works of fiqh in the light of modern needs and challenges and in view of the spirit and goals of the Shari'ah. This is what is referred to as "reopening the door of ijtihad." This view will help in solving some conceptual difficulties concerning the position of the ulama in framing modern Muslim legislation.

The opinions of Muslim jurists are not and never have been law in the modern sense of the term; they were merely a source of law. The importance of fiqh was due, in turn, to its sources, the Qur'an and the Sunnah, with their tremendous influence on Muslims' psychology. Also, the propriety, suitability, or convenience of the opinion relative to Muslims' needs gave weight to this source.

The executive, legislative, and judicial functions of Muslim government during the High Caliphate or classical period were not well defined or systematically carried out. The relationship between these branches of government differed from one time to another, from one dynasty to another, and even from one caliph or sultan to another. In modern times, with the massive change in the structure and organization of the Muslim social system and the pressing need for far more precise and effective organization of the social system and government, modern Muslim political authority has begun to commit itself to Islamic ideals and goals, to develop its political base effectively along the same lines, and to reorganize and systemize the functions of the government. This can never be achieved without reforming the educational system and the constitutional system, incorporating both Islamic goals and values with modern needs and functions.

Certain assumptions for further thought proceed from this situation: the ulama and jurists will participate with and influence the modern legislator and provide him with ideas and opinions. Then, since juristic opinions would no longer be confused (as somehow at odds) with laws, misunderstanding, contradiction, and intolerance on the part of many sections of Muslim society would likely diminish. Hence, the traditional mechanism of government would function much more easily.

In chapter 2, the Islamic works of fiqh and *siyar* concerning jihad will be analyzed. Our purpose is to find out and to understand the Muslim framework for the subject and its dynamism as well as the extent to which Muslims' positive participation in the field of international relations is possible.

CHAPTER 2

THE CLASSICAL THEORY AND ENSUING DEVELOPMENTS

The Classical Theory of *Siyar*

The classical theory of *siyar* and jihad discussed here is gleaned from the pick of Muslim juristic opinions during the golden age of Islamic civilization or High Caliphate. These cover issues of external relations in the works of major Muslim jurists and thinkers like Muhammad ibn Ḥasan al Shaybānī, Muhammad ibn Idrīs al Shāfi'ī, Abū al Ḥasan al Māwardī, Abū Ḥāmid al Ghazālī, and Ibn Taymīyah.

The Nature of the Classical Muslim Theory

Before becoming involved in any analysis of the classical Muslim theory of relations among nations, it is essential that we identify what kind of theory it is, especially since the word "theory" has already been used to convey various meanings in the field of international relations.

In chapter 1, we demonstrated that the classical theory is a normative one. Simply stated, it rests on the authority of divine sources (the Qur'an and the Sunnah) and offers sets of values and standards which indicate how political actors ought to behave. As a matter of fact, the classical theory with its diversity of opinions presents through the works of fiqh the basic historical outlook of Muslims vis-à-vis their friends and foes, and in particular towards non-Muslim minorities, based on the ideological foundation of the Islamic mission.[1] This does not mean that Muslim rulers (caliphs and sultans) in all cases followed the classical theory to the letter. But due to the accepted authority of that theory, it was accorded great respect in shaping Muslim attitudes, policies, and actions for a long time.

Islamic works can be considered either as primary or documentary materials or as secondary materials. This depends on the kind of material sought, because for historical studies the basic works of fiqh, *sīrah*, and history like those by Ibn Hishām, al Ṭabarī and al Wāqidī are primary source and documentary materials. For the analysis of the contents of Islamic thought, faith, and ideology, the Qur'an and the basic elements of the Sunnah serve as the source and documentary materials, while works of fiqh, along with other works, serve as secondary materials. In assessing the content of the classical theory of external relations, works of fiqh will serve as a primary source, while in discussing the Islamic framework (chapter 4) fiqh materials will serve as a secondary source, and the Qur'an and the Sunnah will serve as primary sources.

Basic Definitions

We have already stated that Islamic studies in the field of international relations are full of conceptual confusion due to the failure to identify the function of fiqh as a source of law, and due to its role and significance in Muslim social life as the articulate reflection of Muslim intellectuals. In this way, fiqh did not represent the actual policies or regulations of the Muslim state, as the analysis of the internal relationship discussed earlier has shown. Some contemporary writers have reached erroneous conclusions simply because they did not realize the close relationship between the thinking of the jurists and the concrete social system laid down by the Prophet.

---

[1] See Edward Shils, "The Concept and Foundation of Ideology," *International Encyclopedia of the Social Sciences*, ed. David L. Sills (New York, Free Press, 1968), vol. VII, pp. 66-67; and James E. Dougherty and Robert L. Pfaltzgraff Jr., *Contending Theories of International Relations* (Philadelphia, J.B. Lippincott, 1971), pp. 25-28.

This makes it extremely difficult to generalize the various opinions put forth by different jurists. If any generalization is to be attempted at all, it has to be done with the utmost care. Thus, to obtain a real picture of High Caliphate thought and to rectify some faulty conclusions, we must take a closer look at the basic terms and definitions pertaining to international relations as preferred by Muslim jurists at the time.

Jihad, *Dār al Islām*, *Dār al 'Ahd*, and *Dār al Ḥarb*

These are four interrelated terms in Muslim thought and jurisprudence pertaining to the external relations of the classical Muslim society.

Jihad: In fulfilling his duties to promote and fulfill the cause of Islam, the Muslim should do his best to rectify wrongs. He must do so by his own actions; if he cannot, he must speak out against them; if he cannot he must oppose them in his heart. Jihad is not only an outward act; it is also an inward one to strengthen one's own self and correct one's own mistakes. This rule amply illustrates that jihad does not necessarily involve waging war (offensive or defensive). Different jurists have taken different positions in interpreting it, as will be shown in the succeeding discussion.

Dār al Islām refers to territories in which Muslims are free and secure.[2]

Dār al 'Ahd, alternately called ***Dār al Ṣulḥ,*** is a term that was coined by al Shāfi'ī to indicate non-Muslim territories involved in treaty agreements giving sovereignty to a Muslim state but maintaining local autonomy. These agreements were considered to extend Muslim jurisdiction with some tributory payment related to the land (*kharāj*) payable to a Muslim state to meet the *jizyah* stipulations, according to al Shāfi'ī.[3]

---

[2] See M. Hamidullah, *Muslim Conduct of State*, pp. 85, 129-131; and W. al Zuhaylī, *Āthār al Ḥarb*, pp. 192-196.

[3] Ibn al Qayyim, *Aḥkām Ahl al Dhimmah*, vol. II, pp. 475-490; and al Shāfi'ī, *al Umm*, vol. IV, pp. 103-104.

Dār al Ḥarb is the opposite of *Dār al Islām,* and refers primarily to non-Muslim territories hostile to Muslims and dangerous to their freedom and security.

Some writers, notably Majid Khadduri, have been responsible for a certain amount of confusion resulting from their tendency to be overly selective in their choice of interpretations of some jurists while neglecting others. Khadduri states that jihad was enjoined by God upon all believers to slay the polytheists wherever they may be found, in accordance with the Prophet's utterance to "fight polytheists until they say:'There is no god but God.'" Khadduri alleges that "in Islamic legal theory, jihad was a permanent obligation upon the believers to be carried out by a continuous process of warfare, psychological and political, even if not strictly military," until *Dār al Islām* overcomes *Dār al Ḥarb.* Moreover, he mentions that the "law of Islam" allows only brief spans of peace, guaranteed by a treaty, "not exceeding ten years in duration."[4]

Taking Khadduri's last point first, namely, the concept of a maximum duration of ten years for peace treaties, it seems that he depended for this point on al Shāfi'ī's strict position[5] but ignored the equally authoritative opinion of Abū Ḥanīfah. Ibn Qudāmah quotes Abū Ḥanīfah's argument on this point: "Since a peace treaty is a contract allowed for ten [years] then it is permissible to extend it in the same way as a contract [which has no such time restriction]... the interest of Muslims can be served in peace more so than in war ... the time period being specified in (units of) ten years means that it (also) applies to longer periods."[6]

Ibn Qudāmah and Ibn Rushd attributed to Mālik, Abū Ḥanīfah, and Ibn Ḥanbal (in one of several opinions attributed to him on the subject) the notion that the duration of a peace treaty could be unlimited depending on the interests of the

[4] M. Khadduri's Introduction to al Shaybānī, *The Islamic Law of Nations*, pp. 16-17.

[5] Al Shāfi'ī, Op. Cit., vol. IV, p. 109.

[6] Ibn Qudāmah, *al Mughnī*, vol. IX, p. 286. The meaning here is that since a treaty is a contract, it can be negotiated without time limits or on the basis of renewable time periods.

Muslim state.[7] This illustrates the diversity of opinions among the jurists. In such matters, no one opinion could be singled out as representative of Islamic law.

With regard to Khadduri's point concerning the polytheists, the scope of this term, and Muslims' intolerance of their existence, he admits that "polytheism seems to have been confined narrowly to paganism, with no implied concept of a supreme deity."[8] There is hardly a consensus on this definition. Again, Abū Ḥanīfah understands the term, as referred to in the Qur'an and the Sunnah, to mean only *Arab* polytheists. In an opinion attributed to Mālik, the same term is confined to only one Arab tribe, namely, Quraysh.[9] Al Awzā'ī, al Thawrī, and Mālik, in another opinion attributed to him,[10] considered the term, as referred to in the Qur'an and the Sunnah, in the historical context, maintaining that the term was no longer applicable to pagans. This position sheds light on the degree of tolerance the jurists allowed and illustrates the point that a jurist's opinion can be very far from a consensus of the Muslims.

Khadduri states that jihad, in Islamic legal theory, was a "permanent obligation upon the believers to be carried out by a continuous process."[11] He supports this point by quoting from the Qur'an and the Prophet's Sunnah. Such a quotation from the Qur'an and the Sunnah torn out of its context could easily mislead the reader who is aware of the supreme and final authority of these Islamic sources by making him believe that his understanding of jihad represents a simple and noncontroversial issue in Muslim jurisprudence.[12] Thus the reader could be left with the impression that Muslim jurists reached a consensus on jihad, an all-out, virtually permanent state of war, through which

---

[7] Ibid., Ibn Rushd, *Bidāyat al Mujtahid*, vol. I, p. 313; and W. al Zuhaylī, *Āthār al Ḥarb*, pp. 675-678.

[8] M. Khadduri, *War and Peace*, pp. 74-75.

[9] Ibn Qudāmah, Op. Cit., vol. IX, p. 195.

[10] Ibid.

[11] M. Khadduri, "Introduction" to al Shaybānī, *The Islamic Law of Nations*, p. 16; and M. Khadduri, *War and Peace*, pp. 74-75.

[12] Ibn Rushd, Op. Cit., vol. I, pp. 310-311.

Islam could be forced on most of humanity or, as Khadduri puts it, quoting the Prophet, "fight the polytheists until they say: 'There is no god but God.'"

This is, indeed, not the stand of all Muslim jurists. Many of them have tolerated those pagans who stuck to their beliefs. Upon paying *jizyah* they were not only to be left to pursue their life in peace but also to be protected by the Muslim state. Abū Ḥanīfah, for example, held that *jizyah* should be accepted from all polytheists except Arab pagans.[13] In an opinion attributed to Mālik, *jizyah* was accepted from all polytheists except the Quraysh. Furthermore, al Awzā'ī, al Thawrī, and Mālik advocated the opinion that *jizyah* is acceptable from all polytheists without exception.[14]

Khadduri's understanding and portrayal of the truce duration and of polytheism are not much different from his understanding and portrayal of jihad and of neutrality in Islam. This is not surprising since he relied basically on one juristic opinion, that of al Shāfi'ī. Again, Khadduri's conclusions pertaining to jihad and neutrality would have been valid had there been a consensus of opinion among Muslim jurists. As in the case of truce duration and tolerance toward polytheists, however, there is no consensus of opinion toward the nature of jihad and the presence of neutrality.

Ibn Rushd, better known in the West as Averroes, summarized a few of the various opinions of Muslim jurists on the issues of peace and war in Islam:

> Some of those who approved of peace whenver the imam finds it in the Muslims' interest are Mālik, al Shāfi'ī, and Abū Ḥanīfah. Al Shāfi'ī only does not approve of a peace duration longer that the period which the Prophet, peace be upon him, made with the nonbelievers...the reason for their differences in approving of peace without necessity is the apparent contradiction between His (Allah's) saying (in the Qur'an): "Then, when the sacred months have passed,

---

[13] Abū Ḥanīfah was the founder of the Ḥanafī school of jurisprudence and the teacher of al Shaybānī, the author of the classic work of *Siyar, Kitāb al Siyar al Kabīr* (The Detailed Work of *al Siyar*). The famous commentator on that work, al Sarakhsī, belonged to the Ḥanafī school.

[14] Ibn Qudāmah, Op. Cit., vol. IX, p. 193; and W. al Zuḥaylī, Op. Cit., pp. 712-715.

slay the idolators wherever ye find them," and "Fight those who believe not in Allah nor the Last Day," and His saying: "If they incline to peace, incline thou also to it and trust in Allah." Those who considered that the verse of fighting abrogates the verse of peace did not approve of peace except out of necessity. Those who considered that the verse of peace places limits on that verse (of fighting) did approve of peace if the imam was in favor of it.[15]

This amply demonstrates that jurists approve of peace with non-Muslims even when there is no necessity and for unlimited durations.

Besides Abū Ḥanīfah's favorable position toward peace, al Sarakhsī puts forth the position of al Thawrī, shared by many other juristic authorities such as ibn 'Umar, 'Aṭā', 'Amr ibn Dīnār, and Ibn Shibrimah: "Fighting the idolators is not an obligation unless the initiative comes from them. Then, they must be fought in fulfillment of His (Allah's) clear instructions: 'If they fight you, kill them,' and His saying: 'And fight all the idolators as they fight you.'"[16]

Finally, Khadduri's impression that there is an absence of a concept of neutrality in Islam stems, to a large degree, from his understanding of jihad.[17] Since his understanding of jihad was shown not to be universally held by all jurists, it must follow that his conclusions pertaining to the concept of neutrality, which is inextricably connected with jihad, were also not universally held.[18] Moreover, his interpretation of historical cases as neutralization rather than neutrality may not hold true.

In fact, Hamidullah and al Zuḥaylī have reached quite different conclusions. Through their study of the Qur'an and the Sunnah, they have interpreted the same historical cases as

---

[15] Ibn Rushd, Op. Cit., vol. I, p. 313.

[16] Ibn Qudāmah, Op. Cit., vol. IX, pp. 286-287; al Shaybānī, *al Siyar*, vol. I, p.190-191; and W. al Zuḥaylī, Op. Cit., pp. 86-87.

[17] M. Khadduri, *War and Peace*, pp. 251-267; M. Khadduri's introduction to al Shaybānī, *The Islamic Law of Nations*, pp. 18-19.

[18] For the text of the opposing point of view of Sufyān al Thawrī and Abū Ḥanīfah vis-à-vis al Sarakhsī and al Shāfi'ī, see above. See also M. al Ṭabarī, *Jāmi' al Bayān*, vol. II, pp. 189-190.

evidence for neutrality in Islam.[19] The lesson to be learned from the above discourse is simply that one should be extremely careful when quoting the basic Islamic sources of the Qur'an and the Sunnah and generalizing about Muslim classical thought. This would not only help one avoid any misrepresentation but would also help one attain a better understanding of the Muslim mentality and its relationship to modern thinking and institutions in the field of international relations.

Jihad, as the duty to pursue what is true and right, includes protection of the human rights of life, belief, honor, family, and education. The highest purpose of jihad is to change one's own life so that one will pursue these rights in submission to Allah. The second highest purpose is to defend the rights of others. Jihad in this second sense is also the pursuit of justice for everyone, always, everywhere; and the substance of justice is human rights.

At this point, conceptually speaking, it is very important for us to realize that one cannot deny the existence of any political institution in Islam by the mere fact that it was not historically dominant. The rise of any political institution is a result of the interaction between a doctrine and its environment. If there were no need or practical possibility for a particular institution at one time, then this should not be taken as conclusive evidence of the impossibility of its coming into existence under different circumstances.

Al 'Ahd and *al Amān*

A host of terms in the Arabic language commonly mean agreement or treaty; *'ahd* (pledge), *hudnah* or *muwāda'ah* (truce), *mu'āhadah* (treaty), *mīthāq* (covenant or pact), *ṣulḥ* (peace treaty), and *ḥilf* (alliance) are a few examples.[20]

Legally speaking, *'ahd* indicates consent on lawful matters and the obligation to fulfill the terms of a contract by the

---

[19] M. Hamidullah, Op. Cit., pp. 285-300; and W. al Zuḥaylī, Op. Cit., pp. 197-220.

[20] Ibn Qayyim al Jawzīyah, *Aḥkām Ahl al Dhimmah*, vol. II, p. 475; Ibn Qudāmah, Op. Cit., vol. IX, pp. 284-292; al Shāfi'ī, *al Umm*, vol. IV, pp. 109-114.

respective parties. Jurists advise termination of the *'ahd* either in case of breach of agreement and unilateral renunciation by the other party, and/or in case the terms of agreement are known to violate *al shar'* (lawful standards). The content of the agreement and the concerned juristical school determine the legality or illegality of the *'ahd* in question. For example, if the political authority concluded a truce for more than ten years, there would be no automatic juristic fiat concerning its legality. While al Shāfi'ī would invalidate it for the extra period beyond ten years, others, such as Ḥanafī jurists, would disagree with al Shāfi'ī's opinion. The act of pronouncing the renunciation of the agreement on the Muslim side is called *nabdh*. Muslim jurists do not agree to any unilateral renunciation of the *'ahd* on the part of the Muslims merely on the basis of suspecting that the other party will breach the *'ahd*. Such an action has to be based on a clear case of breach of agreement. With the exception of the Ḥanafī school, jurists do not approve of Muslims initiating the breach of any lawful agreement. If the other party breaches the agreement, with or without being aware of its act, the Muslim party has to inform the other party of the termination of the agreement on the part of the Muslims, unless the other party attacks the Muslims first.[21]

Because of their attitude toward jihad as a means of spreading Islam, some Ḥanafīs would advise the political authority to renounce a truce unilaterally whenever circumstances change to the Muslims' favor. Since they believe that the interests of Islam are best served by undertaking jihad, it behooves the imam, as circumstances change, to renounce the truce (*yanbudh ilayhim*) unilaterally. Other jurists, however, do not agree with this interpretation of *nabdh* because it constitutes a breach of the agreement. To them, the Muslims' interest is a consideration at the time of concluding the agreement, but not

---

[21] See Fakhr al Dīn al Rāzī, *al Tafsīr al Kabīr* (Cairo: 'Abd al Raḥmān Muḥammad, 1938), vol. XV, pp.182-183; al Shāfi'ī, Op. Cit., vol IV, pp. 107-109; al Shaybānī, Op. Cit., vol. I, pp. 190-191; M. al Ṭabarī, *Jāmi' al Bayān 'an Ta'wīl Āy al Qur'ān* (Cairo: Muṣṭafā al Bābī, 1945), vol. X, pp. 26-27.

after that.[22] The *'ahd* was a major diplomatic vehicle which jurists discussed and utilized in order to regulate various aspects of foreign affairs such as peace agreements. Along with *amān* (safe conduct or pledge of security) and *dhimmah* (constitutional agreement with non-Muslim minorities), *'ahd* was also used to facilitate political, cultural, and social communications as well as to regulate trade with non-Muslim peoples and territories.

Al Amān: While political issues of truce, peace, and constitutional agreements with non-Muslims were reserved to the political authorities, professional, economic, and trade matters were, according to classical jurisprudence, permitted to individual Muslim men and women, via *amān*, to decide and conduct on their own. The majority of jurists consider this the right of individual adult Muslims.[23]

With the exception of the Ḥanbalīs, jurists tended to favor the non-Muslims while they were in Muslim lands with regard to their economic interests, social practices, and criminal offences.[24] They demanded that Muslims be fair and ethical with non-Muslims when the latter entered Muslim territories under the pact of *amān*. With *amān*, communication and exchange were made very easy between Muslim and non-Muslim territories.

Al Mushrikūn, al Dhimmah, and *al Jizyah*

The word *mushrikūn* derives from the word *shirk*. Literally, it means making partners; religiously, it refers to the attribution of partners or associates to Allah. In many places in the Qur'an and the Sunnah this term connotes investing associates and partners

---

[22] al Shāfi'ī, Op. Cit., vol. IV, p. 107; al Sarakhsī, *Sharḥ al Siyar*, pp. 187-191; W. al Zuḥaylī, Op. Cit., pp. 358-362.

[23] See Ibn Qudāmah, Op. Cit., vol. IX, pp. 226-233, 284, 312-313; Mālik, *(bi riwāyat)* Saḥnūn, *al Mudawwanah al Kubrā* (Cairo: Matba'at al Sa'ādah, 1965) vol. II, pp. 41-42; M. Khadduri's introduction to *The Islamic Law of Nations*, p. 53; al Shāfi'ī, Op. Cit., vol. IV, pp. 145-146, 196-197; al Shaybānī, Op. Cit., vol. I, p. 306; W. al Zuḥaylī, Op. Cit., pp. 220-334.

[24] M. Khadduri, Op. Cit., pp. 170-174; Ibn Rushd, Op. Cit., vol. I, pp. 308-309; al Shāfi'ī, Op. Cit., vol. IV, pp. 196-197, 290-291, 325-326.

with Allah's divinity. The verses and traditions pertaining to the Muslims' attitudes and conduct in their relations with different groups of *mushrikūn* are most important to this discussion.

In their attempt to settle the intricate issues of who the *mushrikūn* are and who fits in what category, the jurists differed sharply. In terms of theory, at least, their differences were serious. To begin with, the absence of theoretical analysis in classical jurisprudence led to a lack of understanding as to what precisely the term *mushrikūn* meant. The varying definitions given to this term led, in turn, to conceptual contradictions.

Jurists classified *mushrikūn* into two basic categories: the People of the Book and the pagans. According to different jurists, each category would include or exclude some non-Muslim groups. The People of the Book (*ahl al kitāb*) would, in all cases, include the Jews and the Christians. Some jurists went into lengthy discussions as to which specific groups were Jews or Christians.[25] The Magians (Zoroastrians) were treated as People of the Book, either on the assumption that they did have a revealed book or because of the Prophet's tradition ordering that they be treated as People of the Book. The People of the Book were allowed and guaranteed freedom of faith upon the payment of *jizyah*.

The term *mushrikūn* could either be stretched to include all non-Muslims except the People of the Book or be limited according to the different schools of classical jurisprudence to mean the Arab pagans or only the Arab tribe of Quraysh. The jurists also differed on how to treat pagans. Some would give them no choice other than to accept Islam. If they refused, they should be fought. Others would accept *jizyah* from them, thus treating them as the People of the Book.

The position of forcing some groups of *mushrikūn* to convert to Islam and the administering of capital punishment for apostasy was, unless it is correctly understood, bound to result in tense relations with non-Muslim communities. The methodology of abrogation enabled jurists to put certain Qur'anic verses relating to basic conceptions into a deep sleep. Modern interpreters,

---

[25] Ibn Qudāmah, Op. Cit., vol. IX, pp. 194-195.

however, have tried to bring these verses and the concepts to which they relate back into focus. They have reintroduced the issue of apostasy and peace, but they have lacked consistency and methodological systematization, and have therefore failed to bring about a comprehensive conceptual treatment of these inter-related issues.

Al Dhimmah: In classical jurisprudence, this term is defined as a sort of permanent agreement between Muslim political authorities and non-Muslim subjects which provides protection for Muslims and peaceful internal relations with the non-Muslim subjects. In return, the latter accepted Islamic rule and paid the *jizyah* as a substitution for being drafted into the army. Jurists were fully aware that, in turn, the Muslim state was obliged not only to tolerate with sincerity the non-Muslims' faith, religious practices and laws, but also to provide them with protection for their lives and properties: "Their blood is as our blood and their possessions are as ours."[26]

Generally speaking, it is obvious that there was no compulsion in religion. To those jurists who advocated jihad as a permanent duty to be initiated by Muslims, *al dhimmah* enabled Muslims to reach out to non-Muslims. Upon realizing the positive meaning of Islam with its social justice, non-Muslims would be in a better position to judge Islam. Those who were determined to keep their faith, however, could do so.

The conceptual confusion about jihad led to confusion on the part of some jurists as to the meaning and significance of *al dhimmah* and *al jizyah*. Ibn Qayyim al Jawzīyah (1291-1351 AC) agreed that since *al dhimmah* agreements require non-Muslims to pay *jizyah*, these agreements were meant to punish the non-believers. This opinion reflected the prevailing tense relationship between Muslims and others.

Ibn Qayyim's position can be explained on three grounds: first, the cumulative effect of centuries of tension in communal

---

[26] Ibn Qudāmah, Op. Cit., vol. IX, pp. 271-272; Muhammad ibn Ismā'īl, *Subul al Salām; Sharh Bulūgh al Marām* (Cairo: al Matba'ah al Tijārīyah al Kubrā, n.d.) vol IV, p. 65.

relationships within the Muslims' territories;[27] second, the effects of the Mongol and Crusaders' invasions; and third, the general confusion in understanding the theoretical bases of Islam.

In their understanding of early Muslim history, the jurists seemed to be impressed more by the conflicts and animosity between Muslims and non-Muslims than by other elements of Islam. Jurists therefore neglected the many elements which relate to the real meaning of the Islamic mission. For instance, in discussing the relationships between Muslims and non-Muslims, the jurists unduly focused on the word *ṣāghir* which means vanquished or overpowered. This term was mentioned in the Qur'an in the context of hostilities between Muslims and non-Muslims. At the same time, the jurists overlooked the significance of the *dhimmah* agreement between the Prophet and the Christians of Najrān, and the constitutional agreement (*ṣahīfat al Madīnah*) between the Prophet and the Jewish tribes of Madīnah. These agreements, and not the word *ṣāghirūn* alone, should have been taken to portray the state of affairs of the Muslims' relations with non-Muslims.[28]

Ibn al Qayyim's opinion illustrates this absence of a comprehensive theoretical conceptualization of the idea of Muslim society. Classical jurists committed this mistake because of their partial and descriptive study of Islam through the Sunnah which, in turn, led them to think of micro rather than macro aspects of the social system. This point will be pursued further in the next chapter.

Jizyah: The above discussion shows that *jizyah* is an integral part of the *dhimmah* agreements. In this sense, *jizyah* is a sort of taxation of non-Muslim subjects in return for services rendered by the state.

---

[27] Subḥī al Ṣāliḥ, editorial introduction to the work of Ibn al Qayyim, *Aḥkām Ahl al Dhimmah*, vol. I, pp. 8-9, 17; Ibn al Qayyim, Op. Cit., vol. I, pp. 23-25; M. Khadduri, *War and Peace*, pp. 176-177; Ibn Rushd, Op. Cit., vol. I, p. 328; Ibn Qudāmah, Op. Cit., vol. IX, pp. 285-289; al Shāfi'ī, Op. Cit., vol. IV, pp. 110-112.

[28] See Ibn al Qayyim, Op. Cit., vol. II, pp. 22-25; al Shāfi'ī, *al Umm*, vol. IV, pp. 97-99.

The term *jizyah* has been used, however, to connote more than taxation of *ahl al dhimmah*. In the case of *muwāda'ah* (truce), *jizyah* could be paid in order to bring about an end to the fighting. Its payment indicated the serious desire on the part of the enemy to cease hostilities against *dār al Islām*. As such, it did not necessitate offering protection or extending Muslim law. In this sense, *jizyah* can be looked upon as a tribute. In the case of *'ahd*, which requires extension of Muslim jurisprudence but not necessarily protection, *jizyah* is a payment related to land and is called *kharāj*.[29]

Many aspects of *jizyah* were discussed earlier in this chapter. Now the amount of *jizyah* will be discussed. Some jurists, guided by the Prophet's tradition, opted to fix the maximum and the minimum allowable. Others specified only the minimum, while still others left the amount to the discretion of the political authority.[30]

Jizyah was generally collectable only from breadwinners. The poor, women, children, the aged, monks, the blind, *et cetera*, were not liable to pay *jizyah*. Unlike zakāh (the tax collected from every Muslim except the poor), *jizyah* was not allocated for specific purposes. It was left to the political authority to decide how to put the money to use.[31] This may explain the lack of enthusiasm on the part of some Muslim rulers upon seeing converts joining Islam. To many of them conversion was no more than a loss of forthcoming government revenues.

At this point it may be advisable to raise some questions pertaining to the nature of Islamic law and the concept of equality among nations in Muslim external relationships. Some writers have dealt with these questions in haste and confusion. It is claimed that Islamic law, unlike modern Western law, is personal and not territorial. It is also claimed that the Islamic theory and law of nations, as well as those of medieval Christianity, would not provide for the modern concept of

---

[29] al Farrā', *al Aḥkām al Sulṭāniyah*, ed. by M. H. al Fiqī (Cairo: Muṣṭafā al Bābī, 1966), pp. 153-209; al Shāfi'ī, Op. Cit., vol. IV, pp. 103-104.

[30] Ibn Rushd, Op. Cit., vol. I, p. 327.

[31] Ibid., vol. I, pp. 326-327, 329.

equality among sovereign nations which is the basis of a true international system.

In many ways the argument is confused and arbitrary. It is plausible only if it is logically sound to mix the actual historical relations with some classical juristic opinions and/or with some synoptic quotations from the Qur'an and the Sunnah. Such a process could lead to any desirable conclusion or theory a writer wishes to prove. This may explain the unbridgeable gulf among writers, especially if they subscribe to different ideologies or cultures. In this way, it is easy to view Islam as an outdated and rigid set of traditions.

As far as Muslim law is concerned, we can deduce from the above discussions that the classic Muslim thinkers of the High Caliphate worked out a complex system to govern external relations. In a close examination of Muslim thought pertaining to *al dhimmah, dār al Islām, dār al ḥarb,* and *dār al 'ahd,* we find Muslim concepts of territorial and personal laws working side by side in the direction of a theoretical system of governance that is basically a constitutional or treaty agreement that provides for pluralistic arrangements in government structure and the decentralization of political power. These Muslim concepts of territorial and personal laws together enabled non-Muslim communities as subjects of Muslim states to enjoy autonomy in running their religious and personal affairs.

In the area of public law, or in the case of conflict of laws, the Shari'ah was applicable. This was the arrangement worked out between the Prophet and the Jewish tribes in the early Madīnan period of the Muslim state. The arrangement with the Christians of Najrān (about 10AH/631AC), which was effective until the death of the Prophet, offered even territorial autonomy and self-government to the people of Najrān. The same concepts caused Muslim jurists to require Muslims, while in territories under non-Muslim rule, to abide by the Shari'ah in running their affairs. At the same time, Muslims were advised not to violate the laws and practices prevailing in these territories. The jurists were in fact making room for the human and personal elements involved in the process. They would not mind non-Muslims raising pigs and eating pork in Muslim territories, but they would object to non-Muslims engaging in, for example, usurious contracts that violated the Islamic concern for social justice.

Just as they would not permit Muslims to violate non-Muslim public law, they would strongly object to Muslims being forced to violate their Islamic personal law. As far as public law was concerned, jurists would object only to Muslims engaging in or being forced to engage in activities not sanctioned by the Shari'ah. In any case, they would advise Muslims to observe their own laws as much as possible without offending foreign authorities. Basically, this kind of arrangement does not conclusively divide the affairs into personal and territorial realms. The modern state system badly needs the introduction of the concept of personal law to accommodate the cultural and religious needs of subjects, especially those with minority status.

Equality is a more difficult problem. We will develop the argument gradually in order to clarify some of the confusion in the field. If we understand the history of the High Caliphate or classical period, a time when almost all nations were hostile toward the Islamic state, and then if we take into account the fact that all external relations by their very nature involve more than one sovereign state, then clearly it was not the Muslims alone who determined the kinds of relationships that prevailed in those days. Still, it is possible that the "hawkish" interpretation of jihad played a minor role in bringing about the kinds of relationships that existed during the classical period.[32]

At the same time, Muslim thought in the High Caliphate exhibited some "dovish" tendencies, which could be considered a suitable framework for introducing the notion of equality among nations. These include the authoritative interpretations of

---

[32] The following examples illustrate the juristic difference on the issue of jihad. 1. "Fighting against non-Muslims is not an obligation unless the non-Muslims started the war; then it is an obligation to fight them..." al Shaybānī, *al Siyar*, vol. I, p. 187; 2. "If the Muslims have enough strength, I would advise that not a year should pass in which (the Imam) does not send an army or make an attack into the non-Muslim territories, without harming the Muslims...and the minimum allowed is that not a year should pass without (the Imam) sending an expedition (against non-Muslim territories), so that jihad would not be suspended any year without a serious excuse." al Shāfi'ī, *al Umm*, vol. IV, p. 90; See also, Ibn Rushd, Op. Cit., vol. I, p. 313.

jihad by such jurists as Abū Ḥanīfah and al Thawrī. These jurists interpreted jihad in defensive terms that could serve as a proper theoretical base for the development of a law among nations that defines the relations among them in terms of peace and equality. Although this was the case with one important section of Muslim thought, the underlying nature of the actual relationships among the social systems of the major powers did not allow the fruition of this notion. These powers never accepted the emergence and rise of the Muslim state or its ideals, and they certainly never accepted the concept of free choice of belief and religion for their subjects. Instead, they persecuted and punished any one of their subjects who accepted Islam. Therefore, we could say that at least a notable section of classical Muslim thought during its period of global ascendancy was compatible with the notion of equality among nations. This may partially explain the apparent ease with which Muslims have accepted the notion of equality in modern times, and how they still search for ways and means to update the Islamic framework in the field of relations among nations.

The turning point in adopting the notion of equality in relations among nations came with the breakdown of the medieval European Christian social system, the development of Europe's industrial power, and its attendant political control over most of the world. The new European state system was introduced to the rest of the world, and the latter, confronted by superior European power, had no real choice but to adopt it.

With this broad and realistic understanding, there is place neither for accusation nor for exaggerated claims either against or for Islam. Likewise, the Muslim objection that adaptation to the new circumstances might result in loss of identity is also out of place.

Khalīfah, Amīr al Mu'minīn, Imam, and Sultan

These four terms denote political power and authority in the Muslim state and society. All of them, with the exception of the term sultan, were used in a broader sense than the merely political.

Khalīfah (Caliph): In the general Qur'anic sense, this term is an expression of the concept that man was given the ability to manage and control his world as a trust through which he achieves what he is worth and thus decides his eternal destiny in the hereafter. With this in mind, we can better understand the pronouncement of the *khalīfah* al Manṣūr that he was the *khalīfah* of Allah and His shadow on earth.[33] The *khalīfah,* unlike the Pope (the Vicar of Christ), is bound by the Shari'ah (based on the Qur'an and the Sunnah) and has no authority to modify doctrine. His pronouncements represent no more than the attempt to buttress the power and authority of his office under the Shari'ah rather than the individual's exercise of authority among his subjects.[34] In Muslim political thought, *khalīfah* actually indicates the role of the first *khalīfah,* Abū Bakr, *Khalīfat Rasūl Allāh* (successor of the Prophet as head of the Muslim community). In this sense, the *khalīfah* is assumed to take over the leadership of Muslim society. Of course the function of prophecy ended with the death of Muḥammad, and no such function was ever to be associated with the office of the *khalīfah.*

Imam, in contrast with the term *Amīr al Mu'minīn* (Commander of the Faithful, that is, the caliph) signifies leadership with more emphasis on the spiritual affairs of the community. In this sense, a Muslim leading a congregational prayer or a pious Islamic intellectual authority is also called an imam.[35]

The literal meaning of the Arabic word sultan is power or authority. In a political sense, this word signifies power rather

---

[33] Sir Thomas W. Arnold, *The Caliphate*, with a concluding chapter by Sulbia G. Haim (New York: Barnes & Noble, 1965), p. 51: See also, al Farrā', Op. Cit.

[34] 'Abbās Maḥmūd al 'Aqqād, *Ḥaqā'iq al Islām wa Abāṭīl Khuṣūmih* (Cairo: Dār al Qalam, 1966), pp. 236-253; Abū al A'lā al Mawdūdī, *Naẓarīyat al Islām wa Hadyuhu*, trans. from Urdu by Jalīl Ḥasan al Iṣlāḥī (Beirut: Dār al Fikr, 1967), pp. 48-52; Abū Ya'qūb al Anṣārī, *Muqaddimat Kitāb al Kharāj*, in *Nuṣūṣ al Fikr al Siyāsī al Islāmī; al Imāmah 'inda Ahl al Sunnah*, ed. Yusūf Ibish (Beirut: Dār al Ṭalī'ah, 1966), pp. 11-14; A. Hourani, *Arab Thought in the Liberal Age* (London: Oxford University Press, 1970), pp. 14-15; E. J. Rosenthal, *Political Thought in Medieval Islam* (Cambridge University Press, 1958), pp. 21-27; Muhammad Abū Zahrah, *al Mujtama' al Insānī fī Ẓill al Islām* (Beirut: Dār al Fikr, n.d.), pp. 167-170; al Qarāfī, *al Iḥkām*, pp. 84-97; Ibn Kathīr, *Tafsīr al Qur'ān*, vol. I, pp. 70-72; vol. II, pp. 199-200; vol. III, pp. 522-524; T. W. Arnold, Op. Cit., pp. 10-22, 52-57, 170, and 195-197.

[35] See Ibn Kathīr, *Tafsīr al Qur'ān*, vol. III, p. 330.

than the spiritual leadership of the community.[36]

It is not our intention to give a complete description of the development of the institution of *khalīfah*. What concerns us here is the role of the jurists in the development of Muslim political thought with regard to power and authority in Islamic society and the issues of political unity.

In many ways, the basic political thought of Muslim jurists concerning the office of the *khalīfah* was idealistic. They showed great concern about the ability of the office of the *khalīfah* to serve the ideological cause of Islam.[37] The Prophet used all the political power at his disposal to create and develop the Muslim community and state. At the very moment of the Prophet's death, however, Muslim society was shaken by the rebellion of numerous desert Arab tribes. At this point, the Muslim elite (with respect to character, leadership, experience, and sacrifice rather than to wealth and class) in Madīnah (*al Muhājirūn*, the Meccan immigrants) used the political office of the *khalīfah* as an instrument to hold together and consolidate Muslim society. Their rationale was that the appointment of a member of Quraysh, the Prophet's tribe, as the head of state would help secure allegiance from the entire Arab people.[38] Abū Bakr immediately sent Muslim armies to counter all insurrections on strict orders "to accept nothing from anyone except Islam" and the payment of zakāh. Then, without exception, the Muslim elite sided with Abū Bakr in his effort to maintain the integrity of the Muslim state.[39]

The civil war which erupted approximately three decades later between 'Alī and Mu'āwiyah provides another example

---

[36] See E. J. Rosenthal, *Political Thought in Medieval Islam*, pp. 8, 38-39, 54, 241-242, and 244ff; see also an Arabic dictionary article on *sa-la-ta* in Muhammad ibn Abū Bakr al Rāzī, *Mukhtār al Ṣiḥāḥ* (Cairo: Muṣṭafā al Bābī al Ḥalabī, 1950), p. 330.

[37] E. J. Rosenthal, Op. Cit., p. 27; H. A. R. Gibb, *The Civilization of Islam*, pp. 148-149; and T. W. Arnold, *The Caliphate*, pp. 11, 25.

[38] Ibn Hishām, *al Sīrah*, vol. II, pp. 657-660; Ibn al Athīr, *al Kāmil fī al Tārīkh* (Beirut: Dār Beirut li al Ṭibā'ah wa al Nashr, 1965) vol. II, p. 327.

[39] Muhammad Hamidullah, *Majmū'at al Wathā'iq al Siyāsīyah li al 'Ahd al Nabawī*, 3rd rev. ed. (Beirut: Dār al Irshād, 1959), pp. 29, 287-305.

of the Islamic elite's stand in favor of central authority. Basically, the Islamic elite and the jurists were leaning toward 'Alī and his Islamic sentiments. Some of the groups, however, like the Khawārij who initially supported 'Alī, were not prepared to be disciplined by submitting to a central authority. Hence the Ummawīs gained the upper hand, as the Islamic elite and the jurists eventually supported them for the reason that they, the Ummawīs, were in a better position to maintain the centrality and unity of the Muslim state.[40]

Theoretically, Muslim jurists advocated a central idealistic Islamic authority. Out of discretion, however, at times they upheld the status quo, even though it might not have been up to the level of their expectations. The lessons of history had led many jurists to believe that drastic reforms led to revolution, and that revolution would bring about bloodshed and civil war which, in turn, would be destructive to Muslim society. So the Sunni Muslim juristic authorities supported the ideal of the *khalīfah*. But often, whether out of necessity or expediency, they had also to lend their support to authorities who represented something less than the ideal. Still, in their favor it may be said that they often played the role of loyal opposition.[41] Generally speaking, however, the jurists used every possible argument to support central governance and to maintain the political unity of the state in the service of the Shari'ah.[42]

When the Turks and Mamlukes assumed political power, with the attendant weakening of the *khalīfah*, the jurists began turning to the masses in order to maintain the characteristics of an already deep-rooted Islamic identity in society. Their appeal to the people was to support the cause of Islam and to influence the political authorities in that direction even though, traditionally, the authorities claimed loyalty and submission to the

---

[40] See H. A. R. Gibb, Op. Cit., pp. 7-14.

[41] See T. W. Arnold, Op. Cit., p. 25.

[42] E. J. Rosenthal, Op. Cit., pp. 27-47.

Shari'ah in order to obtain the loyalty of the masses.[43]

The courageous stand taken by Ibn Taymīyah in his writings and the position of jurists such as al 'Izz ibn 'Abd al Salām in favor of the Shari'ah exemplify the roles which classical Islamic intellectuals played in the service of Islam and the Muslim peoples.

It is also worth noting that Islamic thought during the High Caliphate tried to reconcile the power struggle between the center and the growing regional units. Muslim jurists gave initial approval to the existence of more than one legitimate independent political unit and authority. Some jurists approved of this when the units were far apart geographically and thus difficult to run under a single administration. The jurists no longer paid much attention to the question of the office of the *khalīfah* when it could no longer be preserved.[44]

Historical and Psychological Background of Classical Muslim Thought in International Relations

Many of the modern writers who study Muslim history tend to look at the immediate physical environment in order to explain history. For example, they stress economic and demographic factors as the reason behind the fast-moving territorial expansion of early Islam. But this oversimplified approach will inevitably lead to faulty perceptions and misleading conclusions.[45] The similarities between the two situations in terms of

---

[43] See E. J. Rosenthal, Op. Cit., pp. 27, 32-35, 51; H. A. R. Gibb, Op. Cit., pp. 4-22, 141-149, 151-164; Muḥammad Ḍiyā' al Dīn, *al Naẓarīyah al Siyāsīyah al Islāmīyah*, 4th ed. (Cairo: Dār al Ma'ārif, 1967), pp. 71, 92-112.

[44] Imām al Ḥaramayn al Juwaynī, *Fasl fī 'Aqd al Imāmah li Shakhṣayn*, in Yūsuf Ibish, Op. Cit., p. 279.

[45] Arnold Toynbee, *Civilization on Trial* and *The World and the West* (Cleveland: World Publishing Co., 1958), p. 325; Francesco Gabrielli, *Muhammad and the Conquests of Islam*, translated from the Italian by V. Luling and R. Linnel (New York: McGraw Hill, 1968), pp. 103-115; J. Hell, *al Ḥaḍārah al 'Arabīyah*, translated from German by I. al 'Adawī and edited by H. Mu'nis (Cairo: Maktabat al Anjlū al Miṣrīyah, 1956), pp. 12-14; John L. Lamonte, *al Harb al Salībīyah*, in *Dirāsāt Islāmīyah*, ed. Nicola Ziyādah (Beirut: Dār al Andalūs, 1960), pp. 103-140; T. W. Arnold, Op. Cit., pp. 23-24; Wilfred Cantwell Smith, *Islam in Modern History* (Princeton, New Jersey: Princeton University Press, 1957), pp. 6-35.

physical appearance or circumstances are themselves not enough to determine why various groups and individuals took a specific course of action. Social, psychological, as well as historical factors decide what attitudes shape the life and history of a nation. We must keep this aspect in mind when studying classical Muslim thought if we are to correctly understand its attitudes, methods, and significance.

We have already indicated that the deep religious concerns espoused by the jurists helped in maintaining the Muslim community and state. In studying the history of the office of the *khalīfah*, one cannot fail to discern the jurists' public role and involvement in pursuing that goal. In reading the works and history of jurists such as Mālik, al Shāfi'ī, al Ghazālī, al Māwardī, and Ibn Taymīyah, one may clearly discern the influence of political and social factors upon their work. Chief among these was their awareness of the importance of a central political authority as an instrument for averting civil and sectarian conflicts. Indeed, the jurists showed realistic and flexible attitudes regarding the issues of political power and authority. Their ideological convictions and the effect of immediate social and political factors upon their thinking do not need further discussion here, for writers on the subject have already shown remarkable awareness of these aspects.

What we would like to bring up, however, is the deep-seated psychological influence on the jurists of the historical experience represented by the life of the Prophet and the sequence of events that followed closely afterwards. Without a clear awareness of this aspect, it will be very difficult to understand the viewpoint of Muslims in their relationships with non-Muslims. For example, without this awareness we can hardly hope to understand the fears the jurists had of the Byzantines. "Can you not see that if you did not fight, Islam would have been destroyed? What would the Byzantines have done?"[46] Most Muslim writers consulted here perceived the first generations of Muslims as

---

[46] Attributed to Aḥmad ibn Ḥanbal. This quotation is mentioned by Ibn Qudāmah, *al Mughnī*, vol. IX, p. 183. Similar feelings were expressed by Imam Mālik. See Mālik (as related by Saḥnūn), *al Mudawwanah al Kubrā* (Cairo: Maṭba'at al Sa'ādah, 1905), vol. IV, p. 5.

weak and endangered people in relation to the non-Muslim world. Many orientalists have handily dismissed this perception as being an apologetic attitude. The oversimplifed explanation that their perception was the result of a persecution complex may very well be inaccurate. There is hardly any logical ground for doubting the sincerity of all of these Muslim writers. Analysis of the Muslim psychological make-up may provide further explanation.

The psychological effect of the early Muslim historical experience, as it was recorded in the memory of Muslims, is an important factor in explaining the attitude of Muslims regarding external relations. The same factor explains the excessive use of the concept of abrogation of Qur'anic verses and of historical precedents that tended to provide a less friendly outlook toward non-Muslims. Furthermore, this psychological reaction to hostility and danger contributes to an explanation of the tendency on the part of Muslim intellectuals toward micro rather than macro analysis of the social system. This last point is reserved for the last chapter, since it is concerned more with the issue of methodology than with the content of thought. The point to be stressed here is that abrogation served to strengthen and legitimize the psychological impact of that historical experience.

The Qur'an, the collections of hadith, and the biography of the Prophet give the impression that the conflict during the early Islamic era was between unselfish, justice-seeking, persecuted Muslims and self-centered, corrupt, oppressive non-Muslim authorities. It is hard for Western writers to fathom the psychological effect of the events that took place during the early Islamic era.[47] This, coupled with the repercussions these events had on the relations between Muslims and non-Muslims, makes it imperative to relate some of them. This helps us to better understand not only the events themselves but also Muslims'

---

[47] See Bernard Lewis, *The Arabs in History* (NY: Harper & Row, 1960), pp. 42-48; Carl Brockelmann, *History of the Islamic Peoples*, translated by J. Carmichael and M. Perlman (NY: Enpriam Books edition, 1960), pp. 22-25; Norman Daniel, *Islam and the West* (Edinburgh, UK: Edinburgh University Press, 1960), pp. 229-307; and Montgomery Watt, *What is Islam?* (NY: Frederick A. Praeger, 1968), p.8.

reaction to non-Muslims, which has basically been one of animosity. Some of these events and their effects are briefly discussed below.

A prolonged economic and social boycott, humiliation, torture, and killing forced the early Muslims to cross the sea to Abyssinia in order to escape from that unbearable plight. The flight of the Prophet to Madīnah did not mean the end of the confrontation between Muslims and non-Muslims. The Muslims prayed for Allah's help when the Quraysh went after Muḥammad, trying to track him down as he migrated to Madīnah.[48] In Madīnah, the pressure and aggression of the Quraysh continued. They contacted Jewish and Arab tribes there so as to recruit them to help put an end to Muhammad's mission.

> They question you [O Muhammad] with regard to warfare in the sacred months. Say: Warfare therein is a great [transgression], but to turn [men] from the way of Allah, and to disbelieve in Him, to prevent access to the inviolable place of worship, and to expel its people thence, is a greater [transgression] with Allah; for persecution [oppression] is worse than killing. And they will not cease from fighting against you until they have made you renegades from your religion, if they can (2:217).

The continuous persecution to which the early Muslims were subjected posed a dilemma: should they wait till the enemy attacks, or should they go out against them? In the case of Badr, they chose the latter although they felt that they were weaker.

> And remember, when you were few and reckoned feeble in the land, and were in fear lest men should extirpate you, how He gave you refuge and strengthened you with His help, and made provision of good things for you, that haply you might be thankful (8:26).

> But Allah willed that He should cause the truth to triumph by His words, and to cut off the roots of the disbelievers, that He might cause

---

[48] It is necessary to point out that beside the historical accounts, such as those of Ibn Hishām or Ibn Athīr, the Qur'an and hadith (especially the six canonicals of al Bukhārī, Muslim, al Tirmidhī, Abū Dāwūd, al Nasā'ī, and Ibn Mājah) are of substantial help as historical sources.

the truth to triumph and bring vanity to naught, however much the guilty might oppose (8:7-8).

When the Lord inspired the angels, saying: I am with you. So make those who believe stand firm. I will throw fear into the hearts of those who disbelieve. Then smite the necks and smite of them each finger. That is because they opposed Allah and His Messenger, and if anyone oppose Allah and His Messenger, for him Allah is severe in punishment. That is the reward, so taste it, and know that for the disbelievers is the torment of the Fire (8:12-14).

You [Muslims] slew them not, but Allah slew them, and you [Muhammad] threw not when you threw, but Allah threw, that He might test the believers by a fair test from Him. Lo! Allah is the Hearer, the Knower (8:17).

It was difficult for the Muslims to feel at ease with non-Muslims, especially in view of incidents such as the Day of al Rajī' and the Well of Ma'ūnah. In both cases, pagan tribes approached the Prophet and asked him to provide them with Muslims to teach them Islam. This proved to be a trick, for as these tribes were returning to their encampments, they attacked and killed their defenseless teachers.[49]

As the sources indicate, the persecution of the Muslim community continued. This time, the tribes of Banū al Nadhīr along with the Quraysh and Ghaṭfān planned to finish off the Muslim community in Madīnah. This alliance was too strong for the Muslims to confront. They dug a ditch around most of Madīnah in order to hinder the advance of the powerful army. To make things worse, the Banū Quraẓah, Muhammad's ally inside the beseiged city of Madīnah, conspired to join the alliance and to attack the Muslims from the rear.[50]

When they [the non-believing allies] came upon you from above you and from below you, and when eyes grew wild and hearts reached to the throats, and you were imagining vain thoughts concerning Allah, then were the believers sorely tried and shaken with a mighty shock.

---

[49] Ibn Hishām, *al Sīrah*, vol. II, pp. 169-185.

[50] Ibid., pp. 214-233.

> And when the hypocrites and those in whose hearts there is a disease were saying: "Allah and His Messenger promised us naught but delusion..." they wished but to flee (33:10-13).

> Of the believers are men who are true to that which they covenanted with Allah. Some of them have paid their vow by death [in battle], and some of them still are waiting; and they have not altered in the least (33:23-24).

The seige came to an abrupt end due to a worsening of weather conditions. The Muslims viewed the failure of the alliance's attack as a manifestation of Allah's help:

> And Allah repulsed the disbelievers in their wrath; they gained no good. Allah averted their attack from the believers. Allah is Strong, Mighty. And He brought those of the People of the Book who supported them [the allies] down from their strongholds and cast panic into their hearts. Some you slew and some you made captive (33:25-26).

The persecution continued even after the peace treaty of Ḥudaybīyah was concluded between the Prophet and the Quraysh. In the sanctuary of Makkah, home of the Quraysh tribe, the Banū Bakr, allies of the Quraysh, massacred the Khuzā'ah, the Muslims' allies.[51] To the Muslims of that time, it appeared that the basic objective of the non-Muslims was simply to take advantage of the situation irrespective of peace agreements. This is expressed in the Qur'anic position on these occasions, which can be seen as a direct reaction to the unrestrained aggressive behavior by non-Muslims:

> How [can there be any treaty for others] when, if they have the upper hand over you, they regard not pact nor honor in respect of you? They satisfy you with their tongues while their hearts refuse. And most of them are wrongdoers (9:7-8).

> And if they break their pledges after their treaty [has been made with you] and assail your religion, then fight the heads of disbelief - lo! they have no binding oaths - in order that they may desist. Will you not fight a folk who broke their solemn pledges, and proposed to

---

[51] Ibid., pp. 389-398.

drive out the Messenger, and did attack you first? What! Do you fear them? Now Allah has more right that you should fear Him, if you are believers. Fight them! Allah will chastise them at your hand, and He will lay them low and give you victory over them, and He will heal the breasts of folks who are believers (9:12-14).

Then, when the sacred months have passed, slay the idolators, wherever you find them, and take them captive and beseige them and prepare for them each ambush. But if they repent and establish worship and pay the zakah, then leave them their way free. Lo! Allah is Forgiving, Merciful (9:5).

How should you not fight for the cause of Allah and of the feeble among men and of women and the children who are crying: Our Lord! Bring us forth from out of this town of which the people are oppressors! Oh, give us from Your presence some protecting friend! Oh, give us from Your presence some defender! (2:193).

Unless we understand the impact of these historical cases, we will find it very difficult to sympathize with the early Muslims' mistrust of non-Muslims. These were the same Muslims who managed to bring about a tremendously humane transformation in the world of their time.

The process of transformation that the Muslims brought about could hardly have been carried out by narrowminded, warlike people. The early Muslims were confronted by unceasing aggression and persecution, and the non-Muslim powers' basic attitude of hostility against Muslim ideals and society never changed. This inevitably left its mark on the thinking of the jurists. Thus, war and fighting became practically an integral and natural part of the relationship with non-Muslims, though some of the jurists did not advocate initiation of fighting by the Muslims. They did, however, advocate retaliation when Muslims were attacked.[52]

The psychological effect of the struggle during the early Muslim era and the continuation of the confrontation with the neighboring powers, especially the Byzantines, partly explain the exaggerated usage of the concept of *naskh* (abrogation), especially in the field of external relations. *Naskh* helped the jurists in their

---

[52] See Ibn Rushd, op. cit., vol. I, p. 313.

effort to gain legitimacy and to rally moral support against the hostile, neighboring non-Muslim powers. It did not help them, however, to think into the future beyond their immediate circumstances.

Naskh: Misinterpretation and Misconception

This discipline has and still does play an important role in the field of Shari'ah studies, especially in the areas of jurisprudence and commentary on the Qur'an. Undoubtedly, the psychological condition of the Muslim jurists has influenced the way this method of abrogation was applied.

In the area of external affairs, the most widely discussed and disputed issue has been the "Verse of the Sword."[53] Influenced by the hostile attitudes on non-Muslims during the early Muslim era, some jurists took an extreme position in interpreting this verse. They claimed that this verse abrogated all preceding verses pertaining to patience (*ṣabr*), persuasion (*ḥusnā*), tolerance (*lā ikrāh*), and right to self-determination (*lasta 'alayhim bi musayṭir*).[54] For instance, Ibn al 'Arabī and Ibn Salāmah believed that the Verse of the Sword had abrogated a total of 124 verses. Muṣṭafā Abū Zayd says that he found the number of verses that were abrogated by the same verse to exceed 140.[55]

[53] The Verse of the Sword is: "Then, when the sacred months have passed, slay the idolaters wherever you find them and take them captive and besiege them and prepare for them every ambush. But if they repent and establish worship and pay the zakah then leave their way free. Lo! Allah is Forgiving, Merciful." See Abū al Qāsim ibn Salāmah, *al Nāsikh wa al Mansūkh* (Cairo: Muṣtafā al Bābī al Ḥalabī, 1967), p.51.

[54] Muhammad 'Abd al 'Azīm al Zarqānī, *Manāhil al 'Irfān fī 'Ulūm al Qur'ān* (Cairo: Dār Iḥyā' al Kutub al 'Arabīyah, n.d.), vol. II, p. 156; Muṣtafā Abū Zayd, *al Nāsikh wa al Mansūkh; Dirāsah Tashrī'īyah, Tārīkhīyah, Naqdīyah* (Cairo: Dār al Fikr al 'Arabī, 1963), vol. I, pp. 289-501, vol. II, pp. 503-583.

[55] See Badr al Dīn al Zarakshī, *al Burhān fī 'Ulūm al Qur'ān*, ed. Muhammad Abū al Faḍl Ibrāhīm (Cairo: Dār Iḥyā' al Kutub al 'Arabīyah, 1957), vol. II, p. 40; Abū Zayd, Op. Cit., vol.II, p.508.

It has been shown that jurists have had various opinions concerning the nature of jihad.[56] Those who stressed the aggressive nature of jihad could only do so by applying abrogation to a wide category of Qur'anic verses. Instead of being concerned with reviving human consciousness for erecting an egalitarian human society, this attitude reduced the Islamic mission to a kind of spiritual totalitarianism. Using abrogation in this manner has indeed narrowed the Qur'anic experience.

If this misconception is removed, then the misinterpretation and application of abrogation can be corrected. In this way, the damaging affects of the method of abrogation would be eliminated. If the meaning of Islam is restricted to the interpretation of events which occurred during a time of hostilities near the very end of the Prophet's era, while the rest of the whole spectrum of Qur'anic and Sunnah texts and the experience of the earlier Makkan and Madīnan periods are ignored, then it will not be possible in the future for mankind to pursue justice or even to survive. Islam has to regain all the dimensions of the Qur'anic experience which make Islam an ideology and a set of values that deal with man in society. This can be done only by reexamining the meaning of the Qur'anic experience and the place of abrogation within it. This will bring about a fundamental change which will limit the scope of abrogation and will alter its familiar meaning in Islamic jurisprudence. [57]

Tolerance and Unity: A Classical Legacy

To shed more light on classical Muslim thought in matters of

---

[56] For further examples of the early jurists' differences of opinion on jihad, see works of commentary on the Qur'an by Ibn Kathīr, Op. Cit., vol. I, pp. 310-311, vol. II, pp.322, 336-337; and Ibn Jarīr al Tabarī, Op. Cit., vol. II, pp. 198-199, 332-335, vol. III, pp. 14-21, vol. IX, pp. 153-155, vol. X, pp. 33-34.

[57] This attempt to deal objectively with Muslim thought and its research methods should not be interpreted by Muslim intellectuals in any way other than to draw their attention to strategic factors that prevented Muslim thought from reaching a broader and more basic understanding of the Qur'anic experience. The intention is the betterment of the conditions of Muslims in the modern world. This broader understanding is an alternative to the formalistic, superficial, and narrow type of intellectual life in which the Muslim world of today is entrapped.

external relations, it will be necessary to examine more closely two of its major aspects: tolerance and the unity of Muslims.

Earlier in this chapter, we introduced and defined the terminology of classical Muslim political thought. But mere introduction and definition are not enough. We must go a step further and link issues within the framework of Muslim political thought to their counterparts in the modern framework of international relations. Unless our readers, especially those attuned to Western thought, go through the process of studying these issues within classical Muslim political thought, they will never be able to comprehend the Muslim view on the internal developments in modern Muslim political thought.

In the Islamic framework, which is basically ideological and personal, the issue of tolerance based on an underlying religious commitment constitutes the basis of the Muslim attitude in external relationships. External relations within the classical framework are relations of Muslims vis-à-vis non-Muslims or vice versa in whatever framework or condition, whether in terms of nations or groups. Even when non-Muslims constitute a minority in a Muslim state, the issue contains some international elements because, it will be recalled, the world for the Muslim is divided into *dār al Islām* and *dār al ḥarb*. It involves an issue of human rights and an issue of political interest of alien governments and organizations. As for the issue of the unity of the Muslim Ummah, the modern system of independent nation status within the Muslim world and the many international problems involving inter-Arab and inter-Muslim relationships would be better understood by studying their roots in classical Muslim political thought, particularly regarding the general subject of the relationship of Muslims to non-Muslim, both domestic and foreign.

In this chapter we will discuss the two major issues of tolerance and unity to determine in what ways classical thought in these areas poses a problem in the context of this thesis. Solutions and alternatives will be treated in chapters 3 and 4.

Tolerance and Respect for Personal Dignity

The issue of tolerance as discussed by Muslims in classical Muslim political thought touched upon the problem of whom to tolerate as well as how to deal respectfully with the tolerated people. All jurists had agreed that the tolerated people were *ahl al kitāb* (People of the Book), meaning primarily Christians and Jews, as well as some other groups who could be linked with them directly or indirectly, such as the Sabeans. The Magians (Zoroastrians) were also included, based on the authority of the hadith.[58]

According to some jurists, Arab pagans were not to be tolerated. They were either to turn to Islam or to be fought. This is the literal meaning or import of the Qur'anic texts and the texts of the Sunnah on the subject. The jurists who advocated this position reasoned so on the grounds that the Arab pagans had no book (scripture), and since they were the people of the Prophet they had to join Islam. Other peoples, especially if they were pagans, were to be treated, according to some jurists, like the Arab pagans.[59]

It is amazing how far removed these jurists were from the meaning of the early Muslim experience relative to non-Muslims. They took the Qur'anic verses out of context and thus destroyed their significance. The Qur'an and the Sunnah ordered all-out war against the Arab pagans who were always referred to as *mushrikūn* (idolaters or associators). Whenever the Qur'an speaks of these Arabs, it stresses their cruelty, treachery, hypocrisy, greed, savagery, *et cetera.* The Arabs who were the subject of these verses were mainly bedouins who continually attacked and persecuted the Muslims and betrayed their agreements and pledges. Thus, Islam viewed them generally as savage, uncivilized people who lacked the necessary requirements for responsible and orderly human interaction. The jurists also missed the significance of calling the Jews and Christians "People of the Book." In the Qur'anic context, reading and writing connote knowledge and civilization. Readers of the Qur'an cannot miss the favorable position that the People of the Book, Christians and Jews, enjoy in terms of knowledge and civilization, in contrast to the bedouins.

---

[58] See Ibn Qudāmah, Op. Cit., vol. IX, pp. 194-195; and al Shāfi'ī, *al Umm*, vol. IV, pp. 94-97.

[59] Ibid., vol. IX, p. 323.

A close examination of all Qur'anic verses in regard to non-Muslims from the beginning in Makkah to the end in Madīnah reveals that the Islamic attitude toward non-Muslims is far more balanced than is indicated by the classical jurists.[60] Islam developed an attitude of all-out war only against the 'Adnānī bedouin and their Qurayshī leadership in their opposition to Islam.[61] This hostile "Islamic" attitude toward the "savage" Arabs came about because the bedouins were considered to be in a stage of social development not capable of any human responsibility or orderly interaction. The "savage" pagans, pursuing in many ways a barbaric course of behavior and life, had to be forced to accept changes that were necessary to put them in the realm of human civilization and orderly social human interaction. A fundamental change indeed was achieved when Islam introduced basic human rights, as Arabia was subdued and started its historic journey of civilization under Islam.

The jurists who failed to comprehend the Islamic attitude toward the bedouin are the same jurists who failed to give proper attention to the significance of the agreement made with the Christians of Najrān after the conquest of Makkah, when they came in what is known as the Covenant of Madīnah (*Ṣaḥīfat al Madīnah*).

Even after the long bloody struggle with the Jewish tribes in Madīnah and Khaybar, during which the Jews' political and military power was destroyed, Jews were allowed to live in peace in Madīnah where they were tolerated and were never forced to accept Islam. They were respected to the extent that they were considered still to have enough social ethics and order to allow human responsibility and orderly human interaction.

---

[60] A. M. al Sa'īdī, *al Ḥurrīyah al Dīnīyah*, pp. 19-173; Abū al A'lā al Mawdūdī, *al Islām fī Muwājahat al Taḥaddīyāt al Mu'āṣirah*, trans. Khalīl Aḥmad al Ḥāmidī (Kuwait: Dār al Qalam, 1971), pp. 39-62 and 171-189; Muḥammad Fatḥī 'Uthmān, *al Fikr al Islāmī wa al Taṭawwur* (Kuwait: al Dār al Kuwaitīyah, 1969), pp. 254-279.

[61] See Ibn Hishām, Op. Cit., vol. I, pp. 264-490; and vol. II, pp. 169-190, 308-328, 389-425, 543-560.

The classical juristic attitude toward the question of tolerance lost some of its flexibility in dealing with non-Muslim communities owing to its narrow interpretation. Where it could have allowed many creative policies to develop, it became rigid and bound by all manner of historical precedents. This situation came about chiefly as a result of excessive abrogation of those Qur'anic verses which support tolerance.

An issue closely related to the concept of tolerance concerns the payment of *jizyah*. The pertinent Qur'anic verse was clearly taken out of context by the classical jurists.

> Fight against such of them who have been given the scripture until they pay the tribute [*jizyah*] readily, having been brought low (9:21).

The bulk of the jurists' emphasis was on how *ṣaghār* (the act of bringing low) is to be applied, rather than why it must be applied at all. The most reasonable interpretation was that *ṣaghār* of the *dhimmis* was accomplished with some by their abiding by the Islamic rule, and with others by the act of paying the *jizyah*.[62] The first part of this argument is clearly not in harmony with the spirit of Islam. Islam stands for a better, purer, and more egalitarian society. Allah "sent you [Muhammad] as a mercy for all peoples" (21:107). The jurists, in this case, did not project Islam as a mercy and betterment for these people, but as a humiliation. It is very difficult to justify this conclusion unless the verse in question (9:29) is taken out of context. In fact, the sequence of verses preceding and following the particular verse cited above does not support the jurists' opinion.

This verse is part of an address to the early Muslims on the subject of confrontation with the aggressive *mushrikūn* as well as with those People of the Book who shared the *mushrikūn*'s qualities and who, at the time, were fighting the Muslims:

> They want to extinguish Allah's light with their utterances; but Allah will not allow this to pass, for He has willed to spread His light in all its fullness, however hateful this may be to all who deny the truth.

---

[62] See Ibn al Qayyim, *Aḥkām ahl al Dhimmah*, vol. I, pp. 16-18; and al Shāfi'ī, Op. Cit., vol. IV, pp. 99-101.

> He it is Who has sent forth His Apostle with the task of spreading guidance and the religion of truth, to the end that He may cause it to prevail over all false religion - however hateful this may be to those who ascribe divinity to aught beside Allah.
>
> O you who have attained to faith! Behold, many of the rabbis and monks do indeed wrongfully devour men's possessions and turn others away from the path of Allah (9:32-34).

The whole section ends as follows:

> And wage war on all the idolaters as they are waging war on all of you, and know that Allah is with those who keep their duty unto Him (9:36).

The jurists simply extended a treatment that was intended for an aggressive and corrupt enemy to include all non-Muslims, regardless of their actual attitudes, and in spite of the universal meaning and basic objective of Islam to guide and serve man. To accept this major conclusion of the classical jurists, we have to forget all about the significance of the constitutional agreements of Madīnah and Najrān. The payment of *jizyah* was divorced from the question of *ṣaghār*. They were completely different issues and served different purposes in dealing with non-Muslims. Finally, it is clear that the question of *saghār* was not intended to apply automatically to all non-Muslims. *Ṣaghār* is not an attitude and punishment for choosing a different belief, but for a hostile and treacherous attitude against Muslim peoples and in opposition to justice and to the Islamic obligation to protect man's right to safety and freedom of belief.

This brief analysis reveals that the classical framework of political thought directed toward external relationships (with non-Muslims within and outside the Muslim state) was in some respects negative in its attitude and lacked genuine understanding and interest in longterm relations with non-Muslim peoples.

This analysis partially explains why the spread of Islam after the first two Muslim generations was accomplished mostly by merchants and Sufi teachers in Africa and Southeast Asia.

The Unity of the Ummah

The word "Ummah" is used in the Qur'an to signify more than one meaning; it has been used to connote excellence, way, length of time, a group, and a people.[63] When the classical jurists dealt with the Islamic Ummah, they spoke of the believers vis-à-vis nonbelievers, which is a philosophical or ideological concept. On the other hand, they spoke of *dār al islām* vis-à-vis *dār al ḥarb*, which is a matter of the extent of Muslim rule or jurisdiction and of *khilāfah* in relation to non-Muslim nations. This usage relates to the organizational and constitutional structure of political authority in Muslim lands.

Although the early Muslims and the classical jurists were intelligent enough to shift emphasis from one aspect to another in order to face concrete problems and to help the growth and continuity of the Muslim Ummah and Islam as a way of life, nonetheless the ambiguity and philosophical aspects led later generations to confusion and contradiction, which contributed to political collapse and regression in the Muslim world.

The early Muslims realized the importance of political authority for the establishment and continuity of the Islamic Ummah. After the death of the Prophet, the Muslim "government" of the first *khalīfah*, Abū Bakr, decided to suppress the tribal uprising against the central political authority of Madīnah in order to maintain the Ummah. The decision was historic, since the issue was both organizational and philosophical. The choice was between anarchy or stability and growth of the nation. This emphasis on "central" authority helped to nourish and unify the increasingly diverse elements of the Muslim community.

With the vast demographic and geographic expansion of the Muslim polity, which brought different racial and cultural groups under its jurisdiction, political reorganization had to be undertaken. Although this had occurred in practice when the Muslim world was divided into a few independent and semi-independent territories, such classical jurists as ʻAbd al Qāhir al Baghdādī, al Māwardī, Abū Yaʻlā, and al Ghazzālī, who wrote

---

[63] For the different usages of the term "Ummah" in the Qur'an, see the following verses: 16:120, 42:8, 43:23, 13:45, 11:8, 7:159, 7:164, 28:23, 3:104, 16:92, 23:34, 35:24, 2:134, and 23:52.

between the eleventh and fourteenth centuries, insisted on a unified supreme central political authority.[64] Although they admitted the existence of a system of multiple sovereignties in the Muslim world, they nevertheless hesitated or refused altogether to help with reorganization and to grant legitimacy to this evolving system.[65] The jurists seem to have been caught between the concrete model of the simple, single government of the Prophet and memories of the sad and bitter historical experience of anarchy and civil wars during the reigns of Abū Bakr, 'Uthmān, 'Alī, and Mu'āwiyah, as well as the civil wars of the Umawīs and the 'Abbāsīs such as the war between 'Abd al Mālik ibn Marwān and 'Abd Allah ibn al Zubayr, and al Manṣūr and Muḥammad ibn al Nafs al Zakīyah.

When, by the twelfth century, the office of the *khalīfah* had for all practical purposes disappeared, the jurists finally turned to the more fundamental concept of philosophical and ideological rather than political and organizational unity in order to help the cause of Islam and the Ummah.[66] Nonetheless they failed to adjust and adapt the political organization to the emerging needs and changes of the Muslim world. As a matter of fact, Muslim writers down to the present have associated power and growth with a central political structure of the Muslim Ummah. Their thinking is marked partly by their lack of understanding of the complex issue of power in the world of politics and by the concrete model of the Prophet and his traditions concerning rebellion and belligerency.[67] These shortcomings continue to be a factor in modern Islamic views on international relations. Most writers, following Western theory, also seem unable to

---

[64] See 'Abd al Qāhir ibn Ṭāhir, *Aḥkām al Imāmah wa Shurūṭ al Za'āmah*, in Yūsuf Ibish, Op. Cit., pp. 126-262. See also, Abū Ḥāmid al Ghazālī, *Fī al Imāmah*, in Yūsuf Ibish, Op. Cit., p. 279.

[65] See Imām al Ḥaramayn al Juwaynī, *Faṣl fī 'Aqd al Imāmah li Shakhṣayn* (Regarding Appointment of Two Persons for *Imāmah*), in Yūsuf Ibish, Op. Cit., p. 279.

[66] Ibn Taymīyah, *al Siyāsah al Shar'iyah* (Beirut: Dār al Kutub al 'Arabīyah, n.d.), pp. 5, 42, 136, 138, 143.

[67] See al Farrā', *Faṣl Shurūṭ al Ṭā'ah li al Imām* (The Relinquishment of Loyalty to the Imam), in Yūsuf Ibish, Op. Cit., pp. 216-218.

conceive of a position between anarchy and central political authority. Nor, it appears, have they been able to understand the changes that occurred when the Muslim state began to extend far beyond the Arab peoples and territories. Their goal has been more utopian than idealistic, and their attitude more negative (condemning anarchy and disintegration) than positive (utilizing available power and political structures for a more unified and politically better organized Muslim world). In short, their approach has failed, due to its negativity, to consider any of the practical and progressive alternatives. In spite of its wishes to the contrary, the Muslim world continues to be in a state of conflict.

Unless conceptual confusion is cleared away in these overlapping areas of philosophy and organization, and more serious work is done on the thought and education of the Ummah, the dilemma that troubles inter-Muslim relationships and Muslim unity will never be resolved.

Highlights of the Classical Theory

Looking at the Muslim world as it stretches from the Atlantic to the outskirts of China, we realize, if we do not allow circumstantial details and legalistic arguments to distract our attention from the overall picture, that the rise of Islam and the influence of Islamic thought brought about revolutionary changes and put into practice a new dimension in human relationships.

Despite the fact that the concept of equality in Islam removed most of the prejudices in regard to race, color, and wealth among Muslims, its ideal goal of total Islamic equality was thwarted by non-Islamic cultural influences which partially survived in the succeeding Muslim dynasties and by the partial approach taken by the classical jurists.[68] In regard to the relations between Muslims and non-Muslims, such relations did improve due to the example set by the early Muslim community which granted communal and legal autonomy to non-Muslims, adopted lenient attitudes, provided better defined rules, and showed a more restrained use of victorious power. Here again, however, the

---

[68] See Appendix, note 4.

concept of equality pertaining to non-Muslims did not go beyond the early examples and therefore did not succeed in achieving the establishment of Islamic ideals.

The limited success of the classical Islamic sense of equality could and should have been directed to reach out to humanity in order to build relationships on the optimistic foundation of *fiṭrah* (nature, or the goodness of human nature) and *da'wah* (invitation or call, specifically to Islam), rather than on the pessimistic foundation of *kufr* (denial of Allah, disbelief, or infidelity). This is true today as well, provided of course that the Muslim world and Islamic *da'wah* (call) are in a position to take this optimistic approach. This is not to say that Muslims in the classical period ever lost touch with the Qur'anic sense of responsibility.

The reader of classical works of jurisprudence cannot help wondering if, with the partial reestablishment of tribalism under the Umawī dynasty which perpetuated its own hostility and destroyed many possible channels of communication, the Islamic sense of responsibility was not confused with arrogance. The Islamic call for social justice, human equality (equity), and submission to the divine will and directions of the Creator requires the deepest and sharpest sense of responsibility, as well as the total absence of human arrogance and egoism, both in internal and external communication.

With the coming of the imperialist powers of Europe in the eighteenth and nineteenth centuries, the classical Muslim attitude toward non-Muslim minorities as well as the actual conditions of these minorities (though most Muslim subjects were in no way better off) were an additional cause for concern to the European powers and an incentive to their interference in the internal affairs of the Muslim states, and especially those of the Ottoman Empire.[69]

Classical thought also insisted emphatically on the concept of unity in the Ummah. This attitude benefited the Muslim peoples in the face of several civil wars and foreign incursions. But in the face of the cultural, political, economic, and military invasions

---

[69] See Appendix, note 5.

by Europeans in the nineteenth century, the lack of clarity in that thought and the inability to analyze the concept of unity for the Ummah backfired in internal struggle, resulting in the absence of effective cooperation and workable institutions.

The major conclusion we derive from our study of classical thought in the field of Muslim international relations is that there is a great deal to improve as well as to utilize. There is a clear need for more earnest and organized efforts in order to establish the preconditions for the growth and participation of Muslim peoples.

The Collapse of Classical Thought

When writers speak of Muslim classical theory, they do not speak of the Qur'an or the Sunnah. Rather, they will usually be found referring to the juridical speculations made at the height of Muslim civilization during the High Caliphate, primarily the 'Abbāsī period (750-1100 AC) which includes major jurists such as the founders of the four Sunnī schools of jurisprudence and other distinguished jurists, including al Shaybānī and al Māwardī. Classical Muslim thought later encompassed such major jurists as Ibn Taymīyah and al Sayūṭī.[70]

Both modern critics and adherents of these schools of thought have generally limited their study and analysis to the conclusions reached by classical jurists, with little regard for the matter of how such conclusions were reached.[71]

Contemporary writers have given little or no attention to the methodology employed by these jurists and the circumstances under which they worked. Critics have dealt with classical Muslim thought within a modern, Western frame of reference, starting with false assumptions and consequently reaching

---

[70] See N. J. Coulson, *A History of Islamic Law*, pp. 75-85; M. Khadduri, "From Religious to National Law," in *Modernization of the Arab World*, ed. J. H. Thompson and R. D. Reischauer (New York: Van Nostrand, 1966), pp. 40-41; M. Y. Mūsā, *al Fiqh al Islāmī*, pp. 27-61; and S. Ramadan, *Islamic Law*, pp. 27-30.

[71] See Fāyez A. Sayegh, "Islam and Neutralism," in *Islam and International Relations*, ed. J. H. Procter, pp. 90-93; M. Khadduri, *War and Peace*, pp. 268-296; Said Ramadan, *Islamic Law; Its Scope and Equity* (London: P.R. Macmillan Ltd., 1961); and W. al Zuhaylī, *Āthār al Ḥarb fī al Islām*.

erroneous conclusions. Although the adherents have tried to face modern challenges by continuing to think in terms of old standards, they have failed to comprehend new and constantly changing circumstances. Thus they have arbitrarily tried to reconstruct the Muslim social system in order to satisfy the emotions of the Muslims, while actually contributing little to the Muslim cause.

Muslim writers tend to attach great importance to external factors in explaining their problems and shortcomings. It is true that the Western attack on and control of the Muslim world seriously challenged the classical approach, but the Western attack revealed and uncovered rather than caused the decay of Muslim thought, and it was only a matter of time before it collapsed, leaving the Muslim people with nothing but the Qur'an, the Sunnah, and memories of glorious Muslim achievements. But the real reason that the attacks were fatal was the state of Muslim thought.[72] Europe, armed with dynamic ideas and efficient methods based on an empirical and rational approach, confronted the static and rigid Muslim frame of mind which rested on textual deduction within the limits of the early Muslim model. The Muslims' thinking had lost touch with reality, and they were incapable of regeneration and reorientation in the light of new developments and demands. It had become moot to argue over defensive versus offensive jihad, personal versus territorial law, neutrality versus neutralization. The new exigencies demanded the acquisition and employment of new methods and tools.

Modern Developments:

Lack of Methodology

When following our line of analysis in trying to explore the background, reasons, and motivations of Muslim thought, one will find the task of analyzing modern developments in Muslim thought in the field of international relations less problematic.

---

[72] See Hisham Sharabi, "Islam and Modernization in the Arab World," in Thompson and Reishauer, Op. Cit., pp. 32-34; T. Naff, "The Setting and Rationale of Ottoman Diplomacy in the Reign of Selim III (1789-1807)," p. 28; and W. M. Watt, Op. Cit., p. 225.

The sharp turns and opposing points of view in the Muslim world today are difficult to understand if one is ignorant of the historical background and circumstances that caused the formation and development of these viewpoints.

Some developments in Muslim thought took place under the actual control or threat of control by non-Muslim Europeans in the twentieth century. These developments took the form either of apology, appealing to the powerful and commanding adversary, or of protest and revolt against the adversary's presence in the Muslims' land. Characteristic of these attitudes were the apologetic appeals to liberalism, peace, freedom, and tolerance promoted by the ruling Muslim aristocracy and by Muslim intellectuals who were under the influence of European thought and power, and ashamed at the same time of Muslim technological backwardness.[73] This was typical of the ruling Ottoman elite and its *tanẓīmāt* of the nineteenth century, and of the intellectuals who came in contact with the West in the times of Ṭahṭāwī (1801-1873).

The point is not whether elite and intellectuals were Islamic or un-Islamic in adopting these attitudes. Actually, the non-aggressive interpretation of jihad made it easy for them to adapt to Western control of Muslim nations. But the overwhelming European pressure was the immediate source of motivation in adopting this "liberal" attitude. The Muslim intellectual emphasis on peace, cooperation, and tolerance was primarily a psychological weapon to put moral pressure on the foreign oppressors and, in addition, to reform the Muslim nations themselves from within.

This "liberal" attitude was also an attempt to unite the internal front of Muslim and non-Muslim peoples living in the same country into a national front, and thus to minimize the manipulation of different religious groups through the use of communal divisions. Furthermore, this attitude also helped to minimize the shock of the extreme situation of Muslims being ruled by non-Muslims and restrained Muslim peoples from ill-advised confrontations, thus providing much-needed time for

---

[73] See Appendix, note 6.

Muslims to introduce some basic reforms and counter European rule. In this light, we can understand and explain the thought and positions of people such as Imam Muhammad 'Abduh of Egypt (d. 1905) in the fields of education, Shari'ah law, and theology, as well as his efforts to maintain friendly relations with the British authorities. Of course, it could be argued that 'Abduh's position made the establishment of imperial rule in Egypt much easier for the British.[74]

There was another kind of response to this non-Muslim imperialistic domination and rule. This response aimed at the liberation of the Muslim land and was organized by the people and their traditional Muslim leadership, such as the Mahdi movement in Sudan, the Jihad movement of Sayyid Aḥmad Barelvī, and the one led by Ismā'īl al Shahīd in India. These movements emphasized the opposite position: jihad, more or less in terms of the classical conceptions of jihad in which Muslims are bound to fight evil and aggressive non-Muslims. But the war cry of jihad to set the world right was like putting the cart before the horse. Such a call to action was bound to fail because very few of the conditions essential for success, including the development of Muslim thought along contemporary lines, were present.[75] The failure of Muslim peoples to attain power and independence in the eighteenth and nineteenth centuries under the traditional leadership of such men as Sayyid Aḥmad Barelvī of India, 'Abd al Qādir al Jazā'irī of Algeria, and Muḥammad al Mahdī of Sudan through military jihad demonstrated the inadequacy of classical thought and leadership as it came into confrontation with the power, technology and secular institutions of modern Europe.

---

[74] See A. Hourani, Op. Cit., pp. 157-160; Muḥammad Ḥusayn, *al Islām wa al Ḥaḍārah al Gharbīyah* (Beirut: Dār al Irshād, 1963), pp. 91-104; and W. C. Smith, *Islam in Modern History* (Princeton University Press, 1957), pp. 55-73.

[75] See Mas'ūd al Nadwī, *Tārīkh al Da'wah al Islāmīyah fī al Hind* (The History of the Call to Islam in India) (Beirut: Dār al 'Arabīyah, n.d.), pp. 167-177, 265-280; Shakīb Arsalān, *Li Mādhā Ta'akhkhara al Muslimūn wa Li Mādhā Taqaddama Ghayruhum?* (Why Are Muslims Declining while Others Are Progressing?) (Beirut: Dār Maktabat al Ḥayāh, 1965), pp. 43-55, 149-161; and W. C. Smith, Op. Cit., pp. 89-92.

The liberal approach to the internal reform of government, to the creation of a free and democratic society, and to a system of international relations of peace and cooperation, especially with the Western powers, also failed.[76] The movement away from the liberal position began early in the twentieth century when the Arabs revolted against their Turkish rulers and joined the allied powers in World War I. They failed, however, to gain the promised independence and fell under direct European occupation in the name of the Mandate System. After World War II, they suffered the loss of Palestine, though some Muslim contries gained independence. These experiences brought disenchantment with Western liberalism, Western institutions, and cooperation with the West. Liberalism failed as the talisman that would bring the blessings of independence from European domination, of stability and prosperity.

Immediately after World War II, the growing trend in the foreign affairs of Muslim states was away from peace and toward open confrontation with the West. Arab countries became involved in the Palestinian question, Muslim Arabs of North Africa rebelled against European occupation, and Indonesian Muslims became involved in guerilla warfare against the Netherlands. All independent Muslim countries joined the United Nations, but they tried to use their membership in the political fight against Western imperialist powers and to help destroy Europe's imperialistic control over Asia and Africa.

With the emergence of the Soviet Union from World War II as a world power, Muslim countries, especially the Arabs, tried to use Soviet economic, technical, and political aid for their

---

[76] See A. Hourani, Op. Cit., pp. 341-373; Bernard Lewis, *The Emergence of Modern Turkey*, 2nd ed. (London: Oxford University Press, 1968) pp. 124-128; H. A. R. Gibb, "The Reaction in the Middle East Against Western Culture," in *The Contemporary Middle East*, ed. B. Rivlin and J. S. Szyliowicz, pp. 132-140; Abū al A'lā al Mawdūdī, Ḥasan al Bannā, and Sayyid Qutub, *al Jihād fī Sabīl Allāh* (Beirut: Ittiḥād al Munaẓẓamāt al Tullābīyah, 1970), pp. 103-134; M. Khadduri, Op. Cit., pp. 294-296; M. al Mubārak, *al Fikr al Islāmī al Ḥadīth*, pp. 50-131; Nadav Safrān, *Egypt in Search of Political Community* (Cambridge, MA: Harvard University Press, 1961), pp. 181-258; T. Naff, *The Setting and Rationale of Ottoman Diplomacy*, pp. 27-28; W. C. Smith, Op. Cit., pp. 58-89; W. M. Watt, *Islamic Political Thought*, pp. 118-119.

cause. These new developments, while speeding up the decline of the liberal approach, introduced to Muslim thought some elements of Marxist theory, notably the concept of wars of liberation (a latter-day form of jihad). But Marxist ideological terminology stems from a philosophy that is in conflict with classical Islamic ideology.[77] Islamic ideology is grounded in the concept of Muslim belief in one, just, supreme God, whereas Marxist ideology is based on the concept of class struggle. Marxist influence on Muslim thought in international relations was minimal, and Marxist terminology was generally a source of increasing confusion. It was never clear to Muslims who was to be liberated or even why. Marxist terminology did come to bear a vague meaning of jihad in the Algerian war of liberation and the civil war in Yemen. The introduction of Marxist influences emphasized the already felt need for social justice, but Marxism helped weaken internal stability by providing an effective rationale for revolution against the old order. Contemporary Muslim jurists and thinkers failed to reestablish Muslim political thought on a basis able to meet modern challenges and to help promote the effective participation of Muslims in contemporary international affairs. The effects of alien Western liberal and Marxist thought on Muslim jurists and thinkers failed to bring about genuine growth in Muslim political thought in the area of international relations.

It is worth noting at this juncture that because of the depressed state of Muslim thought in general and the lack of real Muslim power and influence in international affairs, the topic of international relations has a low priority in contemporary Islamic studies.[78] At this point in our discussion, it is necessary to realize that neither peace, tolerance, defensive jihad, offensive jihad, nor

---

[77] See 'Abd al Ḥamīd Ṣiddīqī, *Tafsīr al Tārīkh*, Kāẓim Jawwād (trans.), (Kuwait: al Dār al Kuwaitīyah, n.d.) pp.87-162; A. K. Brohi, *Islam in the Modern World*, (Karachi: Chirāgh-i-Rāh Publications, 1968) pp. 69-91; H. A. R. Gibb, Op. Cit., pp. 132-149; Jihād Qal'ajī, *al Islām Aqwā* (Kuwait, Dār al Kitāb al 'Arabī, n.d.), pp. 97-167; Khalifa Abdul Hakim, *Islam and Communism*, 3rd ed. (Lahore: Institute of Islamic Culture, 1962), pp. 43-67; M. Rafiuddin, *Ideology of the Future*, 3rd ed.(Lahore: Ashraf, 1970), pp. 355-400, 411-481; and Muḥammad al Ghazālī, *al Islām fī Wajh al Zaḥf al Aḥmar* (Kuwait: Maktabat al Amal, n.d.), pp. 20-58.

[78] See Appendix, notes 7 and 8.

the jihad of liberation have provided a successful or a satisfactory base for modern Muslim involvement in and contribution to the field of international relations. The actual functioning of the international relationships of Muslim peoples and governments is carried out in conformity with the external forms of the modern system, without much understanding of the system, and with an almost total lack of active and effective participation. As a result, Muslims have gained very little from the modern system by discussing historical precedents of neutrality and neutralization etc., for the problem is much greater in scope. It is the dilemma of modern Muslim thought.

Muslims need to realize the problems presented by these new developments in Muslim thought. The question is, how can they adapt themselves to new circumstances and make good use of new and alien ideas as well as classical ones?

The grand approach of jihad clearly represents a powerful dynamic in the Muslim society of the classical period. But this approach in its historical framework will be of little help to modern Muslim statesmen. Liberal or Marxist-socialist approaches are based fundamentally on the alien philosophical, historical, and social experiences and frames of reference of the West. Any idea belonging to one of these approaches, unless adjusted to fit with and respond to the inner conscience and personality of the Islamic Ummah will result in more inner conflict and confusion which, needless to say, could be very detrimental to the Muslim nation's capacity to act and respond constructively to existing needs and conditions.

Muslim intellectuals should fully realize that the problem of classical or traditional thought in modern times cannot be argued or understood in relation to any specific or detailed idea. This requires a total comprehension and understanding of the modern world, a world which cannot be explained in terms of the classical concepts and frame of mind. Thus the problem is elevated to the level of the methodology of generating ideas and solutions and the mechanism of classical Muslim thought in maintaining the social system. The methodology consists of *uṣūl*; and it is clear that Muslims have not re-examined these *uṣūl* critically for the purpose of readjusting the Muslim approach and understanding of the modern world.

The main approach of Islamic thought continues to be legalistic. It has adapted to different methods, for example, *talfīq* (piecing together), only to meet alien standards and to justify historical actions or practices in modern times.[79] Muslim jurists and thinkers have remained sterile in their work because they fail to go back to the origins of Muslim thought (political or otherwise) and reexamine and reform their methods and approaches.[80] Under these conditions, no comprehension, systematization, consensus, originality, or productivity is possible. Consequently, it is necessary to examine the problem of methodolgy (*uṣūl*) in Muslim thought. New bases and directions for Muslim external relations are possible only after the problems of approach and methodology are satisfactorily dealt with.

---

[79] Contemporary Muslim political thought in the field of international relations is not limited to essays related directly to the field. Literature about the biography of the Prophet, for example, is one more important source for this field. It is also worth noting that contemporary Muslim university texts have started making specific reference to international relations, though in most cases the treatment is very brief. See, for example, Muḥammad Ḥāfiẓ Ghānim, *Mabādi' al Qānūn al Dawlī al 'Āmmah*, 3rd ed, (Cairo: Maṭba'at al Nahḍah, 1964), pp. 50-55. See also, 'Alī Manṣūr, *Muqāranah Bayn al Sharī'ah al Islāmīyah wa al Qawānīn al Waḍ'īyah*, (Beirut: Dār al Fatḥ, 1968), vol. XI, pp. 140-235; Muhammad Aḥmad Bā Shumayl, *Banū Qurayẓah*, pp. 236-283: M. Hamidullah, *The Muslim Conduct of State*, pp. vii-viii; W. Zuḥaylī, Op. Cit., pp. 14-27.

[80] Most contemporary works on *uṣūl* are descriptive. Analysis and criticism in most cases are limited to the question of authenticity of the Sunnah and a general call for new ijithad. See A. Khallāf, *'Ilm Uṣūl al Fiqh* (Kuwait: al Dār al Kuwaytīyah, 1968), pp. 8-10; A. Khallāf, *Khulāṣat Tārīkh al Tashrī'*, pp. 103-104; A. Khallaf, *Maṣādir al Tashrī' al Islāmī*, 3rd ed. (Kuwait: Dār al Qalam, 1972), pp. 5-18; Anwar Ahmad Qadri, *Islamic Jurisprudence in the Modern World; A Reflection on Comparative Study of the Law* (Bombay: N. M. Tripathi Pvt. Ltd, 1963), pp. 55-81, 305-324; Fazlur Rahman, *Islamic Methodology*, pp. v-viii, 1-84, and 175-191; M. al Mubārak, *al Fikr al Islāmī al Ḥadīth*, pp. 7-26, 150-151, and 186-191; M. Y. Mūsā, *al Fiqh al Islāmī*, pp. 175-206; and N. J. Coulson, *A History of Islamic Law*, pp. 182-218.

CHAPTER 3

REFORM OF METHODOLOGY

Muslim methodology refers to *uṣūl,* the formal classical methodology of Muslim jurisprudence. Unlike Western positive law, *uṣūl* takes the whole of human conduct as its field and is concerned with both the internal and the external affairs of the Muslim peoples. Classical Muslim methodology provides not only the research method for Muslim thought but also its source material. As was mentioned in chapter 2, Muslim political thought, including the theory of international relations, continues to be classical in its approach through the techniques of *taqlīd* and *talfīq*.

In this connection, H. A. Sharābī says:

> The movement of reform in nineteenth century Islam's awakening was not an intellectual awakening, but a reaction to the military and political threat of Europe. Even after the European impact had been transformed into a cultural challenge, response to it remained largely defensive and negative.

H. A. R. Gibb says:

> It [knowledge] is still dominated by the ideal of authority; and if Western 'authorities' are now recognized alongside Muslim 'authorities,' the result is only to create a confusion of thought...

Malik Bennabi admits this by stating:

> The modern [Muslim cultural] movement in fact has no precise understanding of its goals nor of its means. The whole affair is just a passion for new things. Its only way of [generating reform] is to make Muslim imitators and customers of foreign civilization, thus lacking in originality.

In the conclusion to his study, *Islamic Reform,* Malcolm H. Kerr states:

> The nationalist sentiments of the present day provide no such moral guideline, or 'regulative principle,' as one writer [Albert Hourani] has put it... Nor can the concern for social justice so explosively conspicuous in the Near East today, quite provide such a principle either, as long as it is primarily an instrument and an expression of nationalism.[1]

A comprehensive understanding of classical Muslim methodology as a generator and filter of Muslim political thought throughout its history is a necessary condition for revitalization.[2] An original and adaptable system of political thought is needed to bring about the emergence of a new framework of Muslim international relations capable of answering the needs of present-day Muslim policymakers. In this connection, it is worth noting the comments of H. A. R. Gibb:

> The Koran [Qur'an] and the Tradition are not, as it is often said, the basis of Islamic legal speculation, but only its sources. The real foundation is to be sought in the attitude of mind which determined the methods of utilizing these sources.

He also said, in another work:

> Every scientific argument must always take the same course and reach the same conclusion, unless you change the postulates or invent new tools.[3]

Muslim Methodology: A Space-Time Problem

Before we deal with the problem of space-time in the context of Muslim thought, it is useful to clarify the nature of this problem. The substance and the structure of social institutions at any point of space and time reflect the need and the rationale of a specific society. With the progression of time and the change of space, the substance and structure of social institutions should also change. The degree of failure on the part of institutions to change in response to the accumulation of newly emerging needs affects the degree of the problem of space-time. In this context, we will deal with Muslim political thought and methodology

---

[1] See Appendix, note 8.

[2] See Appendix, note 9.

[3] H. A. R. Gibb, *Muhammadanism: a Historical Survey*, 2nd ed. (New York: Oxford University Press, 1962), p. 91.

and its acute problem of relevance to the needs of Muslims in the contemporary world.

Classical Muslim methodology (*uṣūl*) refers to the basic textual sources and methods used in producing Muslim attitudes in different spheres of life, including international relations. These sources are the Qur'an, the Sunnah, *ijmā'*, and ijtihad (the use of human reason or *'aql* in the elaboration and interpretation of the Shari'ah). Ijtihad includes the fourth major source of Muslim thought, *qiyās* (analogy), along with other supplementary methods such as *istiḥsān* (juristic preference), *maṣlaḥah* or *maṣāliḥ mursalah* (public interest), and *'urf* (customs of a particular society).[4]

Except for the Qur'an, which for the most part expresses itself in terms of general statements as philosophical guidance, including those matters relating to international relations, we find that the *uṣūl* reflect the classical Muslim point of view.[5]

The space-time factor is not limited to the content of the Sunnah in particular and classical Muslim thought in general, but is also present in the *uṣūl* themselves, the way they were established and developed. The contemporary narrow traditionalist examination of the *uṣūl* on the one hand, and the modernist and orientalist overemphasis on the question of the authenticity of the hadith on the other, can only distract us from what seems to be the basic problem of modern Muslim thought.[6] Unless the space-time dimension of the classical methodology is dealt with

---

[4] A. Khallāf, *'Ilm Uṣūl al Fiqh*, p. 149; A. Khallaf, *Maṣādir al Tashrī'*, pp. 19-103; Joseph Schacht, *The Origins of Muhammadan Jurisprudence* (Oxford, UK: University Press, 1950), pp. 120-130; Muhammad Abū Zahrah, *Ibn Hanbal: Ḥayātuhu wa 'Aṣruhu wa Fiqhuh* (Cairo: Dār al Fikr al 'Arabī), pp. 287-332; M. Abū Zahrah, *Mālik*, pp. 324-358; M. Abū Zahrah, *Tārīkh al Madhāhib*, pp. 73-359; al Shāfi'ī, *al Risālah*, pp. 288-290; S. Maḥmaṣānī, *al Awḍā' al Tashrī'īyah*, pp. 150-160; and S. Ramadan, *Islamic Law*, p. 23.

[5] Of the 6,000 verses of the Qur'an, there are between 80 to 500 verses which technically (depending on the definition) meet the criterion of a "legal rule." The remainder consists of broad propositions and a large number of moral precepts of a general nature relating to such matters as unity among humankind, freedom of religion, nonaggression, right of self-defense, distribution of wealth, fairness in commercial dealings, etc. See J. N. D. Anderson and N. J. Coulson, *Islamic Law in Contemporary Cultural Change*, p. 14.

[6] H. Gibb, *Modern Trends in Islam*, p. 124.

and properly proven, Muslim political thought is bound to lack productive and original content and methodology and to continue to be trapped in *taqlīd* and *talfīq*.

The Impact of the Main *Uṣūl* on Muslim Thought

Before we discuss the *uṣūl* of Muslim jurisprudence and the kinds of defects existing in them, we will investigate the function, strategy, and fundamental positions of the basic *uṣūl* in shaping Muslim thought and in building and developing Muslim jurisprudence (fiqh).

Unlike Western positive law and the Western legal system, Islamic jurisprudence takes the whole of human conduct for its field.[7] Not only does it regulate in meticulous detail the ritual practice of the faith, but many of its precepts are also directed solely at the individual's conscience, inasmuch as certain acts are classified as "recommended" and "reprehensible" where performance or omission may be met with divine approval or disapproval, but entails no legal sanctions as such. The popular movements demonstrated that the appeal to the Shari'ah can still be an effective instrument to energize the demand for social justice.[8]

No idea or social institution can win the legitimacy or acceptance of the Sunnī Muslim scholars unless it can pass this traditional methodological test (*uṣūl*). Ideas and institutions failing to pass this test will continue as foreign objects in the body of Muslim thought, generating inner psycholgical tensions. These ideas and institutions lack effective rapport within the inner core of the Muslim personality and motivation. To demonstrate this psychological crisis, I shall recall two major issues handled by a competent and recognized Muslim authority, Rashīd Riḍā. The issues were those of apostasy (*riddah*) and usury (*ribā*).[9]

---

[7] J. N. D. Anderson, *Islamic Law in the Modern World* (New York: New York University Press, 1959), p. 4.

[8] H. Gibb, *Muhammadanism*, pp. 191-192; ed. J. N. D. Anderson and N. J. Coulson, Op. Cit., p. 14.

[9] See A. Hourani, *Arabic Thought*, pp. 237-238, A. al Sa'īdī, *al Ḥurrīyah al Dīnīyah*, pp. 30-33, 160-161.

In the case of apostasy, Riḍā applied the Muslim source-material, *uṣūl*. He discarded *ijmā'* on the ground that it was not based on a clear text of the Qur'an. "On the contrary," he argued, "there is a text which forbids all compulsion in religion" and *ijmā'* is, therefore, in contradiction with "a higher *aṣl* (source or method)." Regarding the issue of usury in the case of bank interest, he observed that Muslims are faced with the danger of "economic penetration and domination by the Western economic system of capitalism." He therefore evoked the principle of *ḍarūrah* (necessity) to allow interest to be charged where applicable.

Neither the authority of Riḍā, combined with the authority of Jamāl al Dīn al Afghānī and the Grand Imam Maḥmūd Shaltūt of al Azhar, could permanently settle the issue of interest on the basis of *ḍarūrah*. The issue of interest is still a source of tension and dispute, leaving the banking system, and in turn the whole economic system in the Muslim world, on shaky grounds. Being uncertain of the Islamic ethics[10] involved, the Muslims have become motivationally weak.

Of course, the answer to such a dilemma is not a formal-legalistic *fatwà* of "yes" or "no," *ḥalāl* or *ḥarām*. This has been tried, and all other possible formal-legalistic positions on the issue of fixed interest rates have been tried. But, then, there are always realities and practicalities which call for workable alternatives. The mere repetition of outdated policies has therefore failed to produce the desired behavior or to put an end to the restlessness and tension.[11]

Comparing Riḍā's conclusion on apostasy with those on usury, we find that his opinion concerning apostasy has gained firm ground and wide acceptance. In the case of usury, however,

---

[10] See J. N. Anderson, Op. Cit., p. 3.

[11] For some examples see: 'Abd al Hādī Ghanāmah, "The Interestless Economy," in *The Contemporary Aspects of Economic and Social Thinking in Islam*, The Muslim Students Association of the United States and Canada (Gary, IN: The Muslim Students Association of the United States and Canada, 1970), pp. 85-100; See also, 'AbdulḤamīd AbūSulaymān, "The Theory of Economics in Islam: The Theory of Tawḥīd," in *The Contemporary Aspects of Economics and Social Thinking in Islam*, the M. S. A., pp. 26-79.

the problem was hardly resolved, creating instead more argument and confusion.

One crucial difference between the two issues under discussion, which ought to be noted, is that while the former did pass a formal test of traditional *uṣūl*, the latter did not. It is primarily in this context that we can understand the meaning of the uneasy coexistence between modern ideas and institutions and the Muslim personality. The modern ideas and institutions did not filter through and pass the *uṣūl* test. They remained alien and continued to exist under the pretext of *ḍarūrah*. The principle of *talfīq* (piecing together) was utilized in order to create a workable relationship, and the result was a continuing absence of originality in contemporary Muslim thought.

It seems as though much effort has been directed toward the content of Muslim thought, while not enough has been done with the problem of methodology. This has led to the borrowing of foreign ideas, ideologies and institutions, all of which have apparently failed to revitalize Muslim thought. Muslim public life has been transformed into a sort of theater where the intelligentsia seem to be playing the roles of Dr. Jekyll and Mr. Hyde. At times they appeal to Islamic motivation, while at others they yield to foreign pressures and to the temptation to chaotically introduce alien ideas and institutions. The front row applauds the excellence of the actors, while the masses are left sleeping in the wings.[12]

The necessary methodological reform was rendered more difficult because both the traditional elite and the modernists have busied themselves with problems of theology and the authenticity of the Sunnah.

This atmosphere of expediency and confusion among intellectuals basically began as a reaction to the Western military and political threat. This reaction led to a new system of education

---

[12] See Malik Bennabi, *Wijhat al A'lām al Islāmī*, p. 57; M. al Bāhī, *Al Fikr al Islāmī*, pp. 490-491; Also, an example of what seems contradictory between what is Islamic and what is modern is the jihad bond which was issued in Egypt. *Al Ahrām*, the Egyptian daily newspaper (containing statements of Egyptian officials) has a page explaining why the government has to pay interest rates for the jihad bond. See *al Ahrām*, April 17, 1971, p. 3, No. 30798 yr. 97.

distinct from the traditional religious system. The result was the formation of two separate groups of intellectuals, the ulama and the *muthaqqafūn* (secular and professional intellectuals), each pursuing its own separate approach and activity. The widening gap between the theological and philosophical reactions of the traditionalists and the reformists, and the simultaneous borrowing and imitation of foreign ideas, ideologies, and institutions by the *muthaqqafūn* precluded any possible genuine revival of Muslim thought, either in assimilating the already existing stream of new ideas or in making the necessary methodological adjustments.[13] Although the door of ijtihad has been declared to be wide open - even if it was claimed to be otherwise earlier - we fail to detect any effective movement toward the revitalization of the Muslim social system or the regeneration of Muslim thought.[14]

The preceding discussion reveals the broad and important nature of Muslim jurisprudence (fiqh) in the traditional system of Muslim thought and the strategic position which *uṣūl* occupies. The discussion further reveals how the failure to understand the function and appreciate the development of *uṣūl* in the system of Muslim thought underlies the intellectual and psychological crisis of the Muslim peoples.

The next step is to study and investigate these *uṣūl* in order to acquire a better understanding of their nature, function, the way in which they are still useful, and the manner in which they should be adjusted to fit the requirements of the contemporary Muslim world.

Uṣūl: The Historical Background

The *uṣūl instinbāṭ al fiqh* (the source material, principles, and methods for deduction of jurisprudence) consist of four basic

---

[13] H. Gibb, *Modern Trends in Islam*, pp. 22, 73, 84, 104, 107; W. M. Watt, *Islamic Political Thought: The Basic Concepts* (Edinburgh, . UK: Edinburgh University Press, 1968), pp. 128-129.

[14] See Fazlur Rahman, *Islamic Methodology in History* (Karachi: Central Institute of Islamic Research, 1965), p. 149; H. Gibb, Op. Cit., pp. 22, 60, 73, 84, 104-105; J. Anderson and N. Coulson, *Islamic Law in Contemporary Cultural Change*, pp. 49, 54; Malik Bennabi, Op. Cit., pp. 83, 185.

uṣūl. The Qur'an and the Sunnah are also called *al aṣlayn* (the Two Sources) since they are the text material of jurisprudence. The Qur'an, the Sunnah, and *ijmāʿ* (consensus) are called *al thalāth al uṣūl* (the Three Sources), distinguishing them from the fourth source, *qiyās* (analogy) or the method for deducing juristic opinions, since *qiyās* belongs to the realm of *'aql* (reasoning) as applied to the text (the Qur'an and the Sunnah).

The Qur'an

The direct revealed word of Allah is the first source of Islamic thought and jurisprudence. It is in Arabic and is divided into one hundred and fourteen *suwar* (chapters), containing more than six thousand verses. The Qur'an is the book that was divinely revealed to the Prophet Muḥammad in verses, during the latter twenty-three years of his life (d. 632 AC), while he lived in the two cities of Makkah and Madīnah in western Arabia. The authenticity of the written text of the Qur'an is beyond dispute.

Watt noted that it became

> clear that the rationally formulated doctrines of the Ashʿarites had less power to evoke responses in ordinary men than the pregnant language of the Qur'an itself. Many Muslims have turned back to the Qur'an and to doctrinal formulations of a Hanbalite type.

The Qur'anic values constitute the basis of the Shariʿah. Through direct contact and religious education and practices, the Qur'an shapes the Muslim outlook and conscience.[15]

The Sunnah

The Sunnah of the Prophet, as Muslim jurists define it, consists of all the authentic reports of pronouncements and acts of the Prophet or such deeds or sayings of other people that had gained his explicit approval. Its subject matter is the life and

---

[15] H. Gibb, Op. Cit., pp. 49-50; Ismāʿīl al Fārūqī, "Islam," in *The Great Asian Religions: An Anthology*, compiled by Wing-tset Chan, et al. (London: Collier-Macmillan Ltd., 1969), p. 336; Muhammad ibn Idrīs al Shāfiʿī, *Islamic Jurisprudence: Shāfiʿī's Risālah*, translated with an introduction, notes and appendices by Majid Khadduri (Baltimore, MD: Johns Hopkins University Press, 1961), pp. 66-80; Muhammad ʿIzzat Darwazah, *Al Dustūr al Qur'ānī fī Shu'ūn al Hayāh* (Cairo: Dār Ihyā' al Kutub al ʿArabīyah, n.d.), pp. 2-80.

actions of the Prophet and the members of his community. The Sunnah of the Prophet, as is reported in the authentic collections of hadith, is the second *aṣl* (singular of *uṣūl*). Muslims believe the Sunnah is divinely inspired, though in meaning rather than letter, whereas the belief in regard to the Qur'an is that both meaning and letter are divine revelation. The Sunnah basically is meant to supplement and to help interpret the Qur'an. This position has been firmly secured for the Sunnah of the Prophet by al Shāfi'ī in his classic work, *al Risālah* (The Message).[16]

The most famous and accepted collections of the Sunnah (hadith) are the six *ṣiḥāḥ* (authentic ones). The *ṣaḥīḥayn* are the two authentic collections of al Bukhārī (194-250 AH) and Muslim (202-261 AH), which are widely accepted by Sunnī jurists and ulama as the most precise and authentic collections. The other four *ṣiḥāḥ* are the four *sunan* of Ibn Mājah, Abū Dāwūd, al Tirmidhī, and al Nasā'ī. The *Muwaṭṭā* of Mālik stands, insofar as the Sunnah part of it is concerned, on almost the same footing in terms of authenticity as the other six, but is not regarded as a collection of Sunnah as such because it was composed primarily as a work of jurisprudence. These are by no means all the collections of Sunnah. There are many others, but they are not considered as authentic as these seven collections. From the above information we can deduce that, in Muslim thought, the Sunnah is considered divinely inspired and that it contains a wealth of source materials.

The subject of Sunnah is a lengthy, difficult, and controversial one. In fact, the controversy starts with the very word Sunnah. What does it mean? Does it refer to the Sunnah of the community (the living Sunnah), or only to the Sunnah of the Prophet? How is the Sunnah of the Prophet related to the Qur'an and to the living Sunnah of the Muslim community? How authentic and precise is the Sunnah? When was the Sunnah documented in writing? How much of it has been preserved? How have the political and theological tensions and struggles affected its authenticity? What are the right criteria to be applied

[16] J. Anderson and N. Coulson, Op. Cit., pp. 23-24; S. Maḥmaṣānī, *Al Awḍā' al Tashrī'īyah*, pp. 146-148.

to the Sunnah? Should criticism be applied to the form or to the content, or to both? How far can man apply reason to measure divine revelation?[17] These are some of the more important questions raised since the *fitnah* (civil war) which started with the murder of 'Uthmān, the third *khalīfah* (656 AC).

Apparently, the question of Sunnah was settled by classical Islam. This was the result of al Shāfi'ī's argument in his *Risālah* on behalf of the Sunnah of the Prophet,[18] and also because of the tremendous efforts made by Muslim scholars in sifting the Sunnah.[19] Besides, there was another major reason why the issue of the Sunnah after al Shāfi'ī seemed to slip into the background as an unimportant and noncontroversial problem. The reason was that, by the time of al Shāfi'ī, Islamic jurisprudence had already been established, its major legal issues had been settled, and the framework of jurisprudence had been laid down, so that controversy about the Sunnah no longer had serious practical implications. This makes us realize that the concern with authenticity and other related questions represented not merely academic and religious concerns, but practical, political, and human interests.

The approach to the problem of the Sunnah depended on the methodology applied and the competence of the scholars in the field.[20] The authenticity of the Sunnah has been settled and its

---

[17] See D. S. Margoliouth, *The Early Development of Muhammadanism* (London, UK: Williams and Norgate, 1914), pp. 79-98; Fazlur Rahman, Op. Cit., pp. 2-84; Joseph Schacht, *The Origins of Muhammadan Jurisprudence* (Oxford, UK: The Clarendon Press, 1950), pp. 1-5, 11-13, 329; Muhammad Abū Zahrah, *Tārīkh al Madhāhib al Islāmīyah* (Cairo: Dār al Fikr, n.d.), vol. II:66-69.

[18] See J. Anderson and N. Coulson, Op. Cit., pp. 22-24; and S. al Maḥmaṣānī, Op. Cit., p. 146.

[19] See H. Gibb, *Muhammadanism*, p. 85; Muhammad Habiballah, *The Earliest Extensive Work on the Hadith: Ṣaḥīfat Hammām ibn Munabbih*, trans. Muhammad Rahimuddin, 5th rev. ed. (Paris: Centre Cultural Islamique, 1961), pp. 1-69; Muhammad Mustafa Azami, *Studies in Early Hadith Literature with a Critical Edition of Some Early Texts* (Beirut: al Maktab al Islāmī, 1968), pp. 246-247, 260-268, 289-292; S. Maḥmaṣānī, Op. Cit., pp. 147-149.

[20] Abū Bakr ibn Mūsā ibn Ḥazm al Hamadānī, *Kitāb al 'Ibar fī al Nāsikh wa al Mansūkh min al Athar*, ed. Rātib al Hakīmī, (Hums, Syria: Maṭba'at al Andalūs, 1966), p. 29, 200-210, 218-219. See also Ṣalāḥ al Dīn al Munajjid and Y. Q. Khūrī, *Fatāwā al Imām Muhammad Rashīd Riḍā* (Beirut: Dār al Kitāb al Jadīd, 1970).

significance as a part of the Sunnī Muslims' mental frame of reference has been permanently established. Other schools of thought, such as the Ẓāhirīyah of the famous Ibn Ḥazm al Andalūsī, either disappeared or slipped away to far-off regions or into minority groups, as in the case of the Shi'ah school of thought.

When we understand the new developments and challenges that the Muslim world has had to undergo and face during the last few centuries, we can understand why the issue of the authenticity of the hadith has again been raised. For the modernists and some reformists, this was primarily a way to do away with an outdated traditional legal opinion. We will show why practically all possible positions on the issue of the authenticity of the hadith, its rejection, acceptance, or sifting have failed to revive either the creativity or the productivity of Muslim thought. To achieve this we have to make explicit the basic assumption involved in the renewed issue of the authenticity of the Sunnah.

To really understand the subject of the Sunnah, one must wade through a huge amount of material. But in order to understand how nearly futile the issue of the authenticity of the hadith is, it is sufficient to glance at two contradictory works on the same subject: the famous work of the late Joseph Schacht, *The Origins of Muhammadan Jurisprudence*, and the work of M. M. Azami, which was supervised by the late A. J. Arberry, *Studies in Early Hadith Literature.* Arberry wrote in his forward to Azami's work, "In the field of Sunnah, Dr. Azami has done a pioneering work of the highest value and exact standards of scholarship."

Two short quotations from each of the above-mentioned works will clarify the picture and help us turn away in this work from what seems a futile effort, and instead look ahead for new answers and directions.

In the epilogue of his work, Schacht says:[21]

> The idea we have gained of the formative period is thoroughly different from the fiction which asserted itself from the early third century A. H. onward.

---

[21] J. Schacht, Op. Cit., p. 329.

In what Azami[22] calls his final conclusion, he says:

> The examples supplied by Schacht tend to refute his own theory. The phenomena of "*isnād*", the number of transmitters belonging to scores of provinces, make the theory of "projecting back" artificial creations and similar statements almost impossible to accept... Traditionalists have taken the utmost care to check errors and discrepancies with sincerity.[23]

Qiyās : Analogy

We cannot understand the widespread usage of *qiyās* and the emergence of the many supplementary *uṣūl* unless we understand the implicit assumptions of the classical period of Islam. The classical thought of the ʿAbbāsī Empire, which was the major power in the world of the High Caliphate, was basically content with the social system and achievements of the model laid down by the Prophet. Thus, the role assigned to both Muslim thought and Muslim methodology was the maintenance of the basic model,[24] in which *qiyās* meant to seek similarities between new situations and early practices, especially those of the Prophet. Classical Muslim thought also succeeded in producing a few supplementary methods, notably that of *maṣlaḥah,* to make up for the growing number of new situations that were difficult to deal with by the direct application of textual material or by analogy with that material. An example of the use of *maṣlaḥah,* not only when there is no text (*naṣṣ*) for reference in ruling on a specific situation but also as a principle used to override a text of consensus (*ijmāʿ*) considered to be

---

[22] M. Azami, Op. Cit., p. 247.

[23] ʿAbd al Wahhāb Khallāf, *ʿIlm Uṣūl al Fiqh* (Kuwait: Al Dār al Kuwaitīyah, 1968), p. 45; M. Abū Zahrah, *Mālik*, pp. 322-341; S. Maḥmaṣānī, Op. Cit., p. 150.

[24] Imam Ibn Kathīr (774/1372) described the role assigned to the Sunnah in the classical jurisprudence when he said, "If some said, what is the best way of interpreting the Qur'an? (The answer) is that the most valid method is to interpret the Qur'an by the Qur'an. What is general in one place has usually been explained in another place. If (this is not the case and) you were unable to do that, then go to the Sunnah. It explains the Qur'an and makes it clear. Not only that, but Imam Abū ʿAbd Allah Muhammad ibn Idrīs al Shāfiʿī said that all the decisions of the Messenger of Allah were from what he understood from the Qur'an..."and whenever we could not find the interpretation in the Qur'an itself, nor in the Sunnah, then we turned to the interpretations (*aqwāl*) of the Companions because they knew better." See Ibn Kathīr, *Tafsīr al Qur'ān*, vol. I, p. 7.

incovenient or unsuitable, was given by Abū Ḥāmid al Ghazzālī in his work *al Muṣtaṣfā*. He ruled that it is proper to kill Muslims who were used in captivity to shield dangerous non-Muslims enemies against a Muslim attack. The public interest (*maṣlaḥah*) necessitated a ruling contrary to the *naṣṣ* and *ijmā'* prohibiting the killing of a Muslim.[25] The further classical Muslim jurists drew away from the time of the Prophet, the more they used and successfully elaborated the method of *maṣlaḥah*, as in the case of the Ḥanbalī jurists in their concept of *siyāsah shar'īyah* (Islamic public policy).[26]

Now that so much time has passed, and so many internal and external changes have accumulated, Muslims can no longer work within the framework of the classical model which required only the simple maintenance of the existing social system. Modern challenges make new demands on the Muslim methodology. The basic requirement now is to generate thought commensurate with the needs of internal and external affairs, and that does not contradict the intents and values of Islam.

The Sunnah and the Space-Time Dimension

Contemporary criticism and dissatisfaction with traditional Muslim thought in the field of international relations usually concentrates on the Sunnah.[27] Traditions that seem to present harsh or outdated practices against non-Muslims usually lend themselves to such disapproval. The standards against which these criticisms are measured are mostly utopian and conceptually and ideologically Western. Likewise, the examples given for such criticism are customarily drawn from such issues as *jizyah*, tactics in foreign relations, and warfare with non-Muslims. Traditionalists and apologists have tried to defend the Sunnah and Muslim jurisprudence by attacking unfavorable examples of Western practice like racial discrimination and modern

---

[25] See A. Khallāf, Op. Cit., pp. 101-102; also see al Farrā', Op. Cit., pp. 37, 43, 49; Ibn Qudāmah, *al Mughnī*, pp. 204-205; W. al Zuḥaylī, *Naẓarīyat al Ḍarūrah*, pp. 163, 168, 243.

[26] See M. Abū Zahrah, *Ibn Ḥanbal*, pp. 218-331.

[27] J. N. D. Anderson and N. J. Coulson, Op. Cit., pp. 23-24; S. Maḥmaṣānī, pp. 146-148.

imperialism. Such a situation was frustrating for both the critics, who were themselves more often than not Westernized, and for the apologists alike.

Contemporary Muslim dissatisfaction with traditional thought in the face of their failure in modern times to prevent Western encroachments and their failure to match Western material achievements could explain to a great extent the efforts by modernists to prove the fallibility of the Sunnah, thereby toppling the structure of traditionalist thought built on the Sunnah. The failure of the modernists, in their turn, to make Muslim political thought more responsive to the needs of the times has resulted in an even more detailed questioning of the Sunnah and its relevance to Muslim dilemmas, especially as regards international relations. Excessive concern with the authenticity of hadith only points up the need to free modern Muslim thought from the negative and inhibiting influences of the traditional Muslim social system, involving space-time elements of a millenium ago. It is important to establish that this element of space-time in the hadith is one of the most important sources of Muslim political thought.

A few examples of the hadith from the field of *siyar* (relations among nations) and related matters reflect elements of space and time:

> Anas reported Allah's messenger as saying "Go in Allah's name, trusting in Allah, and adhering to the religion of Allah's Messenger. Do not kill a decrepit old man, or a young infant, or a woman. Do not be dishonest about booty, but collect your spoils. Do right and act well, for Allah loves those who do well." Abū Dāwūd related it.[28]

> 'Alī related that Allah's Messenger had an Arab bow in his hand and, on seeing another with a Persian bow in his hand, said, "What is this? Throw it away. Stay with these and the like, and with spears with shafts, for Allah will help you to support the religion with them, and establish you in the land." Ibn Mājah related it.[29]

---

[28] Walīy al Dīn al Tabrīzī, *Mishkāt al Maṣābīh*, translated with explanatory notes by James Robson (Lahore: Sh. Muhammad Ashraf, 1963), vol. III, p. 838.

[29] Ibid., vol. III, p. 825.

Abū Usayd reported that the Prophet said to them at the battle of Badr when they drew up in lines to meet the Quraysh, "When they come near you, shoot arrows at them." Another version states, "When they come near you, shoot at them; but do not use all of your arrows." Bukhārī related it.[30]

Looking carefully at these hadith (the whole of classical and traditional political thought has been built upon them), we can see clearly that these are instructions pertaining to the running of a medieval war in the context of a medieval social system, and any reference to them that overlooks the space-time context is misleading. To make any meaningful use of this kind of text we have to understand the aspect of the underlying value involved in such pronouncements, as distinguished from the concrete physical and cultural aspects. It is understandable for the classical jurists to have engaged in literal analysis, a word-for-word and an issue-for-issue comparison and analogy in their arguments along the lines of these traditions. But when contemporary jurists function in the same manner and even repeat the old instructions word for word, there is obviously a lack of appreciation for the changes that have taken place.[31] Today the repetition of old instructions that forbid killing women, children, etc., in war clearly show that modern jurists are not aware of the implications of modern warfare and modern weapons.[32] These kinds of instructions are of no help to the administrators of modern warfare and mean little to them. Often the choice of the kinds of weapons to use, whether it be conventional or nuclear bombs or even exotic weapons, no longer exists. It is often difficult to single out civilians. Under the techniques of modern warfare, the moral questions are no longer whom one should or not kill, but how many one should kill, and what constitutes "over-kill."

---

[30] Ibid., vol. III, pp. 821, 837, 838; al Shaybānī, *al Siyar al Kabīr*, vol. I, p. 87.

[31] See Ibn Rushd, *Bidāyat al Mujtahid*, vol.I, pp. 311-312; Mālik ibn Anas, *al Mudawwanah*, vol. III, p. 8, and al Shaybānī, Op. Cit., vol.I, p. 42.

[32] See Muhammad Abū Zahrah, *Al 'Ilāqāt al Duwalīyah fī al Islām* (Cairo: al Dār al Qawmīyah, 1964), p. 43; S. Sābiq, *Fiqh al Sunnah*, vol. XI, pp. 48-49, 129-132.

It is understandable that al Shāfi'ī, in dealing with foreign relations, advises Muslim rulers to attack the *mushrikūn* in their country at least once a year, if not more often, and not to accept a truce for more than ten years. Indeed, this opinion is based on analogy with the Sunnah of the Prophet, since the latter was engaged with his enemy in a battle at least once a year and did not accept a truce for more than ten years.[33] However, under the extremely dangerous conditions of modern warfare and the fragile international system of today, and in the foreseeable future, no statesman could possibly accept this kind of analogy and understanding.

Imam Ibn Kathīr tells us in his work of *tafsīr* (commentary on the Qur'an):

> When the Messenger of Allah arrived at Makkah, he and his Companions had suffered badly from Yathrib's (Madīnah's) fever and it had exhausted them. The *mushrikūn* expected that the Muslims would be exhausted and seriously weakened from Yathrib's fever. While the mushrikūn were seated near the Black Stone, Allah made known to His Prophet what the *mushrikūn* had been saying among themselves about the Muslims. Therefore, the Prophet ordered his Companions to walk half-running (in the area where the mushrikūn could see them) in the first three circumabulations (of the Ka'bah) in order to show the *mushrikūn* their endurance, and ordered them to walk between the two corners where the *mushrikūn* could not see them. The Prophet spared his companions half the running (*ramal*) in all the circumabulations out of consideration for their exhaustion. The *mushrikūn* said, "Are these the people we thought the fever had exhausted? These are stronger than so and so." This was related in the two *ṣiḥāḥ* by Ḥammād ibn Zaydabah.[34]

For that reason, it is a command of the Sunnah (practiced even today) that Muslims walk half-running in the first three rounds of *ṭawāf*, the circling of the Ka'bah in Makkah.

---

[33] See al Shāfi'ī, *al Umm*, vol. IV, pp. 90-91; and Ibn Rushd, Op. Cit., vol. I, pp. 313-314.

[34] Ibn Kathīr, *Tafsīr al Qur'ān*, vol. IV, p.202. The reader should be aware that the question of time and place in Islam and throughout this thesis deals with questions of social relationships and systems. This has nothing to do with the questions of *'ibādah*, *sha'ā'ir*, and *dhikr*.

It is clear that, in this case, what has been considered tradition and then performed out of love, respect, and adherence to the Sunnah of the Prophet, in itself a good and noble motive, has its origins in a tactic used by the Prophet for deceiving an enemy waiting for the first available opportunity to destroy the Muslim army. This example shows to what extent the Prophet was responsive to the circumstances around him. The effect of the time-place element is not always so evident or simple, and in order to overcome the limitations of this time-place element, a far greater degree of sophistication in analysis is needed.

The real problem underlying the Sunnah, and with it *uṣūl* and the whole of traditional Muslim political thought, is the failure to comprehend the influence of the space-time element. This element must be present, in one way or another, in all instructions concerning the carrying out of any concrete system. This kind of Sunnah and instructions, except for their noble goals, should not be extended beyond their space-time limitations. Such an attitude could not exist except for extreme conservatism, shortsightedness, and unawareness of new realities. The lesson we learn from these examples is that *qiyās* in areas of social interaction should be total and comprehensive wherever applicable. A long passage of time and a radical change of place may leave little practical room for the application of partial and case-to-case *qiyās*.

Concrete Examples Given in the Qur'an

The Qur'an is not exactly like the Sunnah, as we noted before. For the most part, it expresses itself in general statements as philosophical and ideological guidelines. Thus, verses of a general nature form the foundation of Muslim outlook and belief. The Qur'an has played, and continues to play, a major role in forming and maintaining values in the Muslim conscience and social system. Nonetheless, when the Qur'an speaks in terms of specific cases or gives concrete examples, it, like most of the Sunnah, involves a space-time element. In these instances, readers ought to be extremely careful in deducing generalities, especially in the field of external relationships where Muslims do not have full control over events.

Simple and direct deduction from Islamic textual materials, without properly accounting for changes involving the space-time element of the early Muslim period, is a retrogressive practice. The classical jurists could indulge in such practices because the social system of the classical period remained basically unchanged throughout, as both the early Muslim period and the classical Muslim period consisted of predominantly agrarian societies. For the most part, Muslims in the classical period governed as great powers and controlled their part of the classical world and its civilization.

This situation is clearly illustrated by the following examples which include a basic concept in the field of international relations: power. Allah says in the Qur'an:

> O Prophet! Rouse the believers to the fight. If there are twenty among you, patient and persevering, they will vanquish two hundred; if a hundred, they will vanquish a thousand of the unbelievers, for these are a people without understanding. For the present, Allah has lightened your task, for He knows that there is a weak spot in you; but even so, if there a hundred of you, patient and persevering, they will vanquish two hundred, and if a thousand, they will vanquish two thousand, with the leave of Allah; for Allah is with those who patiently persevere (8:66).

It is clear that these verses are instructions to the Prophet regarding mobilization and preparation for fighting. The verses clearly state the ratio of 1:10 and then 1:2 as the number of Muslim soldiers who would be able to defeat the number of enemy soldiers. The verses also speak of qualities - faith, patience, and perseverance. The important point here, however, is that some basic assumptions regarding the ratio of Muslims capable of fighting nonbelievers can be valid only if other factors, such as skills, techniques, and equipment continue to remain constant. The passage makes this point quite clear, after certain factors change ("...for the present... He knows that there is a weak spot in you"), the ratio correspondingly changes drastically from 1:10 to 1:2. Thus, the reader or the jurist should be sensitive to any changes in meaning and their effects on the strategy of confrontation with the enemy. Furthermore, it is evident that if commentators or jurists ignore the implicit assumptions involved in such verses, or draw heavily on merely the ratio in commenting on the above verses, they are in danger of committing a grave mistake, as has happened at times, and distorting the illustration or example given in the Qur'an.

With this in mind, let us compare what a jurist of the late second century AH (eighth century AC) and a jurist of the late fourteenth century (twentieth century AC) have to say on the subject of numerical superiority.

The renowned jurist, al Shāfi'ī (786-820 AC) wrote:

> When this verse was revealed, Ibn 'Abbās explained concerning the verse: "If there are twenty among you, patient and persevering, they will vanquish two hundred," that Allah made it a duty that they (the Muslims) should not flee from the battlefield if they are up against two hundred. Allah Most High revealed, "For the present, Allah has lightened your task, for He knows that there is a weak spot in you; but even so, if there be a hundred of you, patient and persevering, they will vanquish two hundred." Allah made it a duty that they should not flee from two hundred of the enemy's soldiers, and this is as Ibn 'Abbās said; "By Allah's will, with the clear revealed text there is no need for interpretation...When the Muslims go to the battlefield and find their enemy double their number, they are not allowed by Allah (*ḥurrima 'alayhim*) to turn away from them. ... Even if the number of *mushrikūn* is more than double, I would not like them to turn away, but it would not call for the anger of Allah (*sukhṭ*)."[35]

From this quotation, we cannot fail to observe that al Shāfi'ī concentrated almost exclusively on the number of fighters. As mentioned before, considering al Shāfi'ī's time, it is not surprising that he came to such an understanding. Conditions then were still comparable to those of the Prophet's time. Another early jurist, Mālik ibn Anas, did realize in a vague way that the real issue involved in the verses was the concept of power rather than the number of fighting soldiers.[36] One twentieth-century jurist has quoted Mālik to this effect.

Sayyid Sābiq, writing in the second half of the twentieth century on the same subject, has taken the same line.[37] To make the picture clear, we will quote most of the parts dealing with the problem. The title of the section is "Fleeing from Double the Number of Enemies."

---

[35] al Shāfi'ī, *al Umm*, vol. IV, p. 92.

[36] Ibn Rushd, *Bidāyat al Mujtahid*, vol. I, p. 313.

[37] Sayyid Sābiq, *Fiqh al Sunnah*, vol. XI, pp. 127-128.

Previously in this work it was mentioned that it is not permissible (ḥarām) to flee while advancing toward the enemy except in two cases; turning to fight in a different direction, or joining another group of the Muslim army. What is left for us to say is that it is allowed (*yajūzu*) to flee during the battle if the enemy is more than double, but if it is double or less, then fleeing is not allowed (*yaḥrumu*). Allah Most High has said: "For the present Allah has lightened your task..."

The author of al Muhadhdhab says: "If their number is more than double that of the Muslims, fleeing is allowed. But if they think that it is most probable that they will not perish, then it is better (al afḍal) that they stand fast. But if they think that it is most probable that they will perish, then there are two ways. The first: they are obligated to leave because Allah says, 'And be not cast by your own hands to your ruin' (2:195), the second: It is recommended but not a duty, because if they are killed they gain martyrdom.

If the number of non-believers is not more than double of the Muslims, and if the Muslims do not foresee the probability of destruction, they are not allowed to flee. But if they see the probability of destruction, they have two choices. First, fleeing is not allowed because Allah says it is not allowed, and the jurists said that this is the right position because it is the literal meaning of the verse. The second, the opinion of Ibn al Mājishūn related from Mālik ibn Anas, is that "Weakness is not a matter of numbers alone. Rather, it is a lack of power. Therefore, it is allowed even in a one on one situation, that the Muslim flee if the enemy has a better horse, or sword, or a stronger body. Evidently, this is the correct opinion."[38]

This is all that this writer has said on the subject. Moreover, analysis of or research into the concept of power and its application has almost been ignored by Muslim writers in the twentieth century.

How much does, or can, this contemporary but traditional writer's work mean to a twentieth-century statesman? Do such writings have any relevance to the modern world?

With such a level of scholarship on the contemporary meaning of power, it would not be surprising if a Muslim were to conclude that either power is a matter of numbers or, clinging to a traditional belief, that Muslims will automatically be victorious even if they are weaker than their enemy.

---

[38] It is worth mentioning the lack of proper treatment of the concept and factors of power in Muslim works. I could not find Muslim works devoted to an investigation of the subject *per se*.

The most elementary principle of strategy has always been that one can attain victory only if one is more powerful, in the broadest meaning of power (*quwwah*), than one's adversary. Contemporary analyses show clearly that power is a broad concept that includes all elements of human life; military, technological, economic, psychological, moral, and spiritual.

Ibn Rushd made a mistake in treating power as an exclusively materialistic equation when he summarized the opinion of Mālik ibn Anas by saying: "Double is to be considered in terms of power (in the widest sense), not in the number of fighters." But Mālik did not use the term *quwwah*. Such a comparison of power could not hold true or be logically valid unless the concept of power in the mind of Mālik was not limited to physical power. If the power, most broadly construed, of the enemy is double or more than double that of the Muslims, then obviously the Muslims will ultimately be defeated. The crucial element here is the word "power," including tangibles and intangibles. The wording of Mālik, however, may imply a physical meaning in terms of equipment by his latter reference only to the excellence of the enemy's sword and horse. If the enemy were better equipped in sword and horse, thereby possessing greater physical power, a Muslim, according to Mālik, was not obliged anymore to fight him man to man. As mentioned, it is only logical that the more powerful will be victorious and that the weak will be vanquished. But the key to applying this truism is one's defining power to include both the physical sense and the widest possible nonphysical sense of the term.

Another result of insensitivity to the space-time element involved in such verses of the Qur'an is the classical concept of permanent abrogation (*naskh*). Due to this concept, the different principles and values behind the Islamic experience in Makkah and early Madīnah have fallen into disuse and been forgotten. In considering *naskh*, all that mattered to the jurists was the last position of the late Madīnan period, which in most cases fit the situation of a powerful and established society and therefore suited states such as those of the Umawīs and the 'Abbāsīs. It is as if the jurists considered the periods and stages prior to the last Madīnan period as having been historically abrogated, and therefore unworthy of consideration. Contemporary Muslim jurists, though they have attempted to reinterpret many cases of *naskh*, seem to accept the same concept of permanent *naskh*, overlooking the space-time element involved in *naskh*. In their thinking, no attempt was made to disavow the concept, only to reinterpret it. The Verse of the Sword (*āyat al sayf*) is a good example of a *naskh* argument that abrogates all previous principles. The Verse of the Sword, according to most dependable interpretations, is "And fight the pagans all together as they fight you all together" (9:36).[39]

Al Sarakhsī, commenting on al Shaybānī's *siyar*, said:

> To sum up, the command for jihad and fighting had been revealed in stages...the final stage being the absolute order to fight non-believers... This involves an obligation, but this obligation is meant to exalt Islam and to subdue the idolators.[40]

Al Zuhaylī has made it clear that most jurists of the second century AH (eighth century AC) considered war as the rule, rather than the exception, in relations between Muslims and non-Muslims. Moreover, he attributes this attitude to their excesses in using *naskh*.[41] Their understanding of the Qur'an had been less than critical owing to their having stopped at the literal meaning of each verse without making serious efforts to compare and reconcile verses that seemed to contradict one another. Instead, the jurists claimed that certain verses abrogated certain other verses. This juristic understanding is a clear reflection of conditions in their times. Al Zuhaylī thinks that the reason behind the jurists' stand was the overriding need for Muslims in those times to remain in a state of constant preparation for battle in order to protect Islam. Under the political circumstances, it is not very difficult to understand why the technique of abrogation served as an aid in providing for a simple and firm position to strengthen the morale of the Muslims when facing their enemies. War was of limited effect. The enemy never accepted the concept of freedom of religion and belief. The safety and security of Muslims made war both a necessary and acceptable instrument in the classical relationship between *dār al Islām* and *dār al ḥarb*.

---

[39] See Abū Zayd, *al Naskh fī al Qur'ān*, pp. 11, 504.

[40] al Shaybānī, *al Siyar al Kabīr*, vol. I, p. 188.

[41] See W. al Zuhaylī, *Āthār al Harb*, pp. 130-131.

In modern times, the international system is trying to provide some alternative to the continuing hostility among nations, because it is extremely dangerous to accept war as a legitimate means for the resolution of political disputes among nations. In maintaining the classical juristic position, Muslim intellectuals have perpetuated the classical misuse of the technique of abrogation, which almost did away with the various values and positions formulated during the Makkan and early Madīnan periods to direct and guide Muslims in their relations with non-Muslims. Al Zuhaylī concludes:

> The position of the classical jurists that war is the permanent basis (for international relations) is not an authority that is binding on anyone. It has no support from the Qur'an and the Sunnah. It is merely a decision (ruling) of temporary effect.[42]

The Qur'an represents the basic source of values for the Muslim social system and international outlook, and is the basic force shaping the inner conscience and outlook of Muslims throughout the world. Despite the fact that Muslims have by and large failed to live up to the ideal expectations of Islam, it is clear that Muslims, through continuous interaction and contact with the Qur'an, have always been deeply affected by it. Any reform that ignores this fact or suggests otherwise does not show a real awareness of the influence of the Qur'an on Muslims. The time-place element must be taken into account when the Qur'an is used to interpret a contemporary situation.

Ijmā' and the Changing World

Ijmā' simply means "consensus." As an *aṣl* (plural *uṣūl*), it is meant to be applied in cases where there is no *naṣṣ* (text) from the Qur'an or the Sunnah to decide the *ḥukm* (ruling) in a particular case or issue. Needless to say, no *ijmā'* could ever rule contrary to the authentic texts of the Qur'an and the Sunnah. When consensus occurs within these limits, it is binding on all Muslims.

In actuality, however, the only agreement among jurists based on *ijmā'* concerns the prayers being five times a day, the

---

[42] Ibid., p. 135.

obligation of zakāh, etc. These are matters, however, that have been established conclusively by the Qur'an, the Sunnah, and the *ijmā'* of the Companions of the Prophet. In this wise they are, in fact, common knowledge. Beyond these fundamentals, no absolute consensus can be said to have been reached on any issue. Indeed, this continues to be a subject of considerable debate among the different schools of jurisprudence.[43]

There are some writers who seem to be optimistic about the possibility of using the technique of *ijmā'* to develop modern Muslim jurisprudence.[44] But if we understand the real problem involved in the existing conditions of traditional thought, especially in the *uṣūl* aspect, we realize that the problem lies not only in attaining consensus *per se*, but also in an intellectual attitude that has not yet produced a creative and effective methodology. The ideas and institutions inherent in this methodology may or may not call for *ijmā'*.

The traditionalists consider *ijmā'* the consensus of all *mujtahidūn*, which in the contemporary world boils down to the consensus of the authoritative ulama. This view, however, is untenable, because the ulama no longer necessarily represent the mainstream of Muslim intellectual and public involvement. Their system of education is certainly not in touch with the changes that are occurring in the world today. Quite often, therefore, their opinions serve only to add to the confusion.

It is clear that the simplistic, traditional concept of *ijmā'* is no longer suitable for a nonclassical social system. Law and policy-making, especially in the field of international relations, involve complex techniques and considerations that are not in any way amenable to the application of *ijmā'*.

It is also clear that *ijmā'* on different subjects now requires the consensus of other segments of society. In other words, the application of *ijmā'* can no longer be viewed as the exclusive prerogative of the professional ulama. Moreover, in a rapidly changing world, the concept of permanent *ijmā'*, particularly as

---

43 M. Abū Zahrah, *Mālik*, pp. 324-325.

44 A. Khallāf, *'Ilm Uṣūl al Fiqh*, p. 149; and M. Maḥmaṣānī, *al Awḍā' al Tashrī'īyah*, p. 150.

regards the fluid area of international relations, is neither practical nor possible because of the space-time factor.

Basic Shortcomings: Lack of Empiricism and Systematization

We have already shown that classical as well as contemporary Muslim jurists and thinkers for the most part overlooked the concept of space-time and its relation to the structure and application of classical Muslim methodology. There are two additional shortcomings inherent in that methodology: the failure to gather empirical data and, concomitantly, the failure to employ a rigorously systematic approach.

Lack of Empiricism

From the very beginning of *uṣūl,* we find Muslim jurists looking upon deduction from the texts of the Qur'an and the Sunnah as their mainstay in acquiring and in maintaining the principles and particulars of the social system according to the Shari'ah, both in internal and external matters. They called this process *uṣūl instinbāṭ al fiqh* (principles for the deduction of legal rulings).[45] In the physical sciences such as medicine, mathematics, and geography, however, Muslims drew on both text and reason. They were empirical and experimental, and applied both induction and deduction. Social sciences, such as political science, psychology, sociology, and social psychology were absent basically because of the absence of empiricism and the lack of the systematic induction and investigation of man and his social nature and reality. The notable exception was the work of the eighth hijrī century scholar, Ibn Khaldūn (1332-1406 A.C.), who marks the real beginning of the modern social sciences.

Two main reasons for this uneven classical Muslim growth are worth noting. The first was, as we have already mentioned, the general satisfaction with the existing social system as laid down by the Prophet and strengthened by the religious texts. The second reason seems to be the failure of the Mu'tazilah movement to deal properly with the question of reason (*'aql*)

---

[45] A. Khallāf, Op. Cit., pp. 11-12; M. Abū Zahrah, *Ibn Hanbal*, p. 205.

and revelation (*waḥy*) in an Islamic context. As a result, they were unable to establish a permanent basis for the evolution of a rational philosophy in Islam.[46]

There was a general reaction in the ninth and tenth centuries against Greek philosophy and the Islamically unorthodox position of the Mu'tazilah on the relationship between reason and revelation. This reaction put an end to the Mu'tazilah experiment and simultaneously brought about the demise of empiricism and systematic investigation in the field of Islamic social studies.[47] The work entitled *Tahāfut al Falāsifah* (Refutation of the Philosophers) by al Ghazzālī (450-505 AH) in the fifth hijrī century is a landmark in the battle against rationalism.

This attitude is reflected in the traditional, orthodox educational system in which the text was emphasized and not much attention was paid to developing any systematic rational knowledge pertaining to law and social structure.[48] This attitude, which does not really conform to the Qur'anic attitude concerning the humanly comprehensible, (*shahādah*) was easily accepted by those who lived in practical isolation from the mainstream of society and its constantly changing situations, or who were either literalist, or interested in maintaining the status quo. The result was a lack of proper input and feedback into Muslim social studies and decision-making processes and the absence of even the concept of organized social sciences. For these reasons, *siyar* continued to be a formalistic field of study rather than a dynamic Islamic empirical study of international relations.

It is not true that jurists, in approaching the Islamic text, proceed only by divine guidance; in the process they have to draw on their acquired understanding and knowledge. No one could

---

[46] See E. I. J. Rosenthal, *Political Thought*, pp. 114-115; Ignaz Goldzieher, *Mawqif Ahl al Sunnah bi Izā' 'Ulūm al Awā'il*, in *al Turāth al Yūnānī fī al Ḥaḍārah al Islāmiyah: Dirāsāt li Kibār al Mustashriqīn*, 3rd ed. (Cairo: Dār al Nahdah al 'Arabīyah, 1965); Abū Zahrah, *Fī Ẓill al Islām*, pp. 17-30; and T. J. Boer, *Tārīkh al Falsafah fī al Islām*, translated from German by Muhammad 'Abd al Hādī, Abū Rīdah, 4th ed. (Cairo: Lajnat al Ta'līf wa al Tarjamah wa al Nashr, 1957), pp. 95-125.

[47] A. Hourani, *Arabic Thought*, p. 18; H. A. R. Gibb, *Islamic Civilization*, pp. 10-14, 148-149; and W. Watt, *Islamic Thought*, pp. 162-164.

[48] See Fazlur Rahman, *Islamic Methodology*, pp. 168-179.

really engage in such an activity with a blank mind. Lack of rigorous application of empiricism through both deduction and induction and other methods of scientific research in the field of the social sciences is bound to result in grave errors and misunderstandings. It is mainly under the influence of Western challenges, discoveries, and scientific methodology that Muslims have hastily reinterpreted their texts in the face of new realities. Nevertheless, they have failed to establish serious integrated studies and systematic research in the areas of law and the social sciences, including that of international relations. At present, the Muslim system of education still lacks originality in this direction and is only a poor imitation of an alien educational system.

Three examples from the field of international relations will suffice to show how the lack of an empirical approach affects Muslim social studies and the growth of the Islamic social system.

The first example has already been mentioned, that of the ratio between the number of Muslim and non-Muslim combatants mentioned in the Qur'an (at 8:66). An empirical, systematic, and conceptual study of the problem of power would help us to better understand the reason for giving the specific numbers in the Qur'anic verse. Close examination of the verse reveals a component of power other than that of the mere numbers of fighters which is only one aspect of an army's power. As a matter of fact, for reasons due to changes in the components of power among the early Muslims, the Qur'an reduced the ratio of Muslim fighters from 1:10 to 1:2. Modern wars are more complicated and involve many other components of power, depending on the type of confrontation, from guerilla warfare to massive mechanized warfare, and even to total nuclear conflagration.

The second example is the formal legal discussion on the right of the army to cut down trees, destroy houses, and kill cattle. Let us listen to the way Ibn Rushd put the case:

> The reason for their (the jurists') differences (on the issue of laying waste to the land by conquering armies) is (the difference between) what Abū Bakr did and what the Prophet did. It is an established fact that the Prophet burned the Banū al Naḍīr's palm trees. It is also known with certainty that Abū Bakr acted contrary to the Prophet's precedent, though it is assumed that he did so for one of two reasons. Either he knew of an abrogation, or he thought that the action against

the Banū al Naḍīr was a special case. Then, for whatever reason, the jurists upheld Abū Bakr's actions. But those who depend solely on the example of the Prophet would not accept either the words or the deeds of anyone else as an authority. [In this case] he would allow the cutting down of trees. What made Mālik differentiate between animals and trees [was that he saw] in killing animals [an act of] mutilation, and mutilation is prohibited, and it was not reported that the Prophet, peace be upon him, had killed animals. That is the limit allowed [for Muslims] in injuring the non-believers in their persons and their possessions.[49]

To this stand al Sarakhsī answered:

But we say: If [it] is allowed [in war] to kill human beings (*al nufūs*), and that is a matter of greater magnitude, then the destruction of buildings and trees is obviously allowed.[50]

Of course the whole argument, as we see it, is now no longer relevant. In modern wars massive destruction is inevitable. The important thing here is that the argument constitutes poor input in terms of an empirical and rational understanding of war, as well as a lack of feedback on the concept of war strategy and other major issues essential in each battle. Looking back, we can see that neither the Prophet nor Abū Bakr intended in their commandments either to produce a war manual which officers must consult for daily orders or to limit Muslim decision makers' freedom in dealing with foreign powers according to changing circumstances.

It seems obvious that both the Prophet and Abū Bakr, within the Islamic framework as they understood it, were doing something which they saw as necessary in the situation each faced. In the case of Banū al Naḍīr, the Prophet, facing a hostile tribe standing behind their fortresses, had to destroy their sources of livelihood in order to force them to come out and surrender. Under their command were water wells and dates, a long-lasting source of food. Using a strategy of destruction, the Prophet freed his army to face the imminent danger of the Quraysh and other Arab tribes. What Abū Bakr faced was a different situation. He sent his army to a vast land, Syria and Iraq, where nonhostile inhabitants were controlled by unpopular

---

[49] Al Shaybānī, Op. Cit., vol. I, p. 43.

[50] Ibn Rushd, Op. Cit., vol. I, pp. 311-312.

powers: the Romans and the Persians. Destruction of the means of living of an otherwise friendly people would have been a foolish policy, as it would have alienated the people and turned them toward the enemy. Of course, this argument does not nullify but rather reinforces the higher Qur'anic values and ethics against corruption and excess or waste of all kinds including killing (*'adam al ifsād wa 'adam al isrāf*). Nothing may be killed or injured needlessly. These basic values and principles no doubt guided both the Prophet and Abū Bakr in achieving victory and saving human lives. There is no need for any further literal or arbitrary explanation by the jurists.

The third example is the role of the technique of *naskh* in cases such as the Verse of the Sword (*āyat al sayf*) which has caused contemporary Muslim scholars to accuse, wrongly, the classical jurists of unconsciously compromising by subordinating their understanding to their immediate needs.[51] It is very difficult to understand why many contemporary Muslim jurists have committed such an error unless one has some insight into the immediate circumstances under which the classical jurists lived. Those circumstances influenced their understanding of the horizontal dimension of the Qur'anic experience from the very beginning in Makkah to the final end in Madīnah. The classical period of Muslim history was basically an extension of the late Madīnan period (7-11AH/628-632AC) when Muslims held a position of superiority and strength vis-à-vis all their non-Muslim adversaries. The formative period for the establishment of jurisprudence and its *uṣūl* under the Umawī and early 'Abbāsī dynasties (sixth-ninth century AC) was a victorious experience similar to that of the last stage of Madīnah. The approach of most jurists, perhaps understandably, was simply to negate the early experience in Makkah and early Madīnah through the technique of abrogation. No doubt a serious analytical and empirical study of the development of the Islamic movement in Makkah and Madīnah and the development of Muslim-non-Muslim relations in Arabia could have led to a

---

[51] M. Abū Zayd, *al Naskh*, vol. II, pp. 506-508; and W. al Zuhaylī, Op. Cit., pp. 79-81, 108, 113, 135-138, 192.

different understanding and employment of the *naskh* technique and to different legal deductions from relevant Qur'anic verses.

The foregoing examples are understandable in the context of coeval knowledge and needs. But to continue the same attitude and methodological framework in the present is not justifiable, but is antithetical to Muslim interests.

Islamic countries need a new framework for Muslim social thought, one that is based on a systematic and objective investigation of the social aspects of human life. Only then is the achievement of a viable modern system of philosophical and moral Islamic values possible. Together with the fulfillment of this need, inductive and deductive methods must be rigorously applied to Muslim social studies. It is not surprising that ijtihad ceased by the end of the fourth century AH (eleventh century AC), because the source material was the same, the method of deduction was the same, and no fresh input or feedback through new and continuous empirical investigations was available in the fields of jurisprudence and social studies.[52] Unless Islamic social sciences and humanities are genuinely established along with their textual bases through empiricism, and unless both induction and deduction are applied in these fields, ijtihad must, for all practical purposes, continue to be considered as closed, and Muslim thought will lack dynamism and productivity.

Lack of Overall Systemization

In discussing Qur'anic exegesis, *al Shahīd* Ismā'īl Rājī al Fārūqī touched upon the problem of systemization in the works of older jurists and commentators when he said:

> It is needless to point out that our ancestors completed remarkable studies constituting a tremendous wealth of insight, though none of them followed this method [axiological systemization]. We can not do so without their work, nor can we afford to overlook the insight of their research or the wisdom of their vision...[though] none of them achieved the axiological systemization we need today.[53]

---

[52] See H. A. R. Gibb, *Modern Trends in Islam*, p. 124.

[53] Ismā'īl R. al Fārūqī, "Towards a New Methodology for Qur'anic Exegesis," *Islamic Studies* (March, 1962), p. 47.

Fazlur Rahman agrees with this, although he sees it in a different context.

> A most fundamental and striking feature of our fiqh is that its various parts and legal points and enunciations do not actually tie up with one another to make it (a really) well-knit system. Indeed, even a casual student cannot fail to notice this "atomicity" of fiqh, this, in effect, intellectually unrelated development of almost all its enunciations. Therefore, rather than being a system, it is a huge mass of atoms, each atom being a kind of system in itself. Broadly speaking, fiqh constitutes materials for a legal system, but is not a legal system itself. We do not, however, deny that fiqh is endowed with a sufficiently definite character which marks it out from other legal systems...its Islamicity; what we deny is that it is a logically connected, intellectually worked out, and therefore a closely-enough-knit legal system.[54]

The lack of comprehensive systemization is clearly apparent in classical works of jurisprudence and *siyar* on one or more of the issues already discussed. The need for a comprehensive systematic approach in the fields of law and Islamic social sciences is in a real sense a contemporary Muslim problem.[55] To the classical jurists and scholars the problem hardly existed. Their aim was not to abstract a social system or to revolutionize the existing one; their effort was basically intended to work out, make explicit, and adjust the details and parts of the already existing system. The jurists' work was in many ways logical and systematic within the existing conditions and frame of mind. The contemporary Muslim social system, facing new changes, needs, challenges, and pressures, has fallen apart, and the changes are so tremendous that the mere maintenance of an old order is no longer workable or desirable.

Muslim thinkers of the present have to achieve a clear, workable, and abstract framework of the Islamic social system, of the social sciences, and of their relationship to the external world. The model of the social system laid down by the Prophet and his Companions which constitutes the body of the Sunnah is an important aid for understanding and consequently

---

[54] Fazlur Rahman, *Islamic Methodology*, p. 184; see also, M. A. al Zarqā', *al Fiqh al Islāmī*, pp. 1-5.

[55] N. J. Coulson, *A History of Islamic Law*, pp. 1-7 and 220-221.

abstracting the values and the basic outlook of Islam, but it cannot be applied or compared issue by issue with the social system that must be built in order to meet today's needs, realities, and challenges.

The lack of systemization and empiricism is a problem when Muslim students today use *uṣūl* in the old way, while the old intellectual atmosphere and implicit assumptions are no longer valid or present.[56] This situation is at present as much a problem for the modernists as it is for the traditionalists.[57] The imitation of historical systems is just as wrong as the imitation of foreign ones, because both reflect a lack of comprehensive understanding of the existing realities of contemporary Muslim peoples and the Muslim world.

Contemporary Muslim thinkers and scholars should realize that ad hoc and casual reflections on the issues of Muslim social life and system are no longer enough. They have to create Islamic social and human sciences, to systemize the goals and methods of their studies of Islamic life, to concern themselves in their studies with the facts of social life and with its nature and interactions as much as with Islamic texts and regulations, and to create and develop comprehensive inductive and deductive Islamic methodology.

Conclusions

1. The problem of Muslim political thought in general lies not in the content as much as it lies in the methodology.

2. The problem of the authenticity of the Sunnah is basically an expression and reflection of the unhappiness on the part of Muslims with the centuries-old jurisprudence.

3. The problem of ijtihad and the related question of jurisprudence and *siyar* lies in a lack of understanding of the nature of *uṣūl* and in the absence of necessary adjustment.

---

[56] See Appendix, note 9.

[57] See A. Khallāf, Op. Cit., pp. 20-96; Muhammad Yūsuf Mūsā, *al Fiqh al Islāmī, Madkhal li Dirāsatihi; Niẓām al Mu'āmalah fīhi*, 3rd ed. (Cairo: Dār al Kutub al Ḥadīthah, 1958), pp. 48, 65-84, 127-142; S. Maḥmaṣānī, Op. Cit., pp. 90-108; S. Ramaḍān, *Islamic Law*, pp. 11-12 and 184. See also H. A. R. Gibb, *Modern Trends in Islam*, pp. 73, 84, 107, 121-124; I. al Fārūqī, Op. Cit., p. 47; N. J. Coulson, Op. Cit., pp. 202-225.

4. The *uṣūl instinbāṭ al fiqh* (the jurisprudential textual sources and methods for the deduction of Muslim jurisprudence) were devised and developed in response to the needs of maintaining the classical social system during the dynastic period.

5. With the rise of the modern West and the emergence of an industrial society, the classical frame of analysis is no longer workable or acceptable.

6. *Uṣūl* can no longer draw on partial analysis; it has to readjust itself to provide a comprehensive analysis, abstraction, and systemization in order to confront the tasks of rebuilding the Muslim social system and creating Islamic social sciences.

7. The rebuilding of a modern Muslim social system and modern studies in the field of international relations requires the conceptualization and abstraction of values, directions, and basic outlook so that Muslims can resume active participation. *Uṣūl* has to provide for a genuine, comprehensive, and systematic analysis.

8. A genuine establishment of empirical and systematic studies and research from the Islamic point of view in the various fields of the social sciences and humanities is a necessary step for Muslim intellectuals to provide proper and up-to-date input and feedback in Muslim thought, jurisprudence, *siyar*, and social structure.

9. Deduction and induction, the availability of the best possible scientific and objective input, and concern with data feedback are necessary tools in the rebuilding of the social system and in approaching the Islamic source materials of the Qur'an and the Sunnah. With these tools Muslim thinkers, scientists, and jurists, in their studies of the source material of Islamic ideology, will be armed with the necessary information and tools, and the process of feeding back the updated material will continue to guarantee a realistic understanding of future developments in the social system and help in planning and directing the growth of Muslim society.

10. The problem of analysis of the hadith is basically not authenticity but the lack of appreciation, of proper consideration, and of understanding the effects of space-time on concrete systems.

11. *Qiyās* can no longer take an issue-by-issue approach. It has to be systematic, conceptual, abstract, and comprehensive.

12. *Ijmā'* is not a matter of the consensus of a number of experts or jurists. Its meaning and function should be worked out in relation to the legislative function in concrete political systems where it may produce a workable relationship between the ideal and the real, with maximum possible support and participation on the part of the Muslim peoples.

13. A comprehensive and conceptual understanding of the technique of *naskh*, so as to stop the narrowing down of the rich Islamic and Qur'anic experience into a single historical act on the part of a historically concrete social system, is urgently needed. This has to be done on a systematic and conceptual basis, not a legalistic one.

14. Exposure to the proper Islamic literature and insight into matters of the social system's structure, decision-making procedures, and law will provide Muslims with proper and practical guidelines for their building efforts. Education to this effect is the answer to contemporary Muslims' need for positive participation. Nothing positive can come out of the controversy over the authenticity of the hadith and other related questions.

The next chapter is a trial application of the reformed methodology suggested in this chapter. We will approach the basic source material of Islam, the Qur'an and the Sunnah, and with the aid of the systems analysis approach, attempt to understand and conceptualize the source materials, especially the Sunnah, and to remove the space-time effect from the concrete social system of the early period of Islam, mainly the era of the Prophet.

With the proper input and feedback, and through adequate comprehension and conceptualization of modern challenges in the Muslim world and the international system, these insights may help bring about more harmonious interaction and more positive participation.

CHAPTER 4

FROM LEGALISTIC TO POLITICAL THOUGHT

In chapter 2, we reviewed classical Muslim thought and modern developments. If there exists any one word to describe the crisis of Muslim thought in the field of external affairs today, that word is "irrelevance." The aggressive attitude involved in the classical approach to jihad as militancy is clearly irrelevant today to a people who are weak and backward intellectually, politically, and technologically.

The "liberal" approach,[1] which emphasizes thinking in terms of peace, tolerance, and defensiveness, has also proved irrelevant in a world facing ever increasing struggles for political, social, and economic liberation. For Muslims, whose energies are needed almost exclusively in the struggle against the conditions, both internal and external, that contribute to their human misery, this approach has proved to be no longer tolerable or useful.

Modern Muslim thought in the field of external affairs is either irrelevant to the reality of the Muslim psychology and conscience or to the reality of the world in which the Muslims live. It is erroneous to assume that Muslim psychology, consciousness, history, lands, and peoples are shapeless. Muslims must learn how to adjust to modern challenges and institutions and how to respond to and accommodate them from within the general Muslim outlook. By the same token, Muslims have to realize the

---

[1] See chapter 2, footnote 73. See also Charles C. Adams, *Islam and Modernism in Egypt* (New York: Russel & Russel, 1933), pp. 248-268; and Erwin I. J. Rosenthal, *Islam in the Modern National State* (Cambridge, UK: University Press, 1965), pp. xi-xiii.

necessity of adjusting to strategies and policies that fit the different parts of Muslim lands and Muslim peoples at different times. For example, what could be applied to the Turks in the fourteenth and fifteenth centuries is different from what could be applied to them in the nineteenth century. By the same token, policies that suit the Pakistanis, the Iranians, or the Turks of today are different from the policies that will fit, for example, the Egyptians or the Syrians.

The need for the adoption of systematic empirical approaches in the social sciences, as a prerequisite to the creation of a new practical Islamic framework in the highly political field of international relations, has been emphasized in chapters 2 and 3. Legitimacy for this approach in Islamic thought is possible only in reference to the early Islamic sources. To achieve this goal, we must, as a first step, apply the systematic empirical approach to the Prophet's external policies in the state of Madīnah. This will help to eliminate the traditional legalistic interpretation of those policies. The second step is to correct some major defects in the traditional Muslim concept of the relationship between Allah and man. The third step is to develop a basic workable Islamic framework in the field of external relations that frees the Muslim policymaker from the space-time elements involved in the traditional approach. In this way, the policy maker will be better able to deal with the changing realities of the contemporary world. The final step is to test this framework against some major contemporary Muslim foreign policies. We have to bear in mind that the success of an ideological framework is measured by its compatibility with the basic assumptions of that ideology, on the one hand, and by its utility to the policy maker on the other. We will start with the first step, namely, a projection back to the Prophet's attitude and policies as regards external relations.

Reconstruction of History: The Political Rationale of the Prophet's External Policies

We have already discussed (in chapter 2) some of the misconceptions concerning the early Muslims' experience in relation to non-Muslims; misconceptions which brought about tense relations in the classical period. These misconceptions detered both the development of a more dynamic federal system and the acquisition of a broader range of human rights and participation for non-Muslim minorities. Certainly, these misconceptions did not promote an attitude of proper cooperation between Muslims and non-Muslims.

We need not repeat what has already been said in order to explain how this situation came about in Muslim thought, nor need we remind the reader that this does not imply that non-Muslims were innocent or that the attitude of non-Muslims toward Muslims was either tolerant or cooperative.

As a result of this attitude of hostility toward cooperation, modern Muslim writers have often been contradictory and apologetic in their efforts to reinterpret Muslim history, thus failing to utilize the political significance and rationale of the rich and broad experience of Islam. I propose here to examine four basic issues, frequently referred to but misread by traditionalists, which clearly point out the superior political, rather than the purely legalistic, rationale of the Prophet in his conduct of foreign affairs. These four issues are:

1. The prisoners of war captured during the battle of Badr,
2. The Muslim expedition against the Jews of Arabia and in particular the Banū Qurayẓah of Madīnah,
3. Lenient policies toward the Quraysh, the archenemies of the early Muslims, and
4. the continued respect and tolerance shown to the People of the Book.

Prisoners of War from the Battle of Badr

The battle of Badr took place between the Muslims and the tribe of Quraysh in the second year after the hijrah (emigration) of the Prophet from Makkah to Madīnah.[2] The Muslims, about 300 in number, opposed approximately 1,000 Qurayshi warriors and achieved a decisive victory in which most of the Quraysh leaders were either killed or captured. Only two out of about seventy prisoners of war were executed; the remainder were set

---

[2] See Abū Muḥammad 'Abd al Mālik Ibn Hishām al Ma'āfirī, *al Sīrah al Nabawīyah*, ed. M. al Saqqā, I. al Ibiarī, and A. Shalabī, 2nd ed. (Cairo: Muṣṭafā al Bābī al Ḥalabī wa Awlāduh, 1955), vol. I, pp. 605-715; vol. II, pp. 3-43; and Ibn Athīr, *al Kāmil fī al Tārīkh*, vol. II, p. 37.

free upon their paying various amounts of ransom. The Battle of Badr was the first major armed confrontation between the Muslims and the Quraysh and other Arab and Jewish tribes of Arabia. This battle came after twelve years of pressure and severe persecution against the Muslims, many of whom were forced to flee, first to Abyssinia and then to Madīnah.[3]

While the Quraysh tried to persuade the people of Madīnah to expel the Prophet and his Qurayshī followers, the Prophet began to establish and consolidate the Muslim force for the inevitable confrontation.[4] He made an honorable peace arrangement (the Madīnah Pact) between the Muslims and the Jewish tribes of Madīnah, established a brotherhood between the *muhājirūn* and the *anṣār,* and personally sent expeditions to the areas around Madīnah to seek support and establish peace.[5] Ibn Jaḥsh's expedition of surveillance ended with the first attack by Muslims against a Qurayshī caravan. The importance of this expedition is that it led to the march of the Quraysh army toward Madīnah and then to the battle of Badr. The following Qur'anic verse was revealed in relation to this occasion:

> It is not for any prophet to have prisoners until he has thoroughly subdued the land (8:67).

Legalism led Muslim writers to apologize for this verse by arguing the contrast with another verse which reads as follows:

> Therefore, when you meet the unbelievers (in battle), smite at their necks; at length, when you have thoroughly subdued them, bind a bond firmly on them; thereafter (is the time for) either generosity or ransom, until the burden of war may be lifted. (47:4) .[6]

The argument of these writers is that the first verse is "not a permanent legislation" or ruling. It is the second verse that is the permanent and established rule for deciding the fate of prisoners of war. The first is only to blame Muslims for having taken prisoners and to point out that the "real" will of God is not to take prisoners of war.[7]

---

[3] See Ibn Hishām, Op. Cit., vol. I, pp. 265-395, 642-646.

[4] Ibid., pp. 317-390, 419-429, 591-606.

[5] See M. Ḥamīdullāh, *al Wathā'iq al Siyāsiyah*, pp. 39-47; and Ibn Hishām, Op. Cit., vol. I, pp. 501-504, 590-606.

[6] See al Zuḥaylī, Op. Cit., pp. 406-408.

[7] Ibid.

This is the modern way of applying the antiquated and static technique of abrogation. Contemporary writers often take a liberal approach by considering the release of prisoners of war as a safe and sound policy, and dismissing the verse of blame (for not killing all the prisoners of war captured at Badr) as something temporary and pertaining only to the period of the establishment of the early Muslim state.[8] The other way in which modern writers look at the issue is by rationalizing it into a legal case against war criminals rather than mere prisoners of war.[9]

These writers seem to overlook the significance of circumstances in directing punitive measures against adversaries of the Muslims. It is clear that the first verse was revealed at a time of extreme pressure on Muslims, whereas a close examination of the second verse shows that Muslim victory was foreseen.

In order that we may understand the meaning and significance of actions, policies, and pronouncements related to the early period of Madīnah and the circumstances that led to Badr and resulted from it, we must take a closer look at those parts of *Sūrat al Anfāl* which were revealed in relation to the Battle of Badr.[10]

Interestingly enough, some verses advising the Prophet to take extreme measures in order to protect the Muslim community were inserted (on the Prophet's orders) in *Sūrat al Anfāl* instead of *Sūrat al Aḥzāb*. The latter, it should be realized, refers explicitly to the Battle of the Ditch and the subsequent Battle of Banū Qurayẓah, but in the context of a Muslim victory. This shows that *Sūrat al Anfāl* deals with the pressures facing Muslims in early Madīnah only, and is meant to guide Muslims when they are faced with similar circumstances.[11]

---

[8] Ibid.

[9] See Muḥammad Aḥmad Bā Shumayl, *Ghazwat Badr al Kubrā*, vol. I of *Min Ma'ārik al Islām al Fāṣilah*, 4th ed. (Beirut: Dār al Kutub, 1969), pp. 227-229; Muḥammad al Ghazālī, *Fiqh al Sīrah*, 4th ed. (Cairo: Dār al Kutub al Ḥadīthah, 1964), pp. 254-255; and Nadav Safran, *Egypt in Search of Political Community*, p. 213.

[10] See al Naysabūrī, *Asbāb al Nuzūl*, pp. 132-138; Ibn Hishām, Op. Cit., vol. I, pp. 666; and al Ṭabarī, *Jāmi' al Bayān*, vol. IX, pp. 168-250, vol. X, pp. 1-57.

[11] See Ibn Hishām, Op. Cit., vol. II, pp. 245-250; al Ṭabarī, vol. X, pp. 25-35; and the Qur'an (8:19, 26, 30, 38, 39, 45, 57, 58, 60, 67, 70-73, and 81).

Surat al Anfāl reveals to the reader the fears of the Muslims due to their lack of manpower, their need for the employment of psychological warfare, and the free hand of the Prophet to employ all suitable actions to counter the overwhelmingly superior enemy forces. This *sūrah* also illustrates the Muslim call for coexistence and reconciliation on the condition that the persecution of Muslims and hostility against their religion cease.

The verses concerning the prisoners of war taken at the Battle of Badr specifically reveal the employment of a threat of extreme punitive action against the enemy on the battlefield as a restraining device of psychological warfare. The psychological use of a threat in this way explains why the threat was not actually carried out at Badr. The killing of prisoners of war was an extremely rare exception throughout the life of the Prophet. Thus, it is clear that the verses were to serve political rather than legal ends.

Banū Qurayẓah:
Use of Extreme Measures for Security and Psychological Ends

The Banū Qurayẓah were one of the Jewish tribes residing in Madīnah when the Arab tribes of Madīnah turned to Islam. Although the Jewish tribes were inferior in number and military capabilities, they were, as scholars and craftsmen, culturally and economically superior to their Arab neighbors.[12]

The Banū Qurayẓah were a part of the federal arrangement between the Muslims and Jewish tribes of Madīnah. This arrangement provided religious freedom, self-government, and a joint military alliance against the Quraysh, the archenemy of the Muslims.[13]

---

[12] See Bernard Lewis, *The Arabs in History*, p. 40.

[13] Ibid., pp. 42-45; F. Gabrielli, *Muḥammad*, pp. 64-65, 72-76; Muhammad Hamidullah, *The First Written Constitution in the World: An Important Document of the Time of the Prophet* , 2nd rev. ed. (Lahore: Sh. Muhammad Ashraf, 1968), pp. 48-49, 51-52. It is also useful to see the summary and translation by Muḥammad Tal'at al Ghunaymī, *The Muslim Conception of International Law and the Western Approach* (The Hague: Martinus Nijhoff, 1968), p. 37, for a more accurate evaluation of the Prophet and the political atmosphere in which the decision against Banū Qurayẓah took place.

The Quraysh, Ghaṭafān, Qays 'Aylān, and Banū al Naḍīr formed an alliance, assembled a large army, and marched against the Muslims in Madīnah. During the siege of the city, the Banū Qurayẓah revoked their pact with the Muslims and opened negotiations with the attackers. Ḥuyay ibn Aḥṭab of the Banū Naḍīr, the tribe that had already been expelled from Madīnah for its hostile and subversive activities in collaborating with the Quraysh, was the initiator and mediator of these negotiations. The negotiations failed, however, to meet the demands of the Banū Qurayẓah. After the siege collapsed, the confrontation between the Muslims and the Banū Qurayẓah took place.

As we saw in chapter 2, the whole episode of the Battle of the Ditch and the great alliance against Madīnah was a nightmare for the Muslims. The Prophet offered the tribe of Ghaṭafān a third of Madīnah's yearly crops if it would withdraw and relieve some of the pressure on the Muslims. The Qur'an eloquently describes this pressure and the Muslims' fear of total destruction.

Writers have emphasized the moral and legal implications of the Banū Qurayẓah's treacherous breach of its agreement with the Muslims, the propaganda of the religious and political war which the Jewish rabbis waged against Islam, or the alleged desire of the Muslims to confiscate Jewish wealth.[14] After many centuries, writers seem to have overlooked the Qur'an's and the Prophet's perceptions of the extreme danger in such an alliance, as well as the psychological impact on the Muslims of the Jews' withdrawal from the alliance as a motivation for the Muslims to take exceptional and extreme measures. The significance of the action taken against the Banū Qurayẓah lies in the attempt on the part of the Muslims to ensure that no more treachery would take place in the future. No other reasoning explains the severe punitive actions that were taken against the Banū Qurayẓah.

---

[14] See F. Gabrielli, Op. Cit., pp. 64-80; Muḥammad Bā Shumayl, Op. Cit., vol. IV, pp. 238-270; M. al Ghazālī, Op. Cit., pp. 257-264; Maḥmūd S. Khaṭṭāb, *al Rasūl al Qā'id* (Baghdad: Dār Maktabat al Ḥayāh, 1960), pp. 161-162; Sayyid Ameer Ali, *The Spirit of Islam: A History of the Evolution and Ideals of Islam with a Life of the Prophet* (London: Methuen, 1922), pp. 72-82; H. Watt, Op. Cit., pp. 166-175; and M. T. al Ghunaymī, Op. Cit., pp. 38-42.

If the reason were no more than a matter of wealth, it does not explain why other wealthy Jewish and Arab tribes were not dealt with as severely as the Banū Qurayẓah. If the reason, as others claim, was the Jews' breach of the treaty and their subversive activity, one need only point out that other Jewish and Arab tribes before and after the Battle of the Ditch had been accused of the same act, including the Banū al Naḍīr and the Quraysh. It is interesting to note that after the Battle of Uḥud, the Banū al Naḍīr were expelled from Madīnah, while after the Treaty of al Ḥudaybīyah (with the Quraysh), the Jewish tribes of Khaybar only had to pay a tribute of half their crops, which put an end to their financial and political power. Furthermore, one year later the Quraysh, the archenemy of the Muslims, were honorably set free upon their surrender. The political reasons for the different treatment of the Quraysh and the Jewish tribes of Khaybar will be discussed under the next heading.

Although Islam continued to build distinct religious practices (such as fasting in the month of Ramadan and zakāh [the giving of charity]), it never questioned the right of the followers of the earlier scriptures (Jews and Christians) to uphold and practice their religions. The whole issue of the difference in punitive action taken against the enemy was political and signifies the flexibility and realism which, in my judgment, the early Islamic framework exhibited. This is not to say, however, that the Islamic framework of external relations is free from moral restraints, for a look at the Qur'an and the Sunnah of the Prophet will easily show the fallacy of such a claim. The diversity of punitive measures implies that political decisions involving the major interests of the Muslim government and community have to be realistic and flexible within the limits of the Islamic framework. This framework, although asserting moral principles and attitudes, does not narrowly and blindly restrict political leaders and actions.

Increasing Arab-Jewish treachery and attacks, and the fresh memory of the extremely dangerous role of the Banū al Naḍīr who had been expelled and set free, exerted overwhelming pressure on the Muslim community and gave rise to a fear of total destruction. The Prophet therefore now had to use all the political and military means available to destroy the overwhelming power of the enemy in order to secure the Muslims' existence. It was clear that the Prophet could no longer tolerate the settlement of the Banū Qurayẓah in Madīnah; nor could he afford to set them free and add to the strength of his enemies under conditions of extreme danger.[15]

Despite the fact that military and political confrontations forced extreme actions, the Islamic stand on allowing non-Muslim minorities to co-exist with the Muslims, based on both religious and practical grounds, was never denied. On the contrary, the Prophet was firmly determined to hold this stand throughout his life. His victories simply brought about the vindication of his moral but realistic attitude toward external relations. As a matter of fact, he managed throughout to make the strict fulfillment of agreements a condition for establishing any external relationship, thus exerting a moral superiority for his side over his adversaries.[16] Moral commitment and successful planning and execution of foreign policies are necessary for the success of ideologically oriented societies. The employment of these elements of policymaking by the Prophet helps to explain his great success. In our own times, there is little doubt that the lack of moral commitment in international affairs is the real source of danger for world peace.

---

[15] See Ibn Hishām, Op. Cit., vol. II, pp. 51-58, 273-276; M. T. al Ghunaymī, Op. Cit., pp. 38-42; and W. M. Watt, Op. Cit., pp. 144-176. See also Yūsuf 'Alī, *The Holy Qur'an: Text, Translation and Commentary* (Brentwood, MD: Amana Corporation, 1983), footnotes 3701-3704 on pp. 1111-1112.

[16] See the Qur'an (23:8, 17:91, 5:1, 16:91-92, 9:4-14, 2:100, 8:72, 3:76-77, 2:177, 13:20,25, 6:152, 17:34, 33:15, 8:61). Also see A. A. Manṣūr, *Muqāranāt*, pp. 57-61; al Farrā', Op. Cit., pp. 48-49; Ibn Kathīr, Op. Cit., vol. II, p. 320; Abū Zahrah, *al 'Alāqāt al Dawlīyah*, pp. 40-41; Mālik ibn Anas, *al Muwaṭṭā*, vol. I, p. 298; M. Hamidullah, *The Muslim Conduct of State*, pp. 82 and 208; M. Khadduri, *War and Peace*, pp. 218-220; M. T. al Ghunaymī, *Muslim International Law*, p. 161; Muḥammad Rashīd Riḍā, *Tafsīr al Manār*, 4th ed. (Cairo: Dār al Manār, 1954), vol. X, pp. 53-60, 169, 178-203, 217-222, 229-234, and vol. XI, p. 281; al Shāfi'ī, *al Umm*, vol. IV, pp. 184-186; al Ṭabarī, Op. Cit., vol. X pp. 26-27. For examples of the implementation of the principle of fulfillment of agreements, see for the early period of Islam, M. Hamidullah, *al Wathā'iq*, pp. 58-63, 369, 371-372, 387, and 393-394; for the Ottoman period and the Capitulation Treaties, see J. C. Horowitz, *Diplomacy in the Near and Middle East*, vol. I, pp. 1-5 and 7-9.

The significance of policy variations in regard to banishment and retaliation as a dynamic response to the basic interests and needs of the Muslim state in relation to its environment is reinforced by further examination of other political and military activities performed during the last ten years of the Prophet's life as head of the Muslim community and state at Madīnah.

Notable among these activities were the missions to eliminate the enemy's leadership, especially the mission to kill Ka'b ibn al Ashraf of the Banū al Naḍīr.[17] Muslim writers expended a great deal of effort to explain and justify these wars and missions in legal terms. But what is important is that they paid very little attention to the political and strategic significance of those missions.

Since the Prophet and the early Muslims represented a new way of life, they expected a very unfavorable response from the Quraysh and other Arab tribes. Thus they had to be on the defensive. The moral justification of the Muslim response can be easily made, but that does not explain the strategy of the response.

From the very beginning at Madīnah, the Prophet sought to interrupt the major economic interests of the Quraysh. He planned his battles as surprise attacks and even advised Abū Baṣīr to formulate a guerilla approach toward the Qurayshī lines of communication. Missions to eliminate the enemy's political leadership were directed at groups that built alliances against the Muslims. The element of surprise, the guerilla attacks, and the threat of harsh punitive measures and reprisals all succeeded in terrifying the enemy, causing disorder in their ranks, and bringing many of them to the side of the Muslims.

It is this kind of realism, with its wide margin of political maneuverability, rather than legalism and formalism, that explains the Prophet's successful conduct of external affairs.

Quraysh: Honor for the Vanquished

After Khaybar, the Prophet finally put an end to the hostile Jewish power in Madīnah and the surrounding areas by

---

[17] See Ibn Hishām, Op. Cit., vol. II, pp. 389-397.

stopping their valuable political and financial aid to the anxious, disabled, and exhausted Quraysh.

With the failure of the Quraysh to live up to the peace agreement between themselves and the Prophet, and after they committed a massacre in Makkah itself when their allies (the Banū Bakr) fell upon the Khuzā'ah, the Prophet took the opportunity to carry out a surprise master stroke against Makkah.[18] While his psychological warfare succeeded in causing Makkah and the Quraysh to surrender,[19] he ordered no military reprisals, no destruction, and no punishment, even after all the bitter memories and the long nightmare of persecutuion of Muslims at the hands of the Quraysh. On the contrary, the Prophet took all measures to ensure the safety of Makkah and its inhabitants. He did everything in his power to win their hearts and gain their support. He was now master of Arabia and found it possible and fruitful to follow a policy of leniency and far-reaching generosity toward the Quraysh and other tribes, such as the Ḥawāzin of Ṭā'if.[20] The decision also had clear political motives for the Muslims were now strong and secure and, moreover, new plans were already taking shape. After Khaybar, the Prophet realized the inevitability of armed conflict with the great powers of Byzantium and Persia when the first bloody conflict had materialized at Mu'tah between the Muslims and Roman troops. With Arabia and the dominant Quraysh tribe on his side, the Prophet was able to turn north toward the stronghold of Byzantium in northern Arabia. These involvements against northern neighbors also had the advantage of maintaining the cohesion and enthusiasm of the Arab tribes. Armed conflict was inevitable, regardless of any academic argument about whether the new Muslim state should expand.[21]

---

[18] See Ibn al Athīr, Op. Cit., vol. II, pp. 239-240.

[19] See Ibn Hishām, Op. Cit., vol. II, pp. 397-407.

[20] Ibid., pp. 482-486.

[21] See Abdul Rahman Azzam, *The Eternal Message of Islam*, translated from Arabic by Caesar E. Farah (New York: New American Library, 1965), p. 46; Ibn al Athīr, Op. Cit., vol. II, p. 277; Ibn Hishām, Op. Cit., vol. II, pp. 591-592, 606-607, 641-642; M. al Ghazālī, Op. Cit., pp. 395-396, 435-438, 442.

Upon returning to Madīnah from the peaceful conquest of Makkah, the Prophet, in response to the hostile Roman attitude and actions toward the Muslims, led the largest Muslim army of his time northward to Tabūk on the borders of Palestine. This was the last time he led his army before his death. Usāmah's expedition was the last Muslim expedition ordered out before he died. Although it was ready before the Prophet's death, it moved toward its destination in the north only upon renewed orders from the newly appointed *khalīfah*. Later events proved the political wisdom of the Prophet in consolidating the Muslims' power in Arabia before getting involved in armed conflict with the two hostile empires bordering on the north.

Freedom of Religion and Belief

The fourth issue, freedom of religion and belief, is still an important source of confusion and contradiction in contemporary Muslim political thought. Here, too, the traditional approach contributes to the atmosphere of fear and suspicion between Muslim and non-Muslim peoples because it minimizes communication and makes interaction and cooperation more difficult. The traditional position stems from the classical interpretation of the early sources on the issues of apostasy (*riddah*), the historical case of the forced Islamization of pagan Arabs, and the imposition of the poll tax (*jizyah*) on non-Muslims. Once more, these issues reveal the traditional attitude to be an obstacle to introducing a constructive Islamic approach to relationships between Muslims and non-Muslims in the world today, and from within a modern Islamic framework in the field of international relations.

Muslim reformists and modernists such as ʻAbduh, Riḍā, ʻAzzām, al Ṣaʻīdī and many others made strenuous efforts to resolve this problem, but it is still not conceptually clear.[22] Apart from other factors, the issue of freedom of belief in Muslim

[22] See ʻAbd al Karīm ʻUthmān, *al Niẓām al Siyāsī fī al Islām* (Beirut: Dār al Irshād, 1968), pp. 60-67; M. Abū Zahrah, Op. Cit., pp. 142-143; Muḥammad ʻAbduh, *al Islām wa al Naṣrānīyah maʻa al 'Ilm wa al Madanīyah* (Cairo: Maṭbaʻat Muḥammad ʻAlī Ṣabīḥ, 1954), p. 64; M. al Bāhī, *al Fikr al Islāmī*, pp. 130-137; Muḥammad al Ghazālī, Op. Cit., pp. 453-454, 458-464; and ʻA. al Ṣaʻīdī, *al Ḥurrīyah al Dīnīyah*, p. 25, 30.

societies is very much in need of unambiguous articulation.[23] For Muslim societies, the issue is not an internal one alone, for it touches on an important ideological aspect of their relationship with other states and peoples. Clarification is essential if Muslim society is to be a truly open one in which civil rights are guaranteed and made available to all its members in a reciprocal relationship between rights and duties, and along pluralistic lines free from religious and sectarian biases. Loyalty and commitment to the welfare of all people and their different systems of law is the only guarantee for the sincere excercise of rights and duties by individuals and groups. Freedom of ideology and religion, assisted by peaceful and orderly means of practice and expression, is necessary for healthy, stable, expanding, and progressive societies.

In chapter 2 we discussed the classical issue of *jizyah* and the People of the Book. We would like to emphasize here that the overall Islamic framework starts ideologically from a genuine concern for one's fellow man.[24] All Muslims, particularly intellectuals, need to focus on this basic emphasis. The fundamental Islamic attitude concerning relations among human beings is expressed in the Qur'an and the Sunnah in terms of love (*tawaddūhum*), help (*tuḥsinū*), gentleness (*allatī hiya aḥsan*), and protection (*dhimmah*).

This attitude, however, should not be confused with situations of confrontation, particularly that of the historical confrontation faced by the early Muslims in Arabia. It was the Prophet himself who drew up the honorable agreement of *jizyah* with the friendly Christian tribes of Najrān and before that the Madīnan

---

[23] See M. al Ghazālī, *al Ta'aṣṣub wa al Tasāmuḥ bayna al Masīḥīyah wa al Islām* (Kuwait: Dār al Bayān, n.d.), p. 37-66; and W. C. Smith, *Islam in Modern History*, pp. 266-291.

[24] See al Qur'an, 60:8-9, 11:84, 26:135, 46:21, 5:118, 18:87, 26:3, 34:28, 21:107, 3:104, 9:67, 11:116, 16:125, 49:13, 18:87, 26:151-152, 68:10-12, 42:41-43, 16:90-91, 107:1-7, and 90:12-20. See also, al Bukhārī, *Matn al Bukhārī bi Ḥāshīyat al Sindī* (Cairo: Dār Iḥyā' al Kutub al 'Arabīyah, 1960), vol. I, p. 228, and vol. II, pp. 159, 161, 171-172; al Khaṭīb, *Mishkāt al Maṣābīḥ* (ed. al Albānī), vol. II, pp. 605,608, 613; al Fakhr al Rāzī, *al Tafsīr al Kabīr*, vol. XXVI, pp. 54-61; M. Rashīd Riḍā, *Tafsīr al Manār*, vol. IV, pp. 25-45; vol. IX, pp. 290-291; al Ṭabarī, *Jāmi' al Bayān*, vol. XII, pp. 98-105; and Muhammad 'Izzat Darwazah, *al Tafsīr al Ḥadīth* (Cairo: 'Īsā al Bābī al Ḥalabī, 1964), pp. 200-203.

Pact with the Jewish tribes of Madīnah, and it was the Prophet who waged a war of life and death against some of the same Jewish tribes who sought the destruction of the Muslim community. These confrontations were situational and tactical and do not destroy the bases of Islamic ideology. Qur'anic references and the detailed accounts of the Sunnah and the *sīrah* are aids in revealing the realistic, rational approach of Islam. These details are matters of historical record that signify the pragmatic Islamic policies undertaken by the Prophet in order to secure the safety and success of the Muslim mission.

The issue of all-out war against the pagan Arab tribes unless they turned to Islam cannot be understood as ideological oppression. This decision came after the establishment of the Muslim state at Madīnah and after the Muslims had undergone about twenty-two years of persecution and war. It is not acceptable to say, as do the traditionalists, that the Prophet was obligated to force them to accept Islam, because the verse concerning the payment of *jizyah* by the People of the Book had not been revealed at the time the Prophet gave the order to force the Arab bedouins to convert to Islam.[25] In fact, the Prophet never tried at any time to convert the Jewish tribes of Madīnah or the Arab Christians of Najrān by force. The forced Islamization was a decision, after the experience of about twenty years, to protect the human rights of Muslims and Arab peoples alike. The Islamization of the wild bedouin tribes of the Arabian peninsula was to provide them with the framework for a structured social system and orderly intertribal interaction.[26] The change proved to be sincere, responsible, correct, and in the best interest of the Arabs, especially in defending their human rights. Contrary to the cultural legacy of other tribal peoples such as the Mongolians and Germans, the primitive Arab tribes, owing to their exposure to the discipline and rehabilitating effects of Islam, became the bearers of culture and the builders of civilization. The Arabs, along with other Muslim peoples, established the greatest civilization in human history up to that time and contributed a

---

[25] W. al Zuhaylī, Op. Cit., p. 102.

[26] M. Rashīd Riḍā, Op. Cit., vol. X, pp. 178-179.

great deal to the continuity and growth of human culture. Allah says:

> Those who believe, then reject faith, then believe [again] and [again] reject faith and go on increasing in unbelief, Allah will not forgive them nor guide them on the way (4:137).
>
> And they observe toward the believers neither pact nor honor. These are the transgressors. And if they repent and establish worship and pay zakah, then they are your brothers in religion. We detail Our revelations for a people who have knowledge (9:10-11).
>
> They [the desert Arabs] impress on you as a favor that they have embraced Islam. Say, 'Count not your Islam as a favor to me: Nay, God has conferred a favor upon you that He has guided you to the faith' (49:17).
>
> And hold fast all together by the rope which Allah [stretched out to you], and be not divided among yourselves: and remember with gratitude Allah's favor on you; for you were enemies and He joined your hearts in love, so that by His grace you became brothers (3:103).

If forced conversion were simply an exercise to show superiority, or a denial of the right of religious freedom, the Prophet had more reason and time to practice this against the Jewish tribes of Madīnah; however, he never attempted that policy either before or after issuing his orders regarding the Islamization of the Arab tribes. As we mentioned in chapter 2, the Qur'anic terminology is revealing in this respect. Thus, we can see that the case of the Islamization of the bedouin pagan tribes of the peninsula was a case of establishing a necessary civilized framework for human interaction based on human maturity and dignity. Properly understood, it does not destroy but rather reinforces the concept of ideological tolerance and real concern for basic human rights proper for humanity, which is an integral part of the responsibility of the *khalīfah*.[27]

---

[27] See Ibn Khaldūn, translated by Franz Rosenthal, *The Muqaddimah*, ed. N. J. Dawood (Princeton, NJ: Princeton University Press, 1967), pp. 118-122; Ahmad Amīn, *Fajr al Islām*, 9th ed. (Cairo: Maktabat al Nahdah, 1964), pp. 30-38; Jawād 'Alī, *al Mufassal fī Tārīkh al 'Arab Qabla al Islām* (Beirut: Dār al 'Ilm, 1970), vol. IV, p. 334; Muhammad Kāmil Līlah, *al Mujtama' al 'Arabī wa al Qawmīyah al 'Arabīyah* (Cairo: Dār al Fikr al 'Arabī, 1966), pp. 85-91, 108-111: and W. Watt, *Islamic Thought*, pp. 6-7.

Apostasy is theoretically the most interesting of the three issues. We find most traditional writers holding the opinion that denial and renunciation of Islam by adult male Muslims is apostasy, and unless they return to Islam they should be executed.[28] The serious problems arising here are twofold: one is the space-time factor, and the second is the conceptual confusion involved in the issue as it has been treated by Muslim writers.

The space-time impact of the issue of apostasy relates to a conspiracy on the part of some Jewish groups to create chaos and confusion in the young Muslim community by using the tactic of apostasy, that is, professing Islam and then renouncing it as a group. It is worth noting that this conspiracy and its expected consequences were mentioned in the Qur'an:

> A faction of the People of the Book say: Believe in the morning what is revealed to the believers, but reject it at the end of the day; perchance they may [themselves] turn back. And believe no one unless he follows your religion (3:72-73).

The question of apostasy is also related to the very serious question of hypocrisy, with which the Qur'an dealt in many lengthy sections and verses. The hypocrites of Madīnah presented a dual problem for the young Muslim community. They helped the enemy, hindered war preparations and action, waged psychological war against the Muslims, and helped to destroy their morale. In this connection, the Qur'an says:

> Had they gone forth among you, they would have added naught to you save trouble, and would have hurried to and fro among you, seeking to cause sedition among you, and among you there are some who would have listened to them. Allah is aware of the evil-doers. Aforetime they sought to make difficulties for you until the truth came and the decree of Allah was made manifest although they were loathe. Of them is he who says: "Grant me leave (to stay home) and tempt me not." Surely it is into temptation they have fallen. Lo! Hell is all around the disbelievers. If good befalls you (O Muhammad) it afflicts them, and if calamity befalls you, they say: "We took precautions," and they turn away well-pleased. Say: "Nothing befalls us save that which Allah has decreed for us. He is our protecting Friend." In Allah let the believers put their trust. Say, "Can you await for us aught save one of two good things [victory or death in Allah's way], while we wait for

---

[28] See 'A. al Sa'īdī, *al Ḥurrīyah al Dīnīyah*, pp. 25-33.

you that Allah will afflict you with a doom from Him at our hands. Wait then! Lo! We are waiting with you," (9:47-52).

The threat of frightful punishment obviously was to check their activities and the practice of conspiratioral hypocrisy. Hypocrites would be trapped in their role all through their lives. To achieve the effect of checking hypocrisy and destructive activities, the Prophet gave the order to kill 'Abd Allah ibn Abū Sarḥ, which later was waived at the desperate request of 'Uthmān ibn 'Affān. Ibn Abū Sarḥ had been a scribe to the Prophet when he ran away, declaring his disbelief and publicly claiming that he had made some changes in his assigned recording. Such conspiracies of hypocrisy or apostasy are extremely serious crimes, and the weights and punishments assigned for them have important space-time considerations. These factors play a decisive role in determining their legal punishments.

The conceptual confusion occurs in the early period of Islam, when the classical jurists took the act for what it appeared to be and not for what it was meant to be. They mistook political conspiracy for an exercise of the human rights of freedom of belief and responsibility of choice. The jurists seemed to exercise little analysis concerning the whole question, as the word "apostasy" alone determined their position.

This misunderstanding of the significance of the word "apostasy" in the Qur'an and the punishment assigned to it in the hadith of the Prophet destroyed, in the classical jurisprudence, the basis of the Islamic concept of tolerance and human responsibility.

The early Muslim position on apostasy, as we have seen, was directed not against the freedom of conscience and belief, but rather toward enforcing the policy of Islamization on the warring bedouin tribes and toward checking conspiracy.[29] The Islamic

---

[29] 'Afīf 'A. Tabbārah, *al Yahūd fī al Qur'ān: Taḥlīl 'Ilmī li Nuṣūṣ al Qur'ān fī al Yahūd 'Alā Ḍaw' al Aḥdāth al Ḥādirah, Ma'a Qiṣaṣ Anbiyā' Allāh, Ibrāhīm wa Yūsuf wa Mūsā 'Alayhim al Salām* (The Jews and the Qur'an: Scientific Analysis of the Qur'anic Text Pertaining to Jews in the Light of the Contemporary Events with the Stories of the Prophets Abraham, Yusuf and Musa, May Peace Be Upon Them), 2nd ed. (Beirut: Dār al 'Ilm li al Malāyīn, 1966), pp. 30-32; and Muhammad Sayyid Tanṭāwī, *Banū Isrā'īl fī al Qur'ān wa al Sunnah*, pp. 168-

(continued...)

position concerning freedom of religion and belief is clearly stated in the Qur'an. Allah says: "Let there be no compulsion in religion" (2:256),

and,

> Dispute not with the People of the Book, except with means better [than mere disputing], unless it be with those of them who inflict wrong [and injury] (29:46).

Islam always showed full confidence in the truth of its teachings and in the faith of its followers. It always strove to achieve and defend the human right to freedom of choice, conscience, responsibility, and belief.

The conceptual confusion regarding freedom of belief in classical and, consequently, in traditional political thought occured because Muslim scholars did not realize the basic meaning and reason behind the Prophet's policy of Islamizing the untamed desert tribes. Another reason is that these scholars did not take into account the criminal aspects of the question or the security needs which early Muslims faced in cases where the Prophet condemned apostasy. This confusion on the part of the jurists explains their endless conceptual contradictions and their inappropriate resort to the method of abrogation.

The so-called War of Apostasy launched by the bedouin tribes against the first *khalīfah,* Abū Bakr was not an exercise in the freedom of faith or conscience. Rather, it was basically an act of renewed bedouin reaction against all restraints of political and social authority. The issues in that particular act of belligerency against the government of Abū Bakr were the payment of zakāh and the new, central political authority in Arabia.

Among the classical scholars, Ibn al Qayyim seemed to realize the conceptual significance of the orders issued by the Prophet at Madīnah in response to this kind of conspiratorial apostasy. In Ibn al Qayyim's opinion, these were political measures taken against subversive activity and had nothing to do with the exercise of freedom of faith or conscience.[30] It is very

---

[29](...continued)
263. See also Ibn al Athīr, *al Kāmil*, vol.II, p. 249; and Ibn Hishām, *al Sīrah*, vol. II, p. 409.

[30] See A. 'Uthmān, *al Nizām al Siyāsī*, pp. 66-67.

important for Muslims to keep in focus the basic and central values of individual moral responsibility and freedom of belief and conscience in Islam and not to be lost in formal, legalistic, and short-sighted academic arguments about details and textual materials. Ideological freedom is a basic necessity for any constructive, peaceful, and humane ideology, both internally and externally.

Reconstruction of the Continuum in Interpreting the Qur'an

We have already shown in chapters 2 and 3 how the classical jurists wanted to maintain and live in a social system similar to the one established by the Prophet. This is why the classical jurists tended to produce manuals describing detailed Muslim behavior and the social institutions that were to go with them.

With the classical method of *naskh,* we find these jurists tending to narrow the margin of freedom in political action to basically the Sunnah of the last period of the state at Madīnah, which was essentially a secure "big power" policy of self-restraint. However, some policy elements from the early Madīnan period of confrontation between the Muslims and the aggressive, tyrannical, and treacherous ruling elite among the disbelievers are still visible.

The power which the Muslim polity commanded, and the weakness and decay of its adversaries, made it possible for the Muslim Ummah to carry out these sorts of policies, although not without deviations whenever the sultan felt the need, generally one of political expediency, to do so.

Seeking to narrow the Islamic position to a purely defensive, peaceful and tolerant position, the liberal modernists found that the methodology of abrogation is not always helpful and is, in practice, at times a double-edged weapon. In fact, abrogation ends in conceptual confusion. We have to settle the issue of abrogation, especially the particular cases mentioned and discussed in the Qur'an, and show the significance of the internal structure of the Qur'an. Otherwise, the Qur'an and, for that matter, all Islamic ideology and institutions will appear as no more than a traditional and outdated way of life.

Abrogation (*Naskh*)

Looking at the Qur'anic and the early Islamic experience as a whole, we find that it carried the Muslims through eras of major and comprehensive change. It sought justice and peace for man in his world and in his relationship to the incomprehensible dimensions of the universe and his destiny beyond life and death:

> Those who spend [of that which Allah hath given them] in both ease and adversity, those who control their anger and are forgiving toward mankind: Allah loveth good. And those who, when they do an evil deed or wrong themselves, remember Allah and implore forgiveness for their sins - for who other than Allah forgiveth sins? - and will not knowingly repeat [the wrong] they did, the reward for such will be forgiveness from their Lord, and Gardens underneath which rivers flow, an eternal and bountiful reward for [those who] labor (3:134-136).

This Qur'anic experience dealt with man as an individual, and as a member of society as well, and led him from individual and minority status to the level of a society and government, and from humiliation, persecution, and weakness to dignity and power. It achieved much in peace as well as in war. Hardly an experience or a mood in human life and mind was not involved in that colossal historical experience. Seeking to achieve its assigned goals for human life and society, Islam established a basic framework of values, principles, and limits that provided Muslim leadership with a great deal of scope for dynamic and creative political planning and action.

Although jurists and scholars quote the Companions of the Prophet on the abrogation of this or that verse, they do not quote the Prophet himself specifying any verse abrogating any other verse.[31] As a matter of fact, the jurists expended a great deal of effort to prove the very existence of abrogation in the Qur'an.[32] Although they give great importance to the definition of abrogation, even contemporary scholars pay no attention to the

---

[31] M. Abū Zayd, *al Nāsikh*, vol. I, pp. 125-134, vol. II, pp. 553, 563-568, 579-581.

[32] M. Abū Zayd, Op. Cit., vol. 1, pp. 221-285.

framework of abrogation.[33] What we can deduce from their lengthy arguments is that their framework is static, that abrogation is the result of an act which occurred once in history, and that Muslims are trapped in a single position decided by an accident during a course of events that took place some time back in history. It is understandable for the classical jurists to think of Muslim society as powerful and established. But contemporary jurists and scholars are in a state of confusion on the issue. They either speak in vague generalizations, divorced from the actual problems and challenges facing the Muslim peoples and authorities, or they speak from a position of idealistic fantasy, assuming a powerful, established society and authority and ignoring the fact that Muslims no longer live in that time or place. Muslim authorities need an Islamic political thought and scholarship that is comprehensive enough to respond creatively to the realities and challenges of the contemporary world.[34]

It is important to put the concept of abrogation back into its proper context so as to limit it basically to abrogation of the messages and *āyāt* revealed before the message of Islam was complete. All parts and rules of the message and experience of Islam are valid whenever they are required in the light of changing circumstances in the overall flow of human life and experience. The Islamic rules and systems should always qualify for unlimited combinations to fit human needs and circumstances in the light of Islamic goals, values, and principles. *Naskh* should be applied only in cases that are clearly suitable for the concept of *naskh*, such as the changes of *qiblah* once and for all from the direction of Bayt al Maqdis (in Jerusalem) to Makkah.[35]

---

[33] Also we have to mention here that we should not commit an old mistake by confusing the freezing of certain principles (because of a situation calling for others) for *naskh*, which means permanent cancellation of the value or principle. See M. Abū Zayd, *al Naskh*, vol. I, pp. 205-220. M. al Zarqānī, *Manāhil al 'Irfān*, vol. II, pp. 69-76.

[34] M. Abū Zayd. Op. Cit., vol. I, pp. 205-220; M. Zurqānī, *Manāhil al 'Irfān*, vol. II, pp. 69-76.

[35] M. Abū Zayd, Op. Cit.,vol. I, pp. 236-242, 399-501; M. Zarqānī, Op. Cit., vol. II, pp. 152-165.

Muslim intellectuals and authorities have to restore responsible, intellectual, political, and legislative freedom of maneuverability within the Islamic framework. The Makkan revelations and attitudes are as valid and relevant to human situations and relationships today as are the early and later Madīnan period's revelations and attitudes. Gentleness, generosity, forgiveness, and humility are as relevant for human society as force and coercion.

Muslims should always be able to resort to persuasion, *ṣabr* (patience), as well as *qitāl* (fighting), psychological as well as physical etc., according to their immediate needs.

Responsible intellectual, political, and legislative freedom, which allows a dynamic use of the different phases of the multidimensional Qur'anic outlook within the constitutional framework, are always the characteristic of progressive and dynamic societies. This was also the case with the Prophet and at least with his first two successors, though more obviously in the case of the second, 'Umar ibn al Khaṭṭāb. This has to be restored if the enormous space-time gap is ever to be bridged in a constructive manner and within the foreseeable future. To this end, it is very useful to study and consider the position and arguments of Abū Muslim al Isfahānī about the meaning and the proper range of *naskh*.

The Significance of the Internal System of the Qur'an

Readers of Islamic literature feel that the treatment and quotation from Qur'anic materials are used, in many cases, without reference to the context. This phenomenon, we think, is due to more than one reason. One is what we have already mentioned, that is, the application of a static, accidental approach to abrogation. The second is the failure to recognize and appreciate the internal system of the Qur'an, which has led to: a) oversimplification and generalization of concrete cases mentioned in the Qur'an, thus overlooking some aspects of the space-time dimension, and b) overlooking the internal structure and the Qur'anic sequence of verses in each section, which leads to focusing, in derogation of the overall Qur'anic framework, on minor details in an argumentative and legalistic way. This fragmentation leads to a blurred Qur'anic vision and the loss of well-defined Islamic goals and priorities.

The third reason which we think responsible for this partiality, fragmentation, and lack of comprehensive and systematic way of thinking in understanding, dealing with, and quoting the Qur'an is a conceptual misunderstanding of the different roles in Muslim society and government of the judiciary, which judges and disciplines, and of the social institutions, which educate, encourage, and protect.

The Significance of Concrete Cases in the Qur'an

The Qur'an is basically composed of verses concerned with general principles, directions, and philosophy. But along with these verses, other verses refer to specific cases, elaborate on them, and provide the Muslims involved in these cases with specific directions and orders.

Early writers and commentators on the Qur'an used to overlook the significance of the contexts and the characteristics of these verses when they generalized and abstracted meanings and directions from them. *Āyat al Sayf* or *Āyat al Qitāl* (The Verse of the Sword or The Verse of Fighting) is a good example to illustrate the problem at hand. The simple, classic, juristic approach of *naskh* helped the cause of a war already in progress against the big powers of the north before the death of the Prophet. As a matter of fact, this approach had the advantage of a direct and simple explanation. This added tremendous moral power to the war efforts against the stubborn, imperial Roman enemy to the north.

The Verse of the Sword says: Wage war on all the idol-aters as they are waging war on all of you (9:36), and the related verse in the same chapter says: O you who believe! Fight those of the disbelievers who are near to you, and let them find harshness in you (9:123).

These two verses played, in classical jurisprudence, a central role in determining the Islamic position pertaining to the relations among nations. The classic interpretation today is damaging to many aspects of the multidimensional Islamic character of the Qur'anic philosophy and does not fit the needs and challenges of the contemporary world.[36]

---

[36] Ibn Salāmah, *al Nāsikh wa al Mansūkh*, pp. 19, 51; M. Abū Zayd, Op. Cit., vol. II, 503, 583; al Zarkashī, *al Burhān*, p. 40; M. Zarqānī, Op. Cit., vol. II, p. 156; Wahbah al Zuhaylī, Op. Cit., pp. 78-89.

In the light of the total Qur'anic revelation and experience, and considering contemporary needs and challenges, Muslim scholars need to reform their approaches and their methods for understanding and interpreting the Qur'an and the Islamic message to humankind. All concrete cases and examples should be examined closely and with full appreciation for the time-place dimension, in order to grasp their true significance and emphasis within the value framework revealed throughout the Qur'an and manifested in the early Islamic experience.

Upon closer examination, the above verse (*Āyat al Qitāl*) involved a situation where the Muslims were already engaged in an all-out and vicious war against the Quraysh and its allied tribes. The verses instruct the Muslims in the best manner and strategy to deal with this savage enemy in a war that was already in progress. Thus, the verses were dealing with a very specific situation. Their purpose was to complement, not to negate, the general rules, attitudes, and moods of the wider framework and scope of Islam in the field of external relationships.

The Internal Structure of the Qur'an

The failure to recognize and appreciate the internal order and structure of the Qur'an, its chapters, sections, and verses is one of the major shortcomings of the classical methodology. It was not uncommon for a scholar to deal with the verses of the Qur'an as entities independent of each other, with little or no regard for the essential concept of the *sūrah*, entertaining them, their place, and their significance in the order of the *sūrah* (chapter) and of the preceding and following chapters. A verse or a part of a verse could be interpreted and analyzed out of context and without regard for its sequence in the *sūrah* or for its relation to the other verses of the *sūrah.* This method made it possible for individuals to force the Qur'an and its verses to appear to yield some of the narrow interpretations they desired. This method made it possible for those classical jurists using the concept of *naskh* (abrogation) to lift verses, or parts of verses, out of their Qur'anic context in order to fit their own times and circumstances; times when the Muslims were a major world power, often engaged in fighting vicious enemies, and war appeared to be a reasonable means for settling political disputes. In the contemporary world this approach is no longer acceptable.

We have to reconsider our methodology for the study and interpretation of the Qur'an. We have to appreciate the internal order and structure of the Qur'an. We have to appreciate the way the Qur'an was revealed to the Prophet chapter by chapter, and verse by verse, according to the manner and the order directed by Allah.

There was obviously a divine purpose in the way the Prophet was guided by Allah to arrange every verse and every word of the Qur'an in the place and position assigned to them.[37]

The following two examples demonstrate this shortcoming in the classical methodology:

The first example deals with the way in which commentators handled the Qur'anic verse which says:

> Allah forbids you not with regard to those who fight you not for [your] faith nor drive you out of your homes from dealing kindly and justly with them, for Allah loves those who are just (60:8).

Commentators and jurists have long argued whether the Verse of the Sword abrogates this verse (of peace).[38] If we look at the verse in its place of occurence in *Sūrat al Mumtaḥanah*, we find that it represents a general rule for the Muslims about the manner in which they should deal with their peaceful non-Muslim relatives and neighbors. They were ordered and encouraged to be friendly, helpful, and just with them. The verse differentiates very clearly between the state of peace and the state of war. During war and hostile confrontation with non-Muslim enemies, Muslims should guard themselves against their enemies. They should unite against them and lend them no help or support.[39]

The *sūrah* and the verse preceding the verse under discussion teach Muslims the reason behind Islamic manners, general rules of conduct in peace and war toward non-Muslim peoples, and

---

[37] Ibn Kathīr, *Tafsīr al Qur'ān*, vol. II, pp. 331; Mannā' al Qaṭṭān, *Mabāḥith fī 'Ulūm al Qur'ān* (Studies in the Qur'anic Sciences) (Jeddah, Saudi Arabia: al Dār al Su'ūdīyah li al Nashr, n.d.), pp. 49-57.

[38] Ibn Salāmah, Op. Cit., p. 91; M. Abū Zayd, Op. Cit., vol. II, pp. 551-553.

[39] See, for example, the article *walīy* in Arabic dictionaries such as *Mukhtār al Ṣiḥāḥ* by Muhammad ibn Abū Bakr al Rāzī.

show that war is a passing condition. The whole Qur'anic lesson and direction in *Sūrat al Mumtaḥanah* started as follows:

> It may be that Allah will ordain love between you and those of them with whom you are at enmity. Allah is Mighty; and Allah is Forgiving, Merciful (60:7).

The second example deals with another verse also in *Surat al Mumtaḥanah,* which says:

> Say to the bedouins who lagged behind: "You shall be called against a people possessed of great might to fight them, or they shall surrender [yuslimūn, which could also be interpreted literally to mean 'to turn to Islam']. If you obey, Allah will give you a goodly wage, but if you turn your backs, as you turned your backs before, He will chastise you with a painful chastisement" (48:10).[40]

Looking at the major works of *tafsīr,* such as those by al Ṭabarī, Ibn Kathīr, and al Rāzī, we find that their major concern was not with what kind of attitude and discipline this *āyah* is trying to build in people; rather their major concern was in determining to which people the verse referred when it spoke of those who "possess great might." We find that al Ṭabarī provides us with a long list of the best guesses about their identities made by many jurists and scholars. He included in that list almost every possible enemy of the Muslims. The commentators he quoted listed Persia, Rome (Byzantium), the Ḥawāzin, the Ghaṭafān and the Banū Ḥanīfah. Some of the scholars speculated that the verse could be directed against people yet to come. Finally, al Ṭabarī concluded that the verse did not really tell us if any of the guesses made by the different scholars were correct, and that it was enough to know that the people mentioned in the verse are people who "possess great might."[41] Ibn Kathīr made the following additions to the list of guesses: the Thaqīf tribe, all the idolators, the Kurds, and people with small eyes, flat noses, and flat faces who were understood to be Turks.[42] Al Rāzī's comments and analyses, though less detailed, were not really any different from the other commentaries.[43]

---

[40] Fakhr al Dīn al Rāzī, *al Tafsīr al Kabīr*, vol. XXVIII, p. 93; Arthur J. Arberry's translation, *The Koran Interpreted* (New York: The Macmillan Company, 1955), p. 227; Yusuf Ali's translation, *The Qur'an*, pp.1395-1396; M. Pickthall's translation, *The Glorious Qur'an*, p. 366.

[41] Al Ṭabarī, Op. Cit., vol. II, pp. 82-84.

[42] See Ibn Kathīr, Op. Cit., vol. IV, pp. 90-93.

[43] See al Rāzī, Op. Cit., vol. XXVIII, pp. 91-93.

It was more relevant to the order and structure of *Sūrat al Fatḥ* to discuss the troubles and dangers facing Muslims from their external and internal enemies among the hypocrites. The *sūrah* explained these dangers at length, and the conduct, discipline, and strategies required from the Muslims to face these dangers. The *sūrah* went to great lengths in order to teach the bedouins about the proper conduct and discipline expected of them if they were to join the Muslim cause and integrate into Muslim society.

The classical jurists could perhaps afford to pay only limited attention to the internal order and structure of the Qur'an. They might have been able to limit their interest and analysis of the Qur'an to the narrow and limited issues that seemed to occupy their minds. Muslims and Muslim scholars can no longer continue with the same narrow interests and methodology. Instead, they must pay more attention to the basic issues, values, and directions revealed in the Qur'an through its internal sequence and structure.

The classical frame of mind, outlook, and methodology explain the conclusion reached by Ibn Kathīr in commenting on verse 256 of *Sūrat al Baqarah* ("There is no compulsion in religion"). To interpret this verse, he turned to verse 48 of the widely-separated *Sūrat al Fatḥ* and verse 36 of another distant *sūrah, al Tawbah.* Ibn Kathir, commenting on the first part of verse 2:256, says:[44]

> Some jurists said that the verse ("There is no compulsion in religion") was abrogated by the Verse of Fighting (9:36) and that all nations should be called to join the religion of straightforwardness, the religion of Islam. If someone refused to join, did not surrender, or did not pay the *jizyah,* he should be fought until killed. This is the meaning of compulsion. Allah says: "You shall be called against a people possesed of great might to fight them, or they surrender." Allah says: "O Prophet! Strive against the disbelievers and the hypocrites! Be harsh with them."

Muslim scholars need to give greater concern to these aspects of interpretation and to the shortcomings in their traditional methodology and its application.[45]

---

[44] See Ibn Kathīr, Op. Cit., vol. I, pp. 310-311.

[45] See W. al Zuhaylī, Op. Cit., p. 99.

Sayyid Quṭb, in his commentary on the Qur'an, *Fī Ẓilāl al Qur'ān* (In the Shade of the Qur'an), introduced a system of dealing with the Qur'an in paragraphs in order to show the student the significance of the Qur'an's internal structure. This is just one of the many steps that might be taken to introduce a more systematic and comprehensive understanding of the Qur'an through its internal system and structure.

From Fanaticism to Rationalism

The second step in the systematic, empirical approach to the development of Muslim thought in the field of international relations is to correct an important traditional misconception of the relationship between God and man. The importance of this misconception is that under certain conditions it can lead to fanaticism in intercommunal and international relations between Muslims and other peoples.

Fanatics usually assume an extraordinary concern for the decline and corruption of the Muslim social system while developing a very strict attitude for dealing with this decline. The intercommunal and international dimension of this fanaticism is an attitude of self-righteousness, contempt, and a lack of concern for non-Muslims (all of whom are believed to be hostile toward Muslims). Such attitudes are not only harmful to communication and interaction between Muslims and non-Muslims, but are also destructive to the very foundations of the Islamic mission. The Qur'an says: "We sent you not but as a Mercy for all creation" (21:107) and "Allah forbids you [Muslims] not, with regard to those who fight you not for [your] faith nor drive you out of your homes, from dealing kindly and justly with them: for Allah loves those who are just" (60:8).

Two factors on the part of Muslims can contribute to a misguided and fanatical attitude in relations between them and non-Muslims. The first, which we have already mentioned, is the influence of the traumatic historical experience of the early Muslims in their relations with the hostile Arab and Jewish tribes surrounding them. The second is the misconception of the perspective from which the Qur'an speaks. Although the Qur'an and Islam never allow a human being to assume theocratic authority, fanaticism nevertheless emerges when a Muslim allows himself to judge other people by assuming in practice an authority equal to the absolute authority and knowledge of Allah as represented in the Qur'an. [46]

> The unbelievers say: "Listen not to this Qur'an, but talk at random in the midst of its [recitation], that you may gain the upper hand." But We will certainly give the unbelievers a taste of a severe penalty, and We will requite them for the worst of their deeds. Such is the requital of the enemies of Allah, the Fire: therein will be for them the eternal abode, a [fit] requital, for that they were wont to reject Our signs (41:27- 28),

and,

> Allah has promised the hypocrites, men and women, and the rejecters of faith the fire of Hell; therein shall they dwell. Sufficient is it for them, and for them is the curse of Allah and an enduring punishment (9:68).

There are many similar verses, but it is a great mistake for Muslims to assume that their position vis-à-vis non-Muslims is the same as that of Allah in such verses. Allah speaks in those verses with absolute authority and knowledge. Muslims should not interpret verses referring to Allah's confrontation with and condemnation of nonbelievers, and God's advice on the way Muslims should respond to aggression, as the position assigned to all Muslims against all non-Muslims for all time. Such erroneous interpretation would overlook the space-time element in these verses and deal a crushing blow to their role as brokers of the universal mission of Islam. Muslims should read with equal care the other Qur'anic verses which point out their human role as carriers of the Islamic mission. Examples of these follow:

> It may be that Allah will grant love [and friendship] between you and those you [now] hold as enemies . . . Allah forbids you not, with regard to those who fight you not for [your] faith nor drive you out of your homes, from dealing kindly and justly with them: For Allah loves those who are just (60:7-8).

> Mention [heed] one of 'Ād's brethren: behold he warned his people, "Worship none other than Allah; truly I fear for you the penalty of a mighty day (46:21).

---

[46] See Hasan al 'Ishmāwī, *Qalb Ākhir li Ajl al Za'īm* (Another Heart for the Leader) (Beirut: Dār al Fath, 1970), pp. 98-180; M. D. al Rayyis, *al Nazarīyah al Siyāsīyah*, pp. 320-341; and M. Khadduri, *War and Peace*, pp. 7-18.

> Then said the man who believed: "O my people, Truly I fear for you something like the day of [disaster for] the Confederates [in sin], . . and O my people, I fear for you a day when there will be mutual calling [and wailing]" (40:30-32).

> It may be that you fret your soul with grief because they do not become believers (26:3).

> Say: 'O you men, now the truth has come to you from your Lord. Those who receive guidance, do so for the good of their own souls; and those who stray, do so to their own loss: and I am not [set] over you to arrange your affairs' (10:108).

All Muslims should strive to avoid all actions that block channels of communication with other peoples. Historical incidents and renewed conflict should not cause them to respond in a hostile manner to any nonhostile non-Muslim peoples or individuals. Their response to the hostile non-Muslims, as circumstances require, should be rational and restrained. Allah says:

> Fight in the way of Allah those who fight you, but do not transgress limits; for Allah loves not transgressers. . . But if they cease, Allah is Oft-forgiving, Most Merciful. . . So if they cease, let there be no hostility except to those who practice oppression (2:190-93).

> The recompense for an injury is an injury equal thereto [in degree]: but if a person forgives and makes reconciliation, his reward is due from Allah: for Allah loves not those who do wrong. . . The blame is only against those who oppress men with wrong-doing, and who insolently transgress beyond bounds through the land, denying right and justice: for such there will be a grievous penalty. But indeed if any show patience and forgive, that would truly be an exercise of courageous will and resolution in the conduct of affairs (42:40-43)

These examples from the Qur'an show the real danger of fanaticism in relations within Muslim society and with non-Muslims as minorities or foreign entities. If the different positions in these examples are allowed to be interchanged randomly, fanaticism will be the logical conclusion.

To avoid this, Muslims have to differentiate between the role of Allah and the role of man. The Qur'an is meant to speak in absolute terms and directly to the conscience of man. Muslims are assigned the role of *khalīfah* (vicegerent and custodian) with utmost concern for their fellow men. Muslim authority has a duty to facilitate, and not to destroy, this Muslim mission of vicegerency.[47]

Thus, conceptual clarity in approaching the Qur'an, the Sunnah, and the early history of Islam is very important. The desirability of sincere concern and mutual help among people of different races, colors, languages, territories, and ideologies should not be overlooked by any Muslim. Fostered by the Qur'an, traditional Muslim tolerance should again open all possible channels of communication among men. These channels transcend man-made boundaries and grasp at all available opportunities for a better and more just and equitable life for man in this world.

The Islamic Framework

The third step, in addition to respecting the coherence of the Qur'an and maintaining a decent humility among men toward Allah, is to design an Islamic ideological base or framework for a systematic empirical approach to the field of international relations.

When we look at classical Muslim political thought and the administration of the Muslim polity during the classical period, we find that policymakers profited from and were basically guided by the rational Islamic political policies of the Prophet. This was possible and reasonable when the foundations of the world's political systems known to the Muslims were fundamentally the same, and when the diplomatic and military techniques were also the same. But when the systems and techniques changed, the benefits from the early Islamic historical precedents and policies in the field of international relations could no longer be realized. Today, a new venture into free investigation is needed, one designed to serve the Muslim policy maker in the face of contemporary needs and techniques. The Muslim

---

[47] The Qur'an contains many verses that teach Muslims concern and love toward their fellow men and that enhance Muslim authority to do its utmost for the service and aid of man. See, for example, the Qur'an at 3:159, 14:36, 6:8, 3:103-105, and 2:190.

policymaker should be aided by a well established, comprehensive, systematic, empirical Islamic social science. What the Muslim policymaker needs from the early Islamic sources and actual historical policies is an ideological paradigm as a guideline that will enable him to continue a cultural and historic heritage, to respond to the conscience of the Muslim people, and to mobilize their energies. The ideological Islamic framework is required not only to provide Islamic guidelines but to assign basic priorities. The framework should be general enough to remove all unnecessary space-time elements. The Muslim policymaker will thus be able to deal more successfully with concrete realities and options.

At this juncture, it will be necessary to abstract some of the basic principles and values central to Islamic thought.[48] With such basics in mind, one can understand and appreciate many of the decisions and policies of contemporary Muslim decision makers.

Basic Principles

Tawḥīd

The most basic principal of Islam is *tawḥīd,* because it gives purpose to the Islamic framework. *Tawḥīd* refers to the existence, oneness, and uniqueness of Allah, the Creator; the unity and equality of man; and man as the vicegerent and custodian (*khalīfah*) of Allah on earth, who should rule in conformity with Allah's will.

The basic concept and the ideological foundation of Islam stems from the concept of *tawḥīd. Tawḥīd* is the visualization of human life as a direct relationship between the transcendent Creator and His creation, in which life is seen as a test of excellence and worth. This puts the final responsibility and initiative on the human individual in society. It leaves no room for man-made divisions based on distinctions of color, language, or wealth in determining the quality of human relationships or the worthiness of an individual. *Tawḥīd* lays the foundation for a

---

[48] See the Qur'an, 6:101-104, 4:1, 49:13, 67:2, 2:30, 7:32, 21:35, 16:125-126, 3:159, 16:90-91, 3:64, 5:2, 21:94, 9:36, and 2:193. See also, B.E. Smith, *Religion and Political Development* (Boston: Little, Brown & Co., 1970).

human society built on the responsibility of each human being as God's *khalīfah,* where superiority and eminence is reserved exclusively for the Unique One, Allah the Creator. Differences in human life and society pertain to function and performance and not to quality. The concept of *tawḥīd* gives society as well as individuals the freedom of destiny and self-determination. It is also the basis for Muslim tolerance toward non-Muslims.[49]

Justice (*'Adl*)

Fairness and justice are enjoined on Muslims in all dealings, even with their enemies. Allah (SWT) says:

> O you who believe! Be steadfast witnesses for Allah in equity, and let not hatred of any people seduce you into dealing unjustly. Deal justly, that is nearer to your duty. Observe your duty to Allah. Lo! Allah is informed of all that you do (5:8).[50]

Since the concept of justice is a basic principle in Islam, Islam extends Muslim responsibility and commitment to fairness and justice in all external relationships. What constitutes justice in any specific matter, how to arrive at that judgment, and how Muslims today are to influence the world's international system or reconcile themselves to any part of that system's content and procedures are matters to be decided from within the system and by the mutual agreement of the parties concerned.

Peace, Mutual Support, and Cooperation

These are the minimum requirements for Muslim unity in the field of international relations. Allah (SWT) says:

> The believers are naught else than brothers. Therefore make peace between your brethren and observe your duty to Allah, that perchance you may obtain mercy (49:10).

> Help one another unto righteousness and pious duty. But help not one another unto sin and transgression. Keep your duty to Allah. Lo! Allah is severe in punishment (5:3).

---

[49] See also M. Abū Zahrah, Op. Cit., pp. 19-47; and Sayyid Quṭub, *al Salām al 'Ālamī wa al Islām* (Cairo: Dār Iḥyā' al Kutub al 'Arabīyah, 1967), pp. 128-155.

[50] See the Qur'an at 16:90, 57:25, 7:29, 4:48, 49:9, and 60:8.

The Prophet summarized these concepts in a hadith reported by al Bukhārī and Muslim when he said: "A Muslim is a Muslim's brother. He does not wrong or abandon him. If anyone cares for his brother's need, God will care for his need."[51] The Prophet further summarized the essential ingredient of the relationship between Muslims who share the same faith and outlook in a hadith reported by al Bukhari: "A Muslim is he from whose hands and tongue other Muslims are safe."[52]

These verses of the Qur'an and hadith of the Prophet, and many more, provide the basis for relations among Muslims as individuals, groups, and states. These clearly emphasize the minimum requirement of just, brotherly, and peaceful relations among Muslims, the absence of aggression and violence, and the spirit of mutual help and cooperation. Islam also directs Muslims to use all possible peaceful means to preserve peace and establish justice among Muslim peoples. The Qur'an demands that Muslims should, wherever possible, organize themselves and employ a type of collective security, including the use of force against Muslim elements that are disruptive to peace among Muslims. Allah says:

> If two parties of believers fall to fighting, then make peace between them. But if one party of them does wrong to the other, fight the party that is doing the wrong til they return unto the commandments of Allah; then, if they return, make peace between them justly, and act equitably. Lo! Allah loves the equitable (49:9).

Whatever particulars go beyond these minimum requirements must be considered on their individual merit, without misunderstanding or misinterpreting such traditions as have been mentioned above in relation to the conditions of the Muslim state and society at the time of the Prophet and the actions taken by his immediate successors.

The absence of armed conflict and aggression and the spirit of symbiosis among Muslims, although they require political cooperation and organization, do not dictate any specific political

---

[51] Walī al Dīn al Tabrīzī, *Mishkāt al Masābīh*, ed. Nāṣir al Dīn al Albānī (Damascus: al Maktab al Islāmī, 1961), vol. I, p. 606.

[52] M. M. Khan, *The Translation of the Meaning of Sahīh al Bukhārī* (Gujaranwala, Pakistan: Sethi Straw Mills Limited, n.d.), vol. I, pp. 18-19.

structure. Islam encourages Muslims to make every possible effort to carry out constructive and progressive political, cultural, social, and economic endeavors. Only in this way is it possible to achieve the Islamic ideals of duty and responsibility.

The traditional interpretation of early Islamic sources on the issue of Muslim unity and political organization is a confusing factor in modern Muslim thought and must be clarified. Traditional interpretations of Muslim unity speak basically of a central political structure tailored after the early Muslim government of the Prophet and his four immediate successors (622-660 AC). In the main, the traditional position is derived from a few hadith concerning the political organization of the earliest Muslim governments.[53] The traditional interpretation, however, ignored the space-time element involved in these hadith. A discussion of some representative hadiths will suffice to clear the misconceptions of the traditional interpretation and lead to an intelligible understanding of political unity and power in the Islamic political system. Among these are the following:

> 'Arfajah said: I heard the Messenger of Allah (SAAS) say: "There is going to be some trouble there; and whoever wants to split the unity while it is maintained, strike him, whoever he is, with the sword. "[54]

> Jābir said: The Prophet at the Farewell Pilgrimage asked the people to listen. He said: "Do not revert after my death to acting like disbelievers who strike each others' necks (i.e., fight each other)."[55]

> Usāmah Ibn Zayd said, "The Prophet looked out from a Madīnah fortress and then said: 'Do you see what I see?' They said: 'No.' He said: 'I see killing, *fitan*, and anarchy going through your homes like rain.'" [56]

---

[53] Aḥmad Amīn, *Yawm al Islām*, (Cairo: Mu'assasat al Khānjī, 1958), pp. 143-152; 'Azīz Aḥmad, *Islamic Modernism in India and Pakistan; 1857-1954* (London: Oxford University Press,1967), pp. 139-140; Majīd Fakhrī,*Dirāsāt fī al Fikr al 'Arabī* (Beirut, Dār al Nahār, 1970), pp. 250-251; Muhammad 'Abduh, *al Islām wa al Radd 'alā Muntaqidīh* (Cairo: al Maktabah al Tijārīyah al Kubrā, 1928), p. 76;

[54] See al Mundhirī, *Mukhtaṣar Muslim*, vol. II, p. 94.

[55] See al Bukhārī, *al Jāmi' al Ṣaḥīḥ*, vol. XI, pp. 42-43; al Mundhirī, Op. Cit., vol. I, p. 19.

[56] al Bukhārī, Op. Cit., vol. IX, pp. 40-41.

'Abd Allah Ibn 'Amr Ibn al 'Āṣ said: "While we were taking care of some animals, we heard the announcer of the Messenger of Allah (SAAS) calling for a meeting at the mosque. We turned in to meet the Prophet [who] said: 'There was no prophet before me who did not find it his duty to point out to his people the best thing he knew for them, and to warn them about the worst he knew for them. The fortune of your Ummah was decreed at its inception. Near the end, the Ummah will fall upon a catastrophe and things you will not approve of. So, whoever wants to be spared the fires of Hell and enter Heaven, he should treat people the way he would like them to treat him. Whoever gives to an imam (political leader) his allegiance, approval, and loyalty of heart should obey him if he can. If someone else comes to challenge the imam, then strike the neck of the other.[57]

These hadiths clearly refer to the conditions in Arabia shortly before the death of the Prophet. The rebellion of the bedouin tribes was spreading and many false prophets, like Musaylamah and al Aswad al 'Anbasī, had already begun to challenge the Prophet and the central political authority and government in Madīnah. These hadiths refer to issues of rebellion and the maintenance of the political system in the state of Madīnah.

The term "Ummah" is a key word in the above hadiths, as it obviously refers to the generation of the Prophet and his Companions. The generalization which the traditional interpretation deduces from this usage ignores the space-time element involved in these hadiths. If the space-time element were recognized in these hadiths and the meaning of the term Ummah corrected (to indicate the generation and the society of early Madīnah), then these hadiths create no problem of legitimacy for the necessary political forms and involvements of the different parts of the Muslim world in the modern international political system. In terms of contemporary international law, these hadiths deal with belligerency, the right of the state to consider it an internal matter, and to use force to deal with it.[58]

---

[57] See al Farrā', *Kitāb al Imāmah*, in *Nuṣūṣ al Fikr*, ed. Yūsuf al Ibish, p. 218; al Mundhirī, Op. Cit., vol. II, p. 87. Notice that in the last hadith the Prophet was addressing immediate issues and circumstances rather than the future in general.

[58] See Charles G. Fenwick, *International Law*, 3rd rev. ed. (New York: Appleton-Century Grafts, Inc., 1948), pp. 140-148; Hans Kelsen, *Principles of International Law*, 2nd ed. (New York: Holt, Rinehart and Winston, Inc., 1966), pp. 414-418; and Muhammad Ḥāfiz Ghānim, *Mabādi' al Qānūn al Dawlī*, pp. 292-295.

Historically speaking, the classical interpretation of these hadiths as orders for Muslims to establish and maintain one permanent central political authority for all Muslims helped to preserve and expand the emerging Muslim society. Since then, as we noted, Muslim political thought has lagged behind the political realities and developments taking place in the Muslim world. As we saw in chapter 2, jurists were unable to introduce either a new vision or practical remedies, and were therefore forced retrospectively to justify and compromise with the political corruption of military dictators and "illegitimate" new independent sovereigns, until the whole *khilāfah* system of the ʻAbbāsī rulers collapsed.

Since then, they have not genuinely accepted any sort of federal or confederal or multinational political system for the Muslim world, although jurists and writers no longer insist on the immediate establishment of one central authority. Any alternative to one central authority is viewed more as a harsh necessity than a desired situation. With this stand, Muslim thought continues to lag behind the trends and currents of the international system and the political realities of the contemporary world, leaving the Muslim peoples in confusion. Muslim understanding of the dynamics of power and politics still needs to develop to the point where Islamic theoreticians can distinguish between functional unity and artificial uniformity and can therefore accept the evolution of sound and realistic combinations as alternatives to a simple central or semicentral political authority as the symbol of Muslim power and unity.

After World War II, Muslim countries in increasing numbers gained political independence and acquired almost all the institutional links for closer association and cooperation. The League of Arab States set up a financial institution for economic development (the Arab Development Bank), a council for Arab economic union (the Arab Common Market), joint defense and economic cooperation treaties among the states of the Arab

League (Arab Collective Security Pact), and so on.[59] A broader link with the Muslim world was established by joining the International Organization of the Islamic Conference (OIC) along with its permanent secretariat and its many associated cultural, economic, financial, and judicial institutions.

These and other agreements, pacts, conventions, and institutions clearly show that there is hardly any need for still more international institutions to help the Muslim Arab and non-Arab people achieve unity and cooperation and decrease the tension and conflict among themselves,[60] thus achieving independence, power, respect, and the constructive participation in international society which they seem to desire.

Clearly, Muslims lack neither the resources nor the institutions necessary for these goals. From our analysis, what is needed is a change of attitude, one that would allow the accumulation of resources and growth of institutions, ideas, and functions toward the desired goal. The existing political structures in the Muslim world would improve substantially if Muslims approached them with this positive spirit, realistically taking into account as many political and economic issues and problems of social communication and organization as possible.[61]

---

[59] Other such institutions are: the Convention for Facilitating Trade Exchange and the Regulation of Transit Trade between States of the Arab League, the Convention for the Settlement of Payments of Current Transactions and Movements of Capital between States of the Arab League, the Convention on the Privileges and Immunities of the League of Arab States, the Federation of Arab Lawyers, the Arab Journalists' Union, the Arab Teachers' Union, the Federation of Arab Physicians, the Arab League's series of Arab social welfare seminars and Arab health seminars, the Arab Manuscript Institute, the Cultural Museum, the Cooperative Training Center, the Institute of Advanced Arab Studies, the Organization of the Arab Scientific Federation, the Arab Telecommunications Union, the Arab Postal Federation, the Arab Broadcasting Union, the Arab Civil Aviation Council, etc.

[60] See 'Abd al Qādir al Jammal, *Min Mushkilāt al Sharq al Awsat* (Cairo: Maktabat al Anjlū al Misrīyah, 1955), pp. 320-477; Norman D. Palmer and Howard C. Perkins, *International Relations: The World Community in Transition* (Boston: Houghton Miflin, 1969), pp. 580-583; and Robert W. MacDonald, *The League of Arab States: A Study in the Dynamism of Regional Organization* (Princeton, NJ: Princeton University Press, 1965), p. 241.

[61] See, for example, the following: Daniel Katz, "Nationalism and Strategies of International Conflict Resolution," in *International Behavior: A Social-Psychological*

(continued...)

Islamic thinkers, scholars, and decision makers need to achieve a new orientation, a better understanding of the meaning of politics, and of power and its dynamics. It is important to study the modern federal and multinational experience of North America, especially of the United States, and of the [former] Soviet Union and the emerging united Europe.[62] All these major contemporary federal experiences deal with the problems of multinational states in different ways, provide insights into different approaches, and open the way for a new Islamic vision. In the case of the United States, the structural approach and the democratic process for the most part leave local problems and issues to local, city, and state governments. In the case of Europe, the pragmatic aspects of economics and common interests are stressed, while the [former] Soviet Union stressed the ideological approach.

Jihad (Self-Exertion)

For humans to carry out their responsibilities as the custodians or vicegerents of Allah on earth, they have to voluntarily exert their utmost efforts to bring their behavior in line with the guidelines revealed in the Qur'an and the Sunnah to humans by Allah, the Creator and Sustainer of the whole universe. This exertion of the self in all directions, in every effort and act, personal and collective, internal and external, is the essence of jihad and *'ibādah* (obedience to Allah in the choice of the right path) in the Islamic sense, which will be rewarded in the hereafter apart from whatever lawful benefit may result from it in this world. Clearly, jihad is supposed to run through all

---

[61](...continued)
Analysis, ed. Herbert C. Kelman (New York: Holt, Rinehart & Winston, 1965), pp. 354-391; John H. Herz, "The Territorial State Revisited: Reflections on the Future of the Nation-State, in *International Politics and Foreign Policy: A Reader in Research and Theory*, ed. James N. Rosenau (New York: Free Press, 1969), pp. 76-90; and Karl W. Deutsch, *Nationalism and Social Communication: An Inquiry into the Foundation of Nationalsim*, 2nd ed. (Cambridge, MA: Massachusetts Institute of Technology, 1966).).

[62] Karl W. Deutsch and others, *Political Community and the North Atlantic Area: International Organization in the Light of Historical Experience* (Princeton, NJ: Princeton University Press, 1968).

phases of a Muslim's life, as it is his duty to do every possible good in the world and to prevent harm. This can, of course, include combat on the battlefield, but to equate jihad exclusively with war is to be bound only by some aspects of the historical experience of the classical period and to misread the historical experience of the early Muslims.

Both al Bukhārī and Muslim reported a conversation between the Prophet and a man who came to him to join his troops in fighting (jihad). The Prophet asked the man if his parents were alive, and the man said: "Yes." The Prophet then told him: "Then strive in serving and providing for them *(fa fīhimā fa jāhid).*"[63] This answer clearly shows that jihad is the Muslim's striving to fulfill his every responsibility and to serve the Islamic cause and principles in a manner consistent with the Islamic framework. It is not to be taken to mean warfare alone. Jihad in this sense is the active expression of the Islamic commitment, responsibility, and sense of duty wherever it is required in practical life.

To interpret jihad as no more than either an offensive or a defensive war is to misunderstand the meaning of the word and the philosophy behind it. It is equally erroneous to assume, as have traditionalists and modernists alike, that jihad as holy war was the sole basis for relations between the Muslim and non-Muslim worlds in premodern times. We have already shown in chapter 2 that jihad meant more than one thing to the classical jurists. Muslim writers of modern times interpret all acts of jihad in the field of external relations in Muslim history, and especially in the early period, in terms of defense, while many non-Muslim writers explain the same as aggression against other non-Muslim peoples, initiated by Muslims almost entirely for internal reasons. A subjective attitude leaves no final verdict on historical actions that is acceptable to all parties concerned. This is not our concern here, however, and it is enough for us to realize that many things depend on the definitions and assumptions held by each writer. All we are saying here is that the Qur'anic text extends jihad far beyond the efforts and sacrifices made on the

[63] See al Khaṭīb al Tabrīzī, *Mishkāh*, ed. al Albānī, vol. III, p. 354.

battlefield.[64] But it must be remembered that a realistic analysis of the use of the term "jihad" in the actual course of the foreign policy of any Muslim state should not stop at the ideological aspects of the Islamic framework. The actual course of action taken by any Muslim state, whether called jihad or not, always depends on the interaction of internal and external factors as well as the extent of its commitment to Islamic teachings. These interactions have, in some instances and in the absence of the leaders' real commitment to sound Islamic ideology, led to the proclamation of some most unholy wars, wars in which it would not be difficult even for a traditionalist to recognize the absurdity of the claims that those wars were jihad. Although jihad as a basic Islamic principle does not exclude the possibility of armed conflict, students of international relations should pay attention to the variety of its meanings and applications in any specific situation. Only then will a better understanding of the motivation and consequences of any specific course of a Muslim foreign policy be possible.

Respect and Fulfillment of Commitments

This principle is a natural extension of the principle of *tawḥīd.* The sense of the responsibiity of man and the oneness and equality of human beings requires establishment of the moral obligation of Muslims, individually and collectively, to fulfill their personal, national, and international commitments. The genuine establishment of this principle in Islam is clearly in line with all other basic principles and values of Islam. Numerous Qur'anic verses urging Muslims to fulfill their agreements leave no doubt about the positive moral attitude of Islam in this sphere that allows no room for double standards.[65] A Muslim decision maker or statesman can find no refuge in the Islamic framework of thought or in its principles or values to justify the violation of agreements either by intention or by deliberate action.

---

[64] See the Qur'an, 22:77-78, 49:14, 29:69, 25:51, 16:110, 3:157, and 2:190-195.

[65] See footnote 24 above.

We refer back to al Sarakhsī's position that it is permissible for Muslims to agree to a truce with a stronger enemy for the sake of gaining time and then break the agreement as soon as they are able to fight successfully against that enemy. This stand was taken on the grounds that fighting against nonbelievers is a duty and that delaying it is similar to giving more time to a borrower to pay later.[66] This stand is the exception in Muslim jurisprudence, and in my opinion the analogy is a faulty one, for the stand is clearly in violation of both the letter and the spirit of every Qur'anic verse related to the subject. Neither do those verses support the static legalistic interpretation relating to the concrete circumstances concerning the Banū Qurayẓah, in conjunction with which Qur'an 8:58 was revealed, as the standard for the interpretation and implementation of the concept of unilaterally withdrawing from or repudiating an agreement.[67]

In the age of nuclear arms and mass destruction, what constitutes "a fear of treachery" as the Qur'an puts it, or, in political terms, aggression? And by what responsible process should decision makers react in such a situation? These are matters to be decided upon according to the prevailing methods and circumstances. The Qur'anic verses (specifically 8:56-58) offer a concept that allows for a realistic, flexible response in a situation of imminent danger. How are decision makers to assess the security of the state? What measures should they take? How is the Muslim state to resolve the conflict in different systems of law? The situations are tremendously complicated and change continually.[68] Mechanical and legalistic decisions are not applicable to

---

[66] See al Shaybānī, *al Siyar al Kabīr*, vol. I, pp. 190-191.

[67] Ibn Kathīr, *Tafsīr al Qur'ān*, vol. II, p. 320; al Tabarī, *Jāmi' al Bayān*, vol. X, pp. 26-27; see also footnote 24 above.

[68] See A. A. Fatouros, "Participation of the 'New' States in the International Legal Order of the Future," in *The Future of the International Legal Order*, ed. Richard A. Falk and Cyrile E. Black (Princeton, NJ: Princeton University Press, 1969), vol. I, pp. 350-371; Adda B. Bozeman, *The Future of Law in a Multicultural World* (Princeton, NJ: Princeton University Press, 1971), pp. 161-186; B. S. Murty, "Foundation of Universal International Law," in *Asian States and the Development of Universal International Law*, ed. R. P. Anand (Delhi: Vicas Publications, 1972), pp. 173-178; Josef L. Kunz, *The Changing Law of Nations: Essays on International Law* (Columbus: Ohio State University Press, 1968), pp. 3-56; and M. H. Ghānim, Op. Cit., pp. 3-16.

existing conditions. Decision makers must have the freedom to make responsible decisions in such situations.[69] To what extent is a weak party forced into an unfair agreement, as the former colonies experienced vis-à-vis their colonizers, justified in unilaterally repudiating treaties and agreements? To what extent are the "have-nots" justified in calling for change in the status quo? It is important to mention here that the careful planning of commitments is necessary for Muslim states. Serious political mistakes could lead to a breach of agreements, the destruction of a state's credibility, and a threat to world peace. Policy makers should endeavor to avoid such errors.

The Islamic framework will not tolerate pretense or marginal gains in agreements. In relation to serious considerations defined and worked out with a full sense of responsibility, the Islamic framework and the above verses leave no doubt that a positive attitude is required in international relations. The Islamic frame of mind leaves no doubt that responsible commitment is a basic ingredient for orderly interaction. The Qur'an makes it clear that Muslims are required to scrupulously observe this injunction in their internal and external relations. Thus, members of international systems should not overextend the legal aspects of treaties. They should realize that in bilateral and multilateral agreements elements such as good intentions, friendship, and/or basic mutual interest are necessary conditions for the serious implementation of treaties; bad intentions, deception, and serious political conflict of interests are bound to end with enmity, breach of agreements, or eventual armed conflict. Once war erupts, most treaties and pledges are repudiated, and thereafter success on the battlefield, as the Prophet put it, basically depends upon mastering the art of maneuver (*al ḥarb khid'ah*).[70]

Basic Values

Looking closely at the Islamic texts, experience, and history, we find that there are some basic values that color the Muslim attitude and influence the Muslim conscience and strategies for

---

[69] See Inis L. Claude, Jr., *Power and International Relations* (New York: Random House, 1962), pp. 197-204.

[70] See al Khaṭīb al 'Tabrīzī, *Mishkāt*, ed. al Albānī, vol. II, p. 384.

action. The failure of these values to function as effectively as they might is due, as we mentioned earlier, to a misunderstanding of historical experiences and to the rigid legalistic attitudes of the traditionalists who tried to set fixed patterns for Muslim action in all aspects of life, including external relations.

The basic values must be freed from space-time elements and kept in focus if Muslim leadership is to regain the efficiency and dynamism that prevailed under the leadership of the Prophet, Abū Bakr, and 'Umar. These values basically promote moderation and self-restraint. They help policy makers to recognize the limits of a particular course of action and not to lose sight of the goals beyond the means. These values, as exemplified by the Prophet in both internal and external affairs, are: no aggression (*'udwān*), no tyranny (*ṭughyān*), no corruption (*fasād*), no excesses (*isrāf*).

A few Qur'anic verses and hadith are enough to show the great emphasis that Islam places on these values. Allah says:

> And obey not the command of the prodigal [al musrifūn, wasteful or excessive] who spread corruption in the earth, and reform not (26:151-152).

> Neither obey each feeble oath-monger, detracter, spreader abroad of slander, hinderer of the good, transgressor, or malefactor (68:10-12).

> [O mankind!] . . . He [Allah] does not love aggressors. So work not confusion in the earth after the fair ordering [thereof] (7:55-56).

> Go, both of you, to Pharaoh. Lo! he has transgressed [the bounds]. And speak to him a gentle word, that perhaps he may heed or fear. They said: "Our Lord! we fear that he may abuse us or that he may play the tyrant" (20:43-45).

> The blame is only against those who oppress men with wrongdoing and insolently transgress beyond bounds through the land, defying right and justice: for such there will be a grievous penalty. But indeed if any show patience and forgive, that would truly be an exercise of courageous will and resolution in the conduct of affairs (42:41-43).

> And let not your hatred of a folk seduce you to transgress; but help one another unto righteousness and pious duty. Help not one another in sin and transgression, but keep your duty to Allah. Lo! Allah is severe in punishment (5:3).

The Prophet said: "Those who are merciful toward others will have mercy shown to them by the Compassionate One. If you show mercy to those who are on earth, He who is in heaven will show mercy to you."[71] And, "Allah will not show mercy to one who does not show mercy to others [*al nās* means humans]."[72]

The Framework for Muslim Attitudes and Policies in External Relations in the Contemporary World

We have already identified some basic attitudes and reviewed some of the external policies of the Prophet in chapter 2. It is clear that these attitudes were a mixture of friendship and cooperation, and of war and conflict. These attitudes were reflected both in policies and in their implementation. The Muslims engaged in policies of cooperation and mutual aid, economic pressure, psychological warfare, guerilla tactics, and regular warfare. These policies clearly reflected the influence of basic Islamic principles and values enunciated by the Prophet in response to the internal and external factors operative at the time. The ultimate goal of these external policies was to serve the Muslim people and their cause under the prevailing circumstances. Policies are action-oriented to carry out the prevailing attitude within the possible alternatives available to the decision maker. Early Muslim policies and attitudes, as we observed, were bound to reflect the space-time dimension. Contemporary Muslims should be open to change and innovation in the area of policy.

For example, the attitude of neutrality in relations among nations, if it existed at all in the period, was not of major significance because the basic attitude among major powers during the time was one of hostility. Neutrality was a major ingredient in the European political system of the nineteenth century because of the new and far-reaching means of communication and war. Changes since World War II in communications and war technology, together with current political alignments, have now reached a point where neutrality is difficult to practice.

---

[71] al Khaṭīb al 'Ṭabrīzī, *Mishkat*, trans. J. Robson, vol. III, p. 1034.

[72] Ibid., p. 1031; see also the Arabic text, ed. al Albānī, vol. III, p. 605.

Major disparities between newly created environments and the attitudes persisting from past experience, as well as a serious lack of creative policies, threaten to bring about disastrous results. Confusion, misunderstanding of the role of basic principles and values, and a lack of firm adherence to them adversely affect the national conscience of a people and their unity in support of foreign policies. Muslim thought, as we have shown, reflects these serious disparities and the urgent need for self-examination in order to achieve a better understanding of the Islamic framework and of the inner workings of the policy mechanisms involved.

Diagrams 1-3 are intended to delineate the potentially dynamic nature of Muslim states and their attitudes and policies.

Diagram 1 illustrates the traditional superimposed understanding of contemporary international relations in terms of the classical jurisprudence of *siyar* and jihad, which was explained in chapter 2. The classical framework is no longer related to current international affairs. As we see it, this traditional approach in the world politics of today is bound to be static and superficial and offers no help for contemporary Muslim policy makers.

Diagram 2 illustrates the modernists' position. Their position and policies on international affairs, while reflecting the influence of foreign powers and a foreign environment, nevertheless lack the capacity to mobilize the people and their potential. This position of the modernists, which represents the prevailing conditions in Muslim political thought, was also discussed in chapter 2. At the heart of this position is the problem of immature and static Muslim thought. Contemporary Muslim thought has been largely under the influence of the modernist approach, which consists of imitation and piecing together. Positive interaction between ideology and environment, and the possible growth of Muslim power and partnership in international affairs, are not integral attributes of such an approach. Modernists believe that Muslim foreign policies are deficient not because they lack Islamic motivation and goals, but because Muslim policy makers have failed to bring about the economic growth and political power needed to support their policies and improve the conditions of the Muslim people.

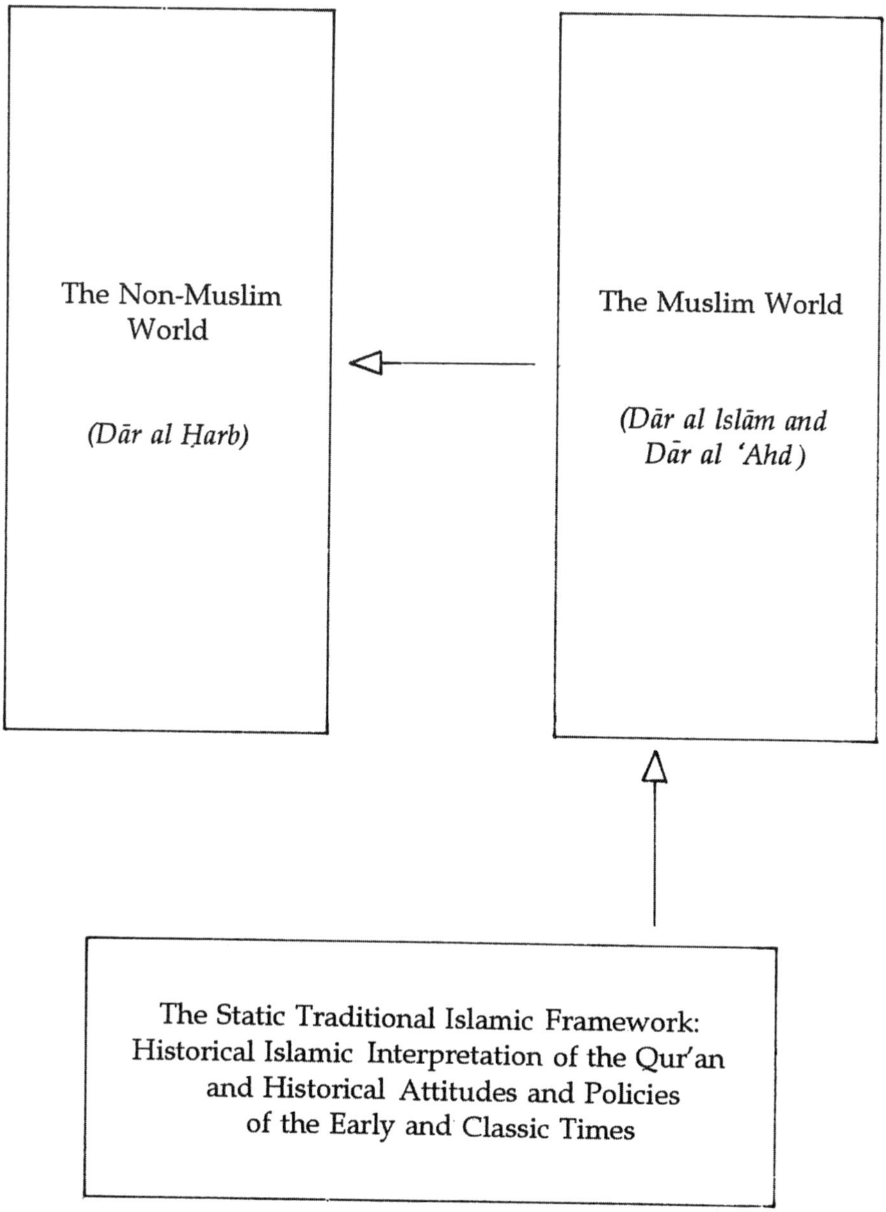

Diagram 1. Traditional Framework

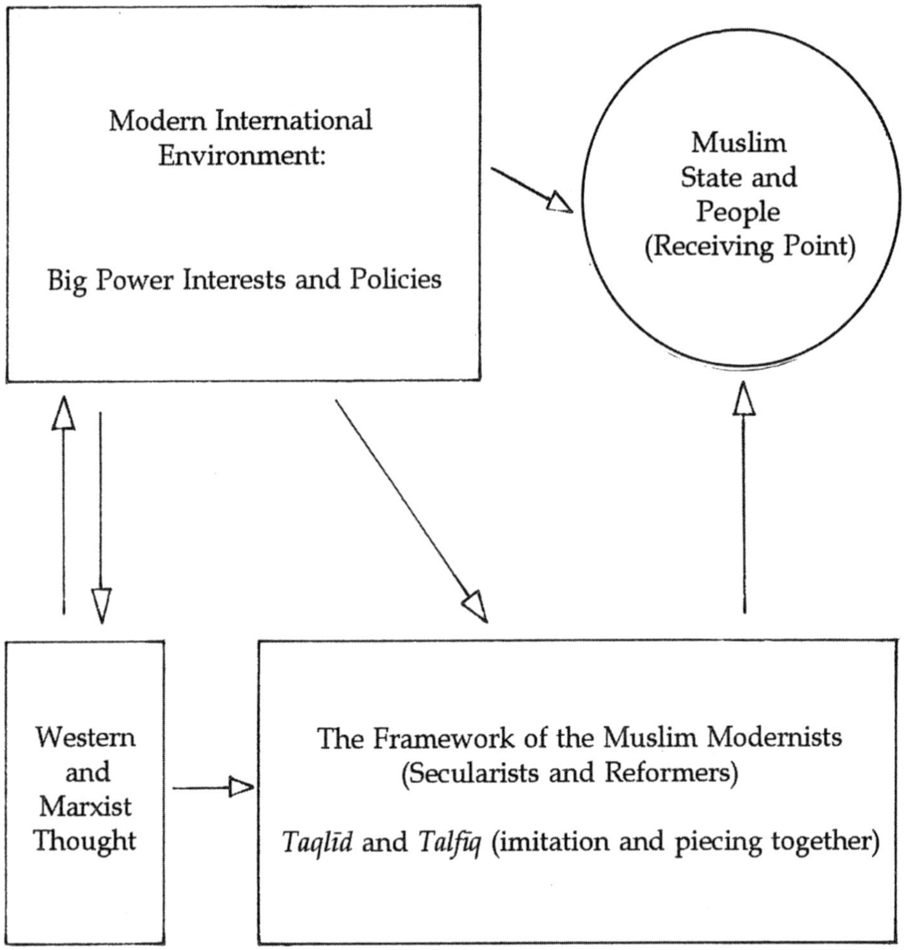

Diagram 2. Modernists and Secularist Framework

Diagram 3 illustrates a proposed Muslim framework in the field of international relations. Islam, in this framework, plays the role of a people's ideology. Islam is presented to the policy makers as a set of abstract principles and values, a framework or a set of guidelines, freed from the major weakness of the traditional approach, namely, the space-time element. The proposed framework also eliminates the other major fault of the traditional approach, its lack of systematic, empirical analysis, since it accounts for dynamic interaction between the ideology and the environment.

The proposed framework, by taking into account the effective use and acceptance of Islamic ideology in the process of policy making, also eliminates the major failure of the modernist approach, namely, the lack of capacity to mobilize the Muslim peoples and their potential. It is clear that the proposed framework is aimed at putting an end to the immobilization of Muslim moral and intellectual powers which occured through the incorrect use of historical and alien experiences. The proposed framework provides policy makers with the necessary freedom to plan and execute rational Islamic courses of foreign policy.

Although the principles and the historical precedents referred to in the diagram are clearly moral, they set no rigid formulas for policy action.

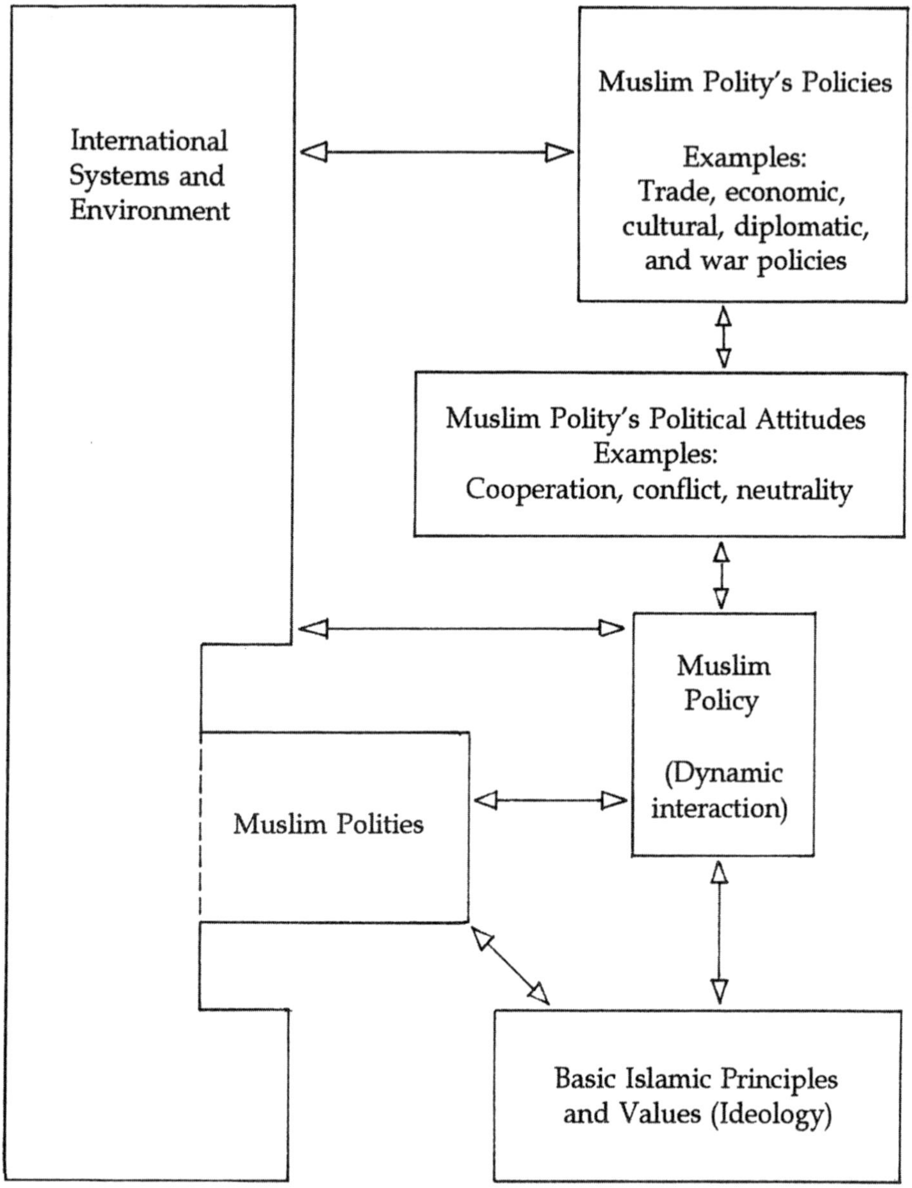

Diagram 3. Modern Dynamic Islamic Framework

Basically, what is required of decision makers is a basic commitment to work within and implement the Islamic framework. Any specific policy devised to meet a specific situation should be undertaken by decision makers in the light of five factors: 1) the basic principles and values of Islam; 2) the character of threats to and opportunities for the pursuit of Islamic goals; 3) the strengths and limitations of Muslim societies; 4) the resources of adversaries and allies; and 5) the limitations of the environment.

Hence, this dynamic framework can accommodate every shade of political strategy from that applied in the established international community to the radicalism of policies used in Algeria during the independence struggle against the colonialist French army and settlers. The nature of policies professed in the Muslim state depends, in the last analysis, on the particular situation at hand. It is therefore simplistic to assume that decision makers can afford to obey the rigid legal provisions of past ages that supposedly govern the conduct of external affairs in Islam.

Major Muslim Policies Examined

The focus of this study now shifts from the early period of Islam to the policies and attitudes of modern Muslim nations. Our purpose in this examination is not to suggest particular changes in any of these policies for any specific country. Rather, our purpose is to point out the irrelevance of the traditional legalistic approach in assessing the value of any course of foreign policy undertaken by a Muslim state as well as the advantages and opportunities available to Muslim policy makers if they adopt an ideological framework free from space-time limitations and built on the solid dynamic basis of the systematic empirical approach suggested in chapter 3.

Three major policies should be analyzed, and their achievements in the service of Muslim states in the field of international relations should be examined. The first policy, already analyzed, is the abandonment of war as the basis of foreign relations with non-Muslims. The second and third are the adoption of diplomatic reciprocity and alliances with non-Muslim states and the principle of positive neutrality.

At the outset, it is important to mention that our concern is not with the detailed development or technical aspects of these policies. What matters, and what we intend to emphasize here, are the causes of these policies and their goals. Only in the light of the rationales and goals of these policies can we assess the assumed conflict of these policies with Islam and the abandonment of Islamic ideology as a possible cause for their failure.

Strategies of Diplomacy and Alliance

Starting with the Ottomans, we find that in the history of the victorious early Ottoman *ghāzīs* (warriors for the faith) against the then inferior hostile powers of Europe, diplomacy had a very limited role and value.[73] With the renaissance of Europe and its successful efforts to reach the trade centers of the Far East, however, new attitudes and policies of cooperation in pursuit of mutual interest emer-ged, as did more diplomatic interaction between the Ottomans and the European powers. In what came to be known as the Treaties of Capitulations, the Ottomans provided more facilities for European traders, and European countries sent diplomatic missions to the Ottoman government (the Ottoman Sublime Porte).[74]

As the contrast between the increasing power and technological capability of Europe and the decaying, corrupt, and stagnant Ottoman cultural, social, and political systems grew, the Ottoman political authorities began to use and rely on diplomacy to counter the militarily superior European enemies who aimed at dismembering an empire that had become increasingly defenseless against their attacks. The Ottomans exchanged diplomatic missions on a permanent basis and entered into treaty and alliance relations with Christian states, though some of these alliances were at the initiative of some European states which wanted to secure better privileges and protect their interests vis-à-vis other European states.[75]

---

[73] See T. Naff, *Reform and Diplomacy*, p. 295.

[74] See R. H. Davison, *Turkey*, pp. 46-47.

[75] See Bernard Lewis, *The Middle East and the West* (New York: Harper & Row, 1966), pp. 116-118; R. H. Davison, *Turkey*, pp. 53-90; T. Naff, *The Setting of Ottoman Diplomacy*, pp. 22, 26; and T. Naff, *The Reform of Diplomacy*, p. 310.

The Ottoman chapter in history closed with World War I and the defeat of the Central Powers. Although Kemalist Turkey continued the Ottoman practice of reciprocal diplomacy, Islam was no longer an approved source for conducting the external relations of the Republic of Turkey. While evaluating the Ottoman policies, some writers took the extreme traditional position for granted and insisted on approaching Islam as a set of traditions and forms, overlooking its fundamental nature as a value system and framework.[76] These writers strictly measured the Ottoman policies against the Ḥanafī jurisprudential manuals and, on that basis, condemned the Ottoman sultans for deviating from Islam.[77] The kind of questions they raised were the like of whether or not Islam allows a treaty of more than ten years, or whether a Muslim subject is allowed to be brought to trial in a non-Muslim court. Ultimately, it was this approach that led them to conclude that deviation from the traditional jurisprudence of one legal school or another is deviation from Islam.

Islam does not accept the concept of the duality of the secular and the religious. Differences in opinion between political authorities and jurists do not necessarily mean that the jurists are Islamic and the political authorities are not. Rather, the matter has to be considered on its merits. While a political authority may tend, under the influence of various political factors, to give less attention to the ideological elements of the system, especially in its rigid juristic form, it is equally as likely that the jurist lacks an understanding of the political factors at play.

The Islamic orientation of the Ottomans is beyond any doubt. Such accusations against the Ottomans are really no more than a matter of opinion. Moreover, criticism of the Ottoman sultans is basically a conservative position. The critics, mainly the ulama, considered any deviation from the classical experience to be a sort of heresy. Classical thought and certain specific historical precedents were not fully acceptable to Ottoman statesmen who were faced with the threat of a rapidly modernizing Europe and its growing power and efficiency. Under such circumstances,

---

[76] See M. Khadduri's introduction to al Shaybānī, *The Islamic Law of Nations*, pp. 62-67; and M. T. al Ghunaymī, *The Muslim International Law*, pp. 18-54.

[77] See M. Khadduri, Op. Cit., pp. 63-64.

then, accusations against the Ottoman statesmen that they were somehow Islamically "deviant" amount ultimately to a denial of their right to exercise the judgment necessary to avoid policies that would lead them to disaster.[78]

The Ottoman sultans of the eighteenth and nineteenth centuries, whose state was formally admitted as a member of the European state system in the Paris peace agreement of 1856, used the diplomatic approach in order to be able to maneuver under new circumstances and developments.[79] This was necessary for their existence and also for the new program of reforms. These basic requirements elevated the question about the "Islamicity" of the Ottoman approach from such legalistic particulars as the legitimacy of a treaty of more than ten years or the empty textual arguments about the permissibility of a policy of alliance with a non-Muslim state, to the more basic question of interaction and efficiency in pursuing Islamic goals.[80] Why then did the Ottoman political authorities introduce the new diplomatic approach? Why did they develop cooperation and coexistence with Christian European powers? And what was the purpose of these new attitudes?

The waning military and economic power of the empire and the growing strength of the European powers was the obvious reason. The purpose was to preserve the empire from dismemberment by manipulating the balance of power among the Europeans. Reform, in the meantime, was supposed to restore sufficient power to the empire to withstand any further encroachments.[81] The success or failure of these policies is reflected in the interaction of various sections of a social system in adjusting and responding to real needs, both internal and external.

---

[78] Note that the Ottomans, in defense of their policies, invoked the classical concept of *maṣlaḥah*, basically in terms of necessity.

[79] See Charles G. Fenwick, *International Law*, p. 18; and Roderic H. Davison, *Reform in the Ottoman Empire: 1850-1870* (New Jersey: Princeton University Press, 1963), p. 4. See also: J. C. Hurewitz, *Diplomacy in the Near and Middle East*, pp. 153-156.

[80] See B. Lewis, *The Middle East*, p. 118; and M. Khadduri, Op. Cit., pp. 63-64.

[81] See R. H. Davison, Op. Cit., pp. 68-77.

Obviously, the Ottoman policy makers failed to achieve their objective of reviving Ottoman military superiority. The only way in which they succeeded was in introducing large numbers of technical and constitutional reforms, some of which were superficially implemented or misapplied. They failed to understand the phenomenon of Europe's growth and development, and Ottoman Sunnī thought failed to abandon legalism and to introduce a genuine systematic and rational application of the value system to new developments in the socio-political sphere. The efforts of more than a century (the nineteenth) resulted in no more than secularization and westernization.[82] Islamic thought and consciousness remained static or was further alienated.

When the Ottoman Empire collapsed and was dismembered at the end of World War I, the gap between the Muslim world and Europe was wider than ever. The fault of the Ottomans was not that they tried to adapt to the changing situation and tried to gain time in order to survive and reform. Rather, the mistake they made was that instead of taking the course of Islamic reform they chose the way of superficial modernist reform.

Most of the Muslim world had to wait until after World War II to gain the degree of independence and freedom that would allow it to participate in world affairs. Some Muslim countries followed a course of alliance with the West, and several have recently aligned themselves with the East. The rest adopted what came to be called positive neutrality and nonalignment.

We now turn to an analytical discussion of these two major contemporary policies to see how much success or failure secular Turkey had in attaining what the Ottomans had aimed at and failed to achieve.

After the end of World War I and the fall of the Ottoman Empire, the Western powers divided the Ottoman territory under the mandate system. In the period between the two world wars, a number of treaties were made between European powers and

---

[82] See T. Naff, Op. Cit., pp. 62-63; Niyazi Berkes, *The Development of Secularism in Turkey* (Montreal: McGill University Press, 1964), pp. 23-289; R. H. Davison, Op. Cit., pp. 62-63 and 53-143; B. Lewis, *The Emergence of Modern Turkey*, pp. 124-128.

Muslim states, full of terms expressing friendship and alliance. But in reality, these treaties did not represent policies or agreements between independent states. They were rather the terms dictated by the victorious European powers vis-à-vis the occupied Muslim territories. Examples of these are the treaties between France and Syria of 1936, France and Lebanon of 1936, Egypt and Britain of 1922 and 1936, and Iraq and Britain of 1922 and 1930.[83]

The policy of alliance assumed importance after World War II, when the Western European powers were no longer the major world powers nor in a position to control the Middle East. This was when the superpowers of the world, the United States and the [former] Soviet Union, began to pursue their global interests in the area. Both the new and the old powers started to compete to gain influence and control the area, and this led to the opening of policy alternatives to the Muslim states of the Middle East.[84]

To understand the various attitudes and policies pursued by the Muslim states of the Middle East, we have to keep in mind the different historical and geopolitical factors involved which divide them into the frontier zone (or what is called the Northern Tier of Turkey, Iran, Pakistan, and Afghanistan) and the Arab world. The threats and dangers to the interests of each area differ; similarly, their attitudes and policies toward the major powers involved in the politics of the area differ. Along the frontier zone are Muslim states facing the [formerly] communist Soviet Union. In the past, when these states were a part of the Ottoman Empire and Iran, they had bitter experiences and

---

[83] See, for example, the Arabic text of the treaties of alliance and friendship between Great Britain and Iraq of 1922 and 1930 in al Sayyid 'Abd al Razzāq al Husaynī, *Tārīkh al 'Irāq al Siyāsī al Hadīth*, 2nd rev. ed. (Sayda, Lebanon: Matba'at al 'Irfān, 1958), vol. II, pp. 30-38, 41-42, 45-81, 204-234; Husayn Fawzī al Najjār, *al Siyāsah wa al Istrātījīyah fī al Sharq al Awsat* (Cairo: Maktabat al Nahdah al Misrīyah, 1953), pp. 501-504, 510-12, 586-610, 470, 471, 476, and for the Treaty of Friendship and Alliance between Egypt and Great Britain, see pp. 592-609 of the same work; and Nicola A. Ziyadeh, *Syria and Lebanon* (Beirut: Lebanon Bookshop, 1968), pp. 53-55.

[84] See J. Hurewitz, "Origins of the Rivalry" in *Soviet American Rivalry*, ed. I. Hurewitz, pp. 1-7.

conflicts with Imperial Russia. Russia projected a threat to these states, and the Western powers, for strategic and geopolitical reasons, usually found it in their interest to cooperate with these Muslim states against Russia. The Russian policy of southward expansion toward the warm seas, culminating in the occupation of some of this frontier zone, also constituted a threat to the interests of the Western colonial powers in Asia and Africa.

The countries of the frontier zone, or what came to be called the Northern Tier - with the exception of Afghanistan, a small landlocked state of high mountains which shares a long border with the [former] Soviet Union - had their reasons to fear the intentions of the then Soviet Union. In the case of Pakistan, its enmity with India and the collaborations between India and the then Soviet Union were two more reasons for the pragmatic policy of alliance between that Muslim state and the West, especially the United States.[85]

The Northern Tier policy was implemented through the involvement of these states in the alliances of CENTO (Baghdad Pact), SEATO, and NATO. The Arab world, however, was in a different situation and had different historical and strategic experiences. The Arab world, with its strategic location, major communication lines, and vital raw materials, experienced from the eighteenth century onward an increasing foreign presence and control of its territories. The World War I alliance of the Arabs with the Western powers against the Ottomans and the Central Powers, in an open bid for their independence, ended with the bitter experience of the mandate regimes. In the aftermath of World War II, the dominant Western powers in the area, France and Britain, were weakened and were no longer able to play the same role. The growing oil interests of the United States and its close relations with the emerging Zionist-Jewish state of Israel, built on the ruins of Arab Palestine as a result of the

---

[85] We should note that in the Baghdad Pact, which after the withdrawal of Iraq changed its name to the Central Treaty Organization (CENTO), Britain was used as the Western connection and the United States was formally only an associate member. Thus, the United States was "in the Pact but not of it, a participant for practical purposes, but without the legal commitments." See N. D. Palmer and H. C. Perkins, *International Relations*, pp. 583-584.

British mandate, gave an impetus to the movement of liberation and independence from Western domination.

Strategies of Neutrality

Arab political attitudes toward the West after World War II continued to be largely bitter and hostile. With the growing policy of cold war between the two major powers and the then Soviet Union's post-Stalin change of strategy toward the developing areas, particularly the Middle East, and its offers of economic and military aid, it became possible for a few years to take advantage of the emergence of new options that came to be known as positive neutrality and nonalignment.[86]

Historic and strategic considerations explain why the alliance with the West came to an end for Pakistan, and why it lost some of its strength in relation to Iran and, to a lesser extent, to Turkey. This happened when the United States provided India, considered the archenemy and a major threat to the existence of Pakistan, with military aid, thus causing serious doubt about the dependability of U.S. commitments to Pakistan.[87] The success of the Egyptian attack on Nūrī al Sa'īd's policy of Iraqi alliance with the West (the Baghdad Pact) can also be explained by the historic and strategic factors analyzed earlier. A policy of alignment with the West against the [former] Soviet Union is contrary to the interests of an area seeking development, liberation, and independence from Western and Zionist control. With the new Soviet approach, the Arab world, especially Egypt, proclaimed the slogan of positive neutrality.[88] This slogan has been misinterpreted and misunderstood. In order to understand it correctly,

---

[86] See Alvin Z. Rubinstein (ed.), *The Foreign Policy of the Soviet Union*, 2nd ed. (New York: Random House, 1966), pp. 379-392, 396-397.

[87] See G. W. Chaudhuri, *Pakistan's Relations with India* (Meerut, India: Meenakshi Prakashan, 1971), pp. 1-8: Muhammed Ahsan, *Pakistan and the Great Powers* (Karachi: Council of Pakistan Studies, 1970), pp. 32-62: Mohammad Ayub Khan, *Pakistan Perspective* (Washington, DC: The Pakistani Embassy, n.d.), pp. 17-34; and Murtaza Rizwi, *The Frontiers of Pakistan* (Karachi: National Publishing House, 1971), pp. 3-11 and 143-168.

[88] Fayez A. Sayegh, "Islam and Neutralism," and P. J. Vaikiotis, "Islam and the Foreign Policy of Egypt," in *Islam and Intertnational Relations*, ed. J. H Proctor, pp. 60-93 and 120-157.

the attitudes and policy underlying this slogan must be explained. Historical developments inevitably turned the Arabs against the West, but at the same time the Arabs were in a position of weakness vis-à-vis the presence of the West in the area. Thus, the Arabs feared the West and had to be cautious in their policies.[89] The [former] Soviet Union, the other superpower and enemy of the West, was therefore a natural ally for the Arabs against the West. Although the Arabs needed Soviet economic and technical aid in their struggle against the West, the ideological differences and the historical experience of their coreligionists in the frontier zone made the Arabs fear the Soviet Union, which is in no way fundamentally different from a Western power. Thus, the Arabs displayed an attitude of caution even while cooperating with the [former] Soviet Union.[90] This explains the bias in the voting pattern of Arab countries, such as Egypt, a nation which claims a policy of positive neutrality toward the [former] Soviet Union while striking at the communist parties on its own territory.

Although positive neutrality represents an attitude of caution on the part of the states that follow it toward the big powers competing in the area, it must be remembered that positive neutrality does not represent the entire foreign policy of these states, which simultaneously follow different attitudes and policies toward other Arab and Muslim states. It would be necessary to consider the ideological, national, and historical factors in interaction with the problems in question, the action required, the other party or parties involved, and other policies pursued by the parties involved in order to understand the variety of attitudes and changing policies pursued within the Muslim world.

The change of strategies and policies between the two superpowers from the Cold War and confrontations to the detente and the subsequent Western abandonment of the Indian Ocean, the South African region, and Afghanistan to the [former]

---

[89] We use the word "West" in this section on contemporary major foreign policies to mean only Western Europe and the United States.

[90] See Bayard Dodge. "The Significance of Religion in Arab Nationalism," in *Islam and International Relations*, ed. J H. Procter, pp. 112-113.

Soviet Union, the fall of the pro-Western regime of the Shah in Iran, and the devastating Iraqi-Iranian War, indicate strategic change. This could bring harm to the Muslim world in general and to the Muslim states of the Middle East in particular, as part of a strategy to provide the [former] Soviet Union with land passage to warm water and the Indian Ocean.

Nonalignment and positive neutrality toward the two superpowers or alliance with either one of them are no longer working policies for the peoples of the Muslim world. Their only option is to find ways and means to achieve a workable unity and cooperation among Muslim countries in politics, economics, and military strategy if they are to avoid more devastating defeats and humiliating control at the hands of the Soviets in the frontier region and at the hands of the West and the Zionist state of Israel in the Arab Middle East.

It is indeed disheartening to note the less than satisfactory reaction of states in the Muslim world to recent developments in the relations between nations, developments that have led to a New World Order in which confrontation has turned to cooperation. The states of the Muslim world have wasted the opportunity to pull together to achieve greater cooperation for the protection of their mutual interests, and to gain greater leverage for bargaining with foreign powers. Thus, at the same time that we witness the emergence of several international groupings in both Europe and Asia, many of the states in the Muslim world, owing to deficiencies in their political systems and the influence of foreign powers, are engaged in bitter disputes with one another.

Today, with the fall of the Soviet empire and its totalitarian Marxist ideology, and with the inability of the secular, liberal, democratic, and capitalist West to deal with the alarming increase in its own moral, social, and economic problems, the Muslim states find themselves face to face with both important opportunities and dangers. Attention must be given to these for, on the basis of favoritism, the future course will be set for several generations to come, and even for the whole of human civilization.

The dangers inherent in a world order in which several groups vie with one another on the basis of particular national interests will certainly lead to world wars and the spread of imperialist ambitions, the chief objective of which will surely be the states of the Muslim world. A study of the global wars and the recent "wars of liberation" that pitted one world power against the other in places like Vietnam, Algeria, and Afghanistan, as well as the fate of the colonial powers and that of the superpowers, will serve to clarify that no single nation will be allowed to wield power on its own. The recent fall of the Soviet Union and the exhaustion experienced by the United States clearly illustrate this point. The lesson that history teaches is that any attempt to seize power exclusively and confront all those with ambitions and interests of their own is certain to result in failure.

The greater likelihood is that the world order will return in one form or another to an international balance of power with localized disputes over the division of territory and spoils. In view of the possibilities afforded by the modern age, however, such a world order will make the tragedies and wars of the twentieth century seem as nothing in comparison to the human and material losses that it will lead to in the twenty-first century. The only way to avoid an all-encompassing war of mass destruction that threatens humanity with extinction is for the world to ransom itself by adopting a new and effective Islamic world order before it is too late.

Undoubtedly, the presence of regions of weakness to which the ambitious are drawn, regions that include the Muslim world as their most important element, serves only to increase the dangers inherent in the dark cloud of the New World Order that now overspreads the horizon.

It would be a great service to humanity if peoples and governments in the Muslim world bring about the sort of fundamental reform that will spare it from having to act out conflicts between foreign powers on its own land. This is a matter that must not escape the conscience of the Muslim populace, or the considered attention of Muslim leaders and intellectuals.

The opportunities open to the Ummah are not confined only to those which will allow it to save itself. On the contrary, many opportunities exist for it to produce Islamic alternatives for civilization based on the principles of *tawḥīd*, *khilāfah*, and the oneness and shared destiny of all of humankind. Such alternatives should join between spirituality and materialism, idealism and pragmatism, the seen and the unseen, and between reason and revelation. Moreover, the purpose of an Islamic alternative for civilization should be to overcome the deficiencies in the present relationship between individuals and society and to settle the conflict between values and approaches. If this is accomplished, freedoms will be regulated by the bounds of objectives and sound human faculties that protect and maintain the rights of the individual and the group, and balance relations between them.

In the difficult stage to come, the essence of national and international politics in the Muslim world must proceed from purely Islamic reformational goals. These, in turn, will require solidarity among Muslim states which will have to overcome their debilitating internal conflicts, learn to set priorities, and insist on intellectual reform before all else. Such reform will naturally be followed by the reform of education and the social order in accordance with sound religious, psychological, and intellectual principles. Thereafter, the political, economic, and other social systems will become effective and productive.

The Islamization of policies within the nations of the Muslim world must not be allowed to come to a halt at the point of implementing the historical Islamic systems and those stipulated in the works of the early jurists. Instead, these should proceed in pursuance of higher Islamic objectives and purposes, while adhering to the basic principles and values of Islam.

Lamentably, many of those who followed the Ottomans fared no better than they had. Despite the soundness of their approaches and policies at the international level, including nonalignment and positive neutrality, the implementation of their policies was plagued by mistakes. In many cases these resulted in bringing about the opposite of what was intended of the policies. Instead of creating the freedom and ability to cooperate, bargain, and manuevre in relation to the influential and covetous foreign powers, more often than not the result was to become further entrenched in the camp of one foreign power or another. Finally, the ideal of unity between Muslim states became illusory as their differing political orientations led them to open conflict.

In this way, the state of the Islamic world was further weakened, so that the economic, technological, and military gap between it and the developed nations grows even more pronounced.

Unless Muslims and their leaders learn to take themselves seriously and develop penetrating and practicable policies, and bring about institutional and intellectual reform based on the higher purposes and values of Islam, they will continue having to extract themselves from deeper and more damaging crises, defeats, and losses. Unless something is done soon, Muslims will have wasted a unique and historic opportunity to deliver themselves and the rest of humanity from a future that threatens all of civilization.

Conclusions

From the above account of the causes and goals of these two basic foreign policies, we find, in accordance with the suggested Islamic framework (diagram 3), that there is nothing in the approaches themselves that makes them un-Islamic or anti-Islamic. According to the traditional approach (diagram 1), of course, it would be very difficult for these approaches to be accepted as Islamic since they do not fit the historical Muslim policies in all aspects. Although the modernist/secular approach (diagram 2) supports these three policies in principle, it assigns little or no value to the revitalization of Islamic thought *(iṣlāḥ* and *tajdīd)* and to the support of Islamic ideology. Thus, the modernist/secular approach as well as the traditional approach both work against these policies if these policies are to be pursued as expressions of the Islamic approach based on the religious, cultural, and historical affiliation of Muslims to Islam. The modernist/secular approach also allows the Muslim world to continue to be basically a sphere of ideological conflict between the different world powers.

A study of Muslim foreign policies within the limits of the suggested Islamic framework (diagram 3) points to the need for a basic reform of Muslim political thought. This framework assumes that we can eliminate both the space-time problem of traditional political thought and the lack of originality and consistency in the modernist approach. The suggested Islamic framework, through emphasis on the basic purpose of *tawḥīd* and on the values, principles, and goals of Islam, makes it possible for the policy maker to utilize the moral power of the Muslim ideology inside and outside the Muslim world. The suggested Islamic framework allows, among other things, a more positive Islamic ideological approach to the positions already taken by Muslim nations (heretofore only partially influenced by Islam) against colonialism, imperialism, and racial discrimination, and for justice toward and within the previously colonized areas of the world.

If it is used rationally in the field of international relations, an Islamic revival could be used in many constructive ways. For example, according to the suggested framework, Islam could be used to bring about more emphasis on issues such as human dignity and human rights by taking a stand against racial and nationalist discrimination, by emphasizing quality and merit, by decentralizing political authority and decision-making bodies, and by advocating wider cooperation and mutual support in economic, technical, social, cultural, and political matters based on principles of human welfare and progress (*iṣlāḥ* and *birr*, in a general sense), equity, merit, and social justice.[91]

From the above analysis, it is clear that Muslims do not lack either the resources, the institutions, or the values for them to attain their legitimate goals. What they need is a change of attitude toward the relevant issues, institutions, and ideas. A dynamic, constructive attitude is necessary to make the resources, institutions, and ideas fulfill the desired goal and achieve the required results.

Change in the approaches and methods of Muslim thought are absolutely necessary for Muslims to create and maintain a successful Islamic social system. These reforms are prerequisites for success in changing the role and condition of Muslims, both internal and external.

---

[91] See Arnold Toynbee, *Civilization on Trial*, and *The World and the West*, (Cleveland: World Publishing Co., 1958), pp. 182-187; D. Smith, *Religion and Development*, pp. 21-22; and M. Abū Zahrah, *al 'Alāqāt al Duwalīyah*, pp. 19-46. Also take note of the Qur'anic verse quoted in this chapter concerning the basic principles and values of Islam.

Muslim peoples and Muslim governments should comprehend the real essence of Muslim unity and progress in various times and in various fields. They should always be ready and able to establish the right attitudes, the proper alternative solutions, and the necessary organizational structures to serve the unity of Muslim peoples and the real goals, objectives, and interests of Islam.

The Muslim Ummah and Muslim peoples should utilize and develop the various international Muslim organizations, especially the Organization of the Islamic Conference and its General Secretariat as well as all affiliated cultural, economic, and technical organizations, in order to protect and serve Islam and Muslim interests and to strengthen Muslim unity.

The conclusion of this research is that Islam, in its principles, values, and goals pertaining to international relations, is still capable of guiding successful and constructive external relationships, provided that Muslims abide by these comprehensive Islamic principles and goals. They should reconstruct their understanding of the early period of Islam and accordingly develop a systematic understanding of the empirical Islamic study of international relations. In this way, Muslim thinkers and statesmen would be able to effectively evaluate the alternative courses of action available to serve their Ummah, man in general, and Islam.

ADDENDA

APPENDIX

Chapter 1

1. See A. Hourani, *Arabic Thought*, pp. 150, 153, 235, and 272; Jerome N.D. Anderson and Norman J. Coulson, "Islamic Law in Contemporary Cultural Change" (unpublished essay written in connection with research work for the *Enzyklopadia des Kuturwandels im 20. Jahrhundert*. The author of this book owes Professor Coulson special thanks for making this paper available to him. See also Majid Khadduri, "From Religious to National Law," *Modernization of the Arab World*, ed. Jack H. Thompson and Robert D. Reischauer (New York: Nostrand, 1966), p. 41.

2. See A. al 'Aqqād, *Ma Yuqāl 'an al Islām*, pp. 129-34; 'Abd al Ḥamīd Mutawallī, *Mabādi' Niẓām al Ḥukm fī al Islām: Ma 'a al Muqāranah bi al Mabādi' al Dastūrīyah al Ḥadīthah (wa bihi bābān tamhīdīyān 'an maṣādir al aḥkām al dastūrīyah fī al sharī'ah al Islāmīyah wa manāhij (aw madāris) al tafsīr fī al fiqh al Islāmī*) (Principals of Political Systems in Islam: in Comparison with Modern Constitutional Principles (with two introductory chapters about "Sources of Constitutional Rules in the Islamic Sharī'ah" and Methods [or Schools] of Interpretation in Islamic Jurisprudence)). (Alexandria, Egypt: Dār al Ma'ārif, 1966), pp. vii-xviii, 7-35,270-273 and 381-389; 'Abd al Wahhāb Khallaf, *'Ilm Uṣūl al Fiqh* (The Science of *Uṣūl al Fiqh*), 8th ed. (Kuwait: al Dār al Kuwaitīyah, 1968), pp. 11-15; 'Abd al Wahhāb Khallāf, *Maṣādir al Tashrī' al Islāmī fī mā lā Naṣṣa fīh* (The Sources for Islamic Legislation in Matters for which there is no Direct Text), 3rd ed. (Kuwait: Dār al Qalam, 1972), pp. 7-17; J.N.D. Anderson, *Islamic Law in the Modern World* (New York: New York University Press, 1959), pp. 2-16; Muḥammad Abū Zahrah, *Uṣūl al Fiqh* (Cairo: Dār al Fikr al 'Arabi, 1957), pp. 3-6 and 379-401; Muṣtafā Aḥmad al Zarqā' *Al Fiqh al Islāmī fī Thawbih al Jadīd: al Madkhal al Fiqhī* (Reintroduction of the Islamic *Fiqh*, vol. 1, Introduction to [Islamic] Jurisprudence), 7th rev. ed. (Beirut: Dār al Fikr, n.d.) pp. 3-5 and 30-32; and N.J. Coulson, *Islamic Law*, pp. 6-20, 75-102 and 223-225.

3. The writings on the science of *fiqh* explain the role and the process of ijtihad and deductions of juristic interpretations and opinions (*al ārā' wa al madhāhib al fiqhīyah*) from the basic sources (Qur'an and Sunnah) in leading to diverse positions. Later on in the course of Muslim history this diversity and duality became more of a factor in the decisions taken by the sultans. They sanctioned

and authorized one opinion or another or acted on their own. Thus there usually existed a gap between what the manuals of *fiqh* said and what was done by the Muslim laymen and the authorities. Consequently works of *fiqh* in the modern western sense should be regarded as sources of law. This is very clear in the political sphere as well in the field of *siyar* works (relations among nations). See: ʻAbd al Wahhāb Khallāf, *Khulāṣat Tārīkh al Tashrīʻ al Islāmī* (The Essence of the History of Islamic Law), 9th ed. (Kuwait: Dār al Qalam, 1971), pp. 23-49 and 65-82; Muhammad Abū Zahrah, *Al Imām Zayd: Ḥayātuh wa ʻAṣruh wa Ārā'uh wa Fiqhuh* (Imām Zayd: His Life, His Age, His Opinions and His *Fiqh*) (Cairo: Dār al Fikr al Arabī, 1959), pp. 11-17, 173-179, and 463-481; Muhammad Yūsuf Mūsā, *Al Fiqh al Islāmī: Madkhal li Dirāsatih; Niẓām al Mu'āmalāt fīhi* (Islamic Jurisprudence: An Introduction for its Study and its Approach to Legal Interactions), 3rd ed. (Cairo: Dār al Kutub al Ḥadīthah, 1958), pp. 11-83; N.J. Couslon, *Islamic Law,* pp. 86-88 and 147-148; Sa'īd Ramaḍān, *Three Major Problems Confronting the World of Islam* (Takoma Park, Crescent Publications, n.d.), pp. 1-6; Shihāb al Dīn Abū al ʻAbbās Ahmad Ibn Idrīs al Qarāfī, *Al Iḥkām fī Tamyīz al Fatāwā ʻan al Aḥkām wa Taṣarrufāt al Qāḍī wa al Imām* (The Perfect Work - Distinguishing Legal Opinions from [Judicial and Executive] Decisions and Functions of the Judge and the Imām), ed. ʻAbd al Fattāḥ Abū Ghuddah, (Halah, Syria: Maktab al Maṭbūʻāt al Islamīyah, 1967), pp. 75-85; Wahbah al Zuḥaylī, *Āthār al Ḥarb fī al Fiqh al Islāmī: Dirāsah Muqāranah,* (Damascus: Al Maktabah al Ḥadīthah, 1965), pp. 130, 135.

Chapter 2

4. See: Albert H. Hourani, "Minorities," in *The Comtemporary Middle East: Tradition and Innovation,* Benjamin Rivlin and Joseph S. Szyliowicz (New York: Random House, 1965), pp. 205-217; Amīr Hassān Ṣiddīqī, *Non-Muslim Rule* (Karachi: Jamiyatul Falah Publications), pp. 55-63; M. al Bahī, *Al Fikr al Islāmī,* p. 487; Roderic H. Davison, *Turkey* (England Cliffs, NJ: Prentice Hall, 1968), pp. 78-108; Sidney Nettleton Fisher, *The Middle East: A History,* 2nd ed. (New York: Alfred A. Knopf, 1969), pp. 295-320; and Thomas Naff, "Reform and the Conduct of Ottoman Diplomacy in the Reign of Selim III: 1789-1807," *Journal of the American Oriental Society* 83:6 (1963), pp. 301-302; also see for documents on capitulations and minorities, J. C. Hurwitz, *Diplomacy in the Middle East: A Documentary Record:* 1535-1914 (New York: 1956), vol. 1, pp. 20, 24-32, 113-116, 149-53, 164-165, and vol. ll, pp. 2-3 and 127-28. For the Syrian Lebanese Case, see the three-volume work of Philip and Fred al Khāzin, *Majmū'at al Muḥarrarāt al Siyāsīyah wa al Mufāwaḍāt al Dawlīyah ʻan Sūrīyā wa Lubnān: 1840-1910* (Collection of International Political Documents and Negotiations about Syria and Lebanon: 1840-1910) (Beirut: Maṭbaʻat al Ṣabr, 1910).

5. See N.J. Coulson, *A History of Islamic Law,* pp. 75-85 and 2[illegible]. M. Khadduri, "From Religious to National Law," in *Modernization of the Arab World*

ed. J.H. Thompson and E.R.D. Reischauer (New York: Van Nostrand, 1966), pp. 40-41; N.Y. Mūsā, *Al Fiqh al Islāmī*, pp. 27-61; and S. Ramaḍān, *Islamic Law*, 27-30.

6. See A. Hourani, *Arabic Thought*, pp. 157-160; Muhammad Husayn, *Al Islām wa al Haḍārah al Gharbīyah* (Islam and Western Civilization) (Beirut: Dār al Irshād, 1969), pp. 91-104; and W.C. Smith, *Islam*, pp. 55-73.

7. It is to be noted that *ḍarūrah* (necessity), being part of the principle of *maṣlaḥah* (public interest) in the classical methodology, and *taqlīd* worked together in the process of borrowing political ideas and institutions from the West. See for *ḍarūrah* and *maṣlaḥah*, Wahbah al Zuḥaylī, *Naẓarīyat al Ḍarūrah al Shar'īyah Muqāranah Ma'a al Qānūn al Waḍ'ī* (The Theory of Necessity in Islamic Law compared with Man Made Law) (Damascus: Maktabat al Fārābī, 1969), pp. 49-53, 64-69 and 140-272.

Chapter 3

8. H. A. Sharabi, "Islam and Modernization in the Arab World," in *Modernization of the Arab World*, J.H. Thompson and R.O. Reischauer ed. p. 32; H.A.R. Gibb, *Modern Trends in Islam*, p. 66; Malik Bennabi, *Wijhat al 'Ālam al Islāmī* (The Direction of the Muslim World), 'Abd al Ṣabūr Shāhīn, trans., *Mushkilat al Haḍārah*, 2nd ed. (Beirut; Dār al Fikr, 1970), p. 77; also A. Hourani, *Arabic Thought*, pp. 372-372, for a brief introduction to Malik Bennabi; Malcolm H. Kerr, *Islamic Reform; The Political and Legal Theories of Muhammad 'Abduh and Rashīd Riḍā* (Berkley: Univ. of California Press, 1966), pp. 221-222; A. A. Maḥmūd, *Al Da'wah al Islāmīyah*, pp. 317-342; M. F. Abū Ḥadīd, "*Risālat al Salām wa al Taḥrīr*" (The Mission of Peace and Liberation) in *Al Muḥāḍarāt al 'Āmmah*, 2nd ed. The Public Administration for Islamic Culture at al Azhar, pp. 367-391; and Maḥmūd Shaltūt, *Al Islām wa al 'Alāqāt al Duwalīyah fī al Silm wa al Ḥarb* (Cairo; Maktab Shaykh al Jāmi' al Azhar li al Shu'ūn al 'Āmmah, 1951), pp. 26-69.

9. See 'Allāl al Fāsī, *Maqāṣid al Sharī'ah al Islāmīyah wa Makārimuhā* (The Higher Purposes of the Shariah and its Virtues) (Casablanca, Morocco: Maktabat al Waḥdah al 'Arabīyah, 1963), pp. 82-194; and Muhammad Ma'rūf al Dawālībī, *Al Madkhal Ilā 'Ilm Uṣūl al Fiqh* (Introduction to the Science of Islamic Juridical Methodology), 5th rev. ed. (Beirut: Dar al 'Ilm li al Malāyīn, 1965), pp. 256-348.

GLOSSARY

In what follows definitions are given to some of the most frequently used Arabic terms in the text.

'Adl: justice
'Ahd: pledge, treaty
Ahl al Kitāb: the tolerated, respected and protected people, the people of the Book (mainly Christians and Jews)
Amān: safe conduct, or pledge of security
Amīr al Mu'minīn: Commander of the Faithful, the Caliph
Asbāb al Nuzūl: the occasions and reasons for the revelation of verses from the Qur'an, the historical circumstances and background for the revelation of specific verses or chapters
Aṣl: singular of *uṣūl*, a juridical principle, a point of jurisprudence
Āthār: traditions, narratives, sometimes used interchangeably with hadith
Dār al 'Ahd: (alternatively, *Dār al Ṣulḥ*) non-Muslim territories involved in treaty agreements with a Muslim state (term coined by al Shāfi'ī).
Dār al Ḥarb: non-Muslim territories hostile to Muslims (opposite of *Dār al Islām*)
Dār al Ṣulḥ: see *Dār al 'Ahd*
Dhimmah, al: permanent constitutional arrangement between Muslim political authorities and non-Muslim subjects whereby subjects receive protection and peaceful relations in exchange for acceptance of Muslim rule and payment of *jizyah* tax
Dhimmī: non-Muslim subject of an Islamic state, pl. *dhimmīyūn*
Fatwà: A legal opinion, or interpretation of religious law, pl. *fatāwà*
Fiqh: the rules and injunctions deduced from the Qur'an and the Sunnah: the sum of Muslim legal decisions and opinions; Muslim jurisprudence; the principal vehicle of reflection for classical and traditional Muslim intellectuals
Hadith: (used as a collective noun) saying or sayings, esp. something that the Prophet said; a tradition of the Prophet
Ḥarbī: an enemy subject
Ḥilf: alliance
Hudnah: truce
Ijmā': consensus
Ijtihad: expending effort; esp. in the use of reason for the purpose of interpreting Shari'ah texts; original juristic opinion(s)
Imam: a leader; Caliph; one who leads the congregational prayer; a pious intellectual authority
Imāmah: Caliphate
Istiḥsān: juristic preference of one deduction over another
Jihad: struggle; a Muslim's striving to fulfill his Islamic responsibility, both in outward actions and in inward correction of his own mistakes; working or fighting in the cause of Allah

Jizyah: tax paid by non-Muslim subjects to the Muslim state, in return for state services; often called poll tax

Khilāfah: the caliphate; vicegerency on earth

Khalīfat Rasūl Allāh: the Successor of Allah's Messenger; caliph

Kharāj: land tax paid by non-Muslims to the Muslim state

Khulafā' al Rāshidūn, al: the Rightly-Guided Caliphs, Abū Bakr, 'Umar, 'Uthmān, and 'Alī

Maṣlaḥah, al: the public interest; also *al Maṣāliḥ al Mursalah*

Mithāq: covenant, pact

Mu'āhadah: treaty, agreement

Mushrikūn: those who attribute partners to Allah; therefore, idolators and pagans

Musta'man: enemy subject granted safe conduct to enter Muslim territory

Nabdh: termination of agreement by the Muslim side

Naskh: abrogation: nullification or suspension of a previously revealed injunction

Naṣṣ: text

Qiyās: analogy

Qur'an: the Holy Book of Islam; the Eternal Word of Allah

Quraysh: the leading Arab tribe of Makkah

Riddah: apostasy

Ṣaghār: humiliation

Ṣaḥīfat al Madīnah: constitutional agreement between the Prophet and the Jewish tribes of Madīnah

Shari'ah: the will of God for human conduct revealed through the Prophet Muhammad (PBUH)

Siyar: account of Muslim external achievements; juristic source for Muslim law of nations

Ṣulḥ: peace treaty, truce

Sunnah: the approved ways; the reported sayings of the Prophet and all actions performed or consented to by the Prophet; *al ḥadīth*

Sunni: orthodox; a follower of one of the four schools of Muslim jurisprudence based on the *sunnah;* true followers of the Prophet; majority of Muslim peoples

Talfīq: piecing-together

Taqlīd: imitation

Ulama: Muslim scholars, theologians, and learned men; sing. *'Ālim*

Ummah: community, people, nation, group of people

'Urf, al: the mores of a society; customary law

Uṣūl: source and method of classical Muslim jurisprudence, i.e., the Qur'an, the Sunnah, *qiyās, ijmā'*, and other rules and measures of ijtihad

Uṣūl al Fiqh: see *uṣūl*

Zakah: the poor-due; alms tax paid by Muslims on excess assets

BIBLIOGRAPHY

References (Arabic)

Bukhārī, Abū 'Abd Allāh Muhammad ibn Ismā'īl, al, *Matn al Bukhārī bi Ḥāshiyat al Sindī* (Bukhari's Collection of Ḥadith with the Commentary of al Sindi) (Cairo: Dār Iḥyā' al Kutub al 'Arabīyah, 1960).

Hamidullah, Muhammad, *Majmū'at al Wathā'iq al Siyāsīyah li al 'Ahd al Nabawī wa al Khilāfah al Rāshidah* (Political Documents Concerning the Period of the Prophet and the Rightly-Guided Caliphs) (Beirut: Dār al Irshād, 1959).

Ibn Manẓūr, al Imām al 'Allāmah Abū al Faḍl Jamāl al Dīn Muhammad Ibn Muqarrin, *Lisān al 'Arab* (The Arab Language) (Cairo: Al Maṭba'ah al Kubrà, 1882).

Kaḥḥālah, 'Umar Riḍā, *Mu'jam al Mu'allifīn: Tarājim Muṣannifī al Kutub al 'Arabīyah* (Index of Authors: Bibliography of Authors of Arabic Books) (Damascus: Al Maktabah al 'Arabīyah, 1957).

Khāzin, Philip al and Fred al, *Majmū'at al Muḥarrarāt al Siyāsīyah wa al Mufāwaḍāt al Duwalīyah 'an Sūrīyā wa Lubnān: 1840-1910* (Collection of International Political Documents and Negotiations About Syria and Lebanon: 1840-1910) (Beirut: Maṭba'at al Ṣabr, 1910).

Mujaddidī, al Muftī al Sayyid Muḥammad Amīn al Iḥsān, al, (ed.), *Qawā'id al Fiqh* (The Rules [and Definitions of Terms] of Muslim [Ḥanāfī] Jurisprudence) (Dhaka: The Secretary, Research and Publication Committee, Madrasah-i-Aliah, 1961).

Mundhirī, al Ḥāfiẓ 'Abd al 'Aẓīm ibn 'Abd al Qawī, al, *Mukhtaṣar Saḥīḥ Muslim* (Summary of Muslim's [Selection of the] Authentic Sunnah), ed. Nāṣir al Dīn al Albānī (Kuwait: The Ministry of Endowments and Islamic Affairs, 1969).

Nuṣayr, 'Āyadah Ibrāhīm, *Al Kutub al 'Arabīyah allatī Nushirat fī al Jumhūrīyah al 'Arabīyah al Muttiḥidah (Miṣr) Bayna 'Āmay 1926-1940* (The Arabic Books Published in the United Arab Republic [Egypt] between 1926-1940) (Cairo: The American University of Cairo, 1969).

Rāzī, Muhammad ibn Abī Bakr, al, *Mukhtār al Ṣiḥāḥ* (Selection of Correct Definitions [an Arabic dictionary]) (Cairo: Muṣṭafā al Bābī al Ḥalabī wa Awlāduh, 1950).

Tabrīzī, Walī al Dīn Muhammad ibn 'Abd Allah al Khaṭīb al, *Mishkāt al Maṣābīḥ* (Collection of Authentic Traditions of the Prophet), ed. Muhammad Nāṣir al Dīn al Albānī (Damascus: Al Maktab al Islāmī, 1961).

References (English)

'Alī, 'Abd Allah Yusuf, *The Holy Qur'an, Text, Translation and Commentary* (Washington, DC: The American International Printing Co., 1945).

The Encyclopedia of Islam, 2nd ed. (Leiden: E.J. Brill, Luzac and Co., 1960-).

Hurewitz, J.C., *Diplomacy in the Near and Middle East: A Documentary Record 1535-1914* (New York: Van Nostrand, 1956).

Khān, Muḥammad Muḥsin, *The Translation of the Meaning Sāhīh al Bukhārī* (Gujaranwala, Pakistan: Sethi Straw Board Mills Conversions, Ltd., n.d.).

Index Islamicus: A Catalogue of Articles on Islamic Subjects in Periodicals and Other Collective Publications (Cambridge: W. Heffer and Sons, Ltd., 1972).

Peaslee, Amos J., *Constitutions of Nations*, prepared by Dorothy Peaslee Xydis (The Hague: Martinus Nijhoff, 1965).

Pickthall, Muḥammad Marmaduke, *The Meaning of the Glorious Korān* (New York: New American Library, n.d.).

Tabrīzī, Walī al Dīn Muḥammad ibn 'Abd Allah al Khaṭīb al 'Imārī, al, *Mishkāt al Maṣābīḥ,* translated with explanatory notes by James Robson (Lahore, Pakistan: Sh. Muḥammad Ashraf, 1963).

Works Consulted (Arabic)

'Abduh, Muḥammad, *Al Islām wa al Naṣrānīyah Ma'a al 'Ilm wa al Madanīyah* (Islam and Christianity with Regard to Knowledge and Civilization) (Cairo: Maktabat wa Maṭba'at Muḥammad 'Alī Sabīḥ wa Awlāduh, 1954).

'Abduh, Muḥammad; *Al Islām wa al Radd 'Alā Muntaqidīh* (Islam and Answers for Its Critics) (Cairo: Al Maktabah al Tijārīyah al Kubrà, 1928).

Abū Zahrah, Muḥammad, *Al 'Alāqāt al Duwalīyah fī al Islām* (International Relations in Islam), Al Maktabah al 'Arabīyah (Cairo: Al Dār al Qawmīyah li al Ṭibā'ah wa al Nashr, 1964).

Abū Zahrah, Muḥammad, *Al Imām Zāyd: Ḥayātuh wa 'Aṣruh wa Ārā'uh wa Fiqhuh* (Imām Zayd: His Life, His Age, His Opinions and His Fiqh) (Cairo: Dār al Fikr al 'Arabī, 1959).

Abū Zahrah, Muḥammad, *Al Mujtama' al Insānī fī Ẓill al Islām* (Human Society under the Rule of Islam) (Beirut: Dār al Fikr, n.d.).

Abū Zahrah, Muḥammad, *Ibn Ḥanbal: Ḥayātuh wa 'Aṣruh wa Ārā'uh wa Fiqhuh* (Ibn Ḥanbal: His Life, His Age, His Opinions and His Fiqh) (Cairo: Dār al Fikr al 'Arabī, 1947).

Abū Zahrah, Muḥammad, *Mālik: Ḥayātuh wa 'Aṣruh wa Ārā'uh wa Fiqhuh* (Mālik: His Life, His Age, His Opinions and His Fiqh) (Cairo: Dār al Fikr al 'Arabī, 1963).

Abū Zahrah, Muḥammad, *Uṣūl al Fiqh* (Methodology of Muslim Jurisprudence) (Cairo: Dār al Fikr al 'Arabī, 1957).

Abū Zayd, Muṣṭafā, *Al Nāsikh wa al Mansūkh: Dirāsah Tashrī'īyah Tārīkhīyah Naqdīyah* (The Abrogating and the Abrogated: A Juristic, Historical and Critical Study) (Cairo: Dār al Fikr al 'Arabī, 1963).

'Alī, Jawād, *Al Mufaṣṣal fī Tārīkh al 'Arab Qabl al Islām* (Detailed Account of Arab History before Islam) (Beirut: Dār al 'Ilm li al Malāyīn, 1970).

Amīn, Aḥmad, *Fajr al Islām: Yabḥath 'an al Ḥayāt al 'Aqlīyāh fī Ṣadr al Islām ilā Ākhir al Dāwlah al Umawīyah* (The Dawn of Islam: Discussion on Intellectual Life in the Early Period of Islam until the End of the Umayyad Dynasty), 9th ed. (Cairo: Maktabat al Nahḍah al Miṣrīyah, 1964).

Amīn, Aḥmed, *Yawm al Islām* (The Day of Islam) (Cairo: Mu'assasat al Khānjī, 1958).

'Aqqād, 'Abbās Maḥmūd, al, *Ḥaqā'iq al Islām wa Abāṭīl Khuṣūmih* (The Facts of Islam and the Allegations of its Adversaries), 3rd ed. (Cairo: Dār al Qalam, 1966).

'Aqqād, 'Abbās M., al, *Al Islām fī al Qarn al 'Ishrīn: Ḥāḍiruh wa Mustaqbaluh* (Islam in the Twentieth Century: Its Present and Its Future), 2nd ed. (Beirūt: Dār al Kitāb al 'Arabī, 1969).

'Aqqād, 'Abbās Maḥmūd, al, *Mā Yuqālu 'an al Islām* (On What has been Said about Islam), 2nd ed. (Beirūt: Dār al Kitāb al 'Arabī, 1966).

Arsalān, Shakīb, *Li Mādhā Ta'akhkhara al Muslimūm wa Li Mādhā Taqaddama Ghāyruhum* (Why Muslims are Declining and Why Others are Progressing) (Beirūt: Dār Maktabat al Ḥayāh, 1965).

Badawī, 'Abd al Raḥmān, ed. *Al Turāth al Yūnānī fī al Ḥaḍārah al Islāmīyah: Dirāsāt li Kibār al Mustashriqīn* (The Greek Heritage in Islamic Civilization: Studies by Prominent Orientalists) (Cairo: Dār al Nahḍah al 'Arabīyāh, 1965).

Al Bahī, Muḥammad, *Al Fikr al Islāmī al Ḥadīth wa Ṣilātuh bi al Isti'mār al Gharbī* (Contemporary Islamic Thought and Its Relation to Western Imperialism), 4th ed. (Cairo: Maktabat Wahbah, 1964).

Boer, T.J., *Tārīkh al Falsafah fī al Islām* (History of Philosophy in Islam), translated from the German by Muḥammad 'Abd al Hādī Abū Rīdah, 4th ed. (Cairo: Lajnat al Ta'līf wa al Tarjamah wa al Nashr, 1957).

Darwazah, Muḥammad 'Izzat, *Al Tafsīr al Ḥadīth* (Contemporary Interpretation of the Qur'an) (Cairo: 'Isā al Bābī al Ḥalabī, 1964).

Fakhrī, Majīd, *Dirāsah fī al Fikr al 'Arabī* (A Study in Arabic Thought) (Beirut: Dār al Nahār, 1970).

Farrā', Abū Ya'là Muḥammad Ibn Ḥusayn, al, *Al Aḥkām al Sulṭānīyah* (The Ordinance of Government), ed. Muḥammad Ḥāmid al Faqī (Cairo: Muṣṭafā al Bābī al Ḥalabī, 1966).

Ghānim, Muḥammad Ḥāfiẓ, *Mabādi' al Qānūn al Duwalī al 'Āmm* (Principles of International Law), 4th ed. (Cairo: Maṭba'at Nahḍat Miṣr, 1964).

Ghazālī, Muḥammad, al, *Al Islām fī Wajh al Zaḥf al Aḥmar* (Islam Fighting Communist Expansion) (Kuwait: Maktabat al Amal, n.d.).

Ghazālī, Muḥammad, al, *Al Ta'aṣṣub wa al Tasāmuḥ Bayn al Masīḥīyah wa al Islām: Daḥḍ Shubuhāt wa Radd Muftarayāt* (Fanaticism and Tolerence Between Christianity and Islam: Rebutting and Answering Misunderstandings and False Accusations) (Kuwait: Dār al Bayān, n.d.).

Ghazālī, Muḥammad, al, *Fiqh al Sīrah* (Normative Understanding of the Sīrah), 4th ed. (Cairo: Dār al Kutub al Ḥadīthah, 1964).

Ḥamadhānī, Abū Bakr Muḥammad ibn Mūsā Ibn Ḥazm, al, *Kitāb al I'tibār fī al Nāsikh wa al Mansūkh Min al Āthār* (Book of Lessons About the Abrogator and the Abrogated of the Traditions), ed. Rātib al Ḥakīm (Ḥimṣ, Syria: Maṭba'at al Andalus, 1966).

Hawātmah, Nāyif, *Azmat al Thawrah fī al Janūb al 'Arabī: Naqd wa Taḥlīl* (The Crisis of the Revolution in South Yemen: Analysis and Criticism) (Beirut: Dār al Ṭalī'ah, 1968).

Hell, J., *Al Ḥaḍārah al 'Arabīyah* (Arab Civilization), translated from German by I. al 'Adawī, ed. H. Mu'nis, Al Alf Kitāb no. 88 (Cairo: Maktabat al Anjlū al Miṣrīyah, 1956).

Ḥusāyn, Muḥammad, *Al Islām wa al Ḥaḍārah al Gharbīyah* (Islam and Western Civilization) (Beirut: Dār al Irshād, 1969).

Ḥusaynī, Sayyid 'Abd al Razzāq, al, *Tārīkh al 'Irāq al Siyāsī al Ḥadīth* (The Modern Political History of Iraq), 2nd rev. ed. (Ṣaydā, Lebanon: Maṭba'at al 'Irfān, 1958).

Ibish, Yūsuf, *Nuṣūṣ al Fikr al Siyāsī al Islāmī: Al Imāmah 'Inda al Sunnah* (Readings in Islamic Political Theory: The Sunni Doctrine of the *Imāmah*) (Beirut: Dār al Ṭalī'ah, 1966).

Ibn al Athīr, 'Izz al Dīn Abū al Ḥasan 'Alī Ibn Abī al Karam Muḥammad Ibn 'Abd al Karīm Ibn 'Abd al Wāḥid al Shaybānī, *Al Kāmil fī al Tārīkh* (The Comprehensive [Study] of History) (Beirut: Dār Bayrūt li al Ṭibā'ah wa al Nashr, 1965).

Ibn Hishām, Abū Muḥammad 'Abd al Mālik, *Al Sīrah al Nabawīyah* (The Biography of the Prophet), ed. M. al Saqqā, I. al 'Ibyārī and A. Shalabī, 2nd ed. (Cairo: Muṣṭafā al Bābī al Ḥalabī, 1955).

Ibn al Qayyim, Shams al Dīn Abū 'Abd Allah Muḥammad ibn Abū Bakr, *Aḥkām Ahl al Dhimmah* (Rules for Non-Muslim Subjects of the Islamic State), ed. Ṣubḥī al Ṣāliḥ (Damascus: Maṭba'at Jāmi'at Dimashq, 1961).

Ibn Qudāmah, Abū Muḥammad 'Abd Allah ibn Aḥmad, *Al Mughnī* (The Sufficient) (Cairo: Maṭba'at al 'Āṣimah, n.d.).

Ibn Rushd al Ḥafīd (Averröes), Abū al Walīd Muḥammad ibn Aḥmad ibn Muḥammad ibn Rushd al Qurṭubī al Andalusī, *Bidāyat al Mujtahid wa Nihāyat al Muqtaṣid* (A Beginning for the Independent Legal Interpreter and an End for the Limited), ed. Muḥammad Amīn al Khānjī (Cairo: Maktabat al Khānjī, n.d.).

Ibn Salāmah, Abū al Qāsim Hibat Allāh, *Al Nāsikh wa al Mansūkh* (The Abrogating and the Abrogated), 2nd ed. (Cairo: Al Ḥalabī wa Awlāduh bi Miṣr, 1967).

Ibn Taymīyah, Taqīy al Dīn Aḥmad ibn 'Abd al Ḥalīm, *Al Siyāsah al Shar'īyah fī Iṣlāḥ al Rā'ī wa al Ra'īyah* (Policies of the Shariah in Reforming the Affairs of the Ruler and the Ruled) (Beirut: Dār al Kutub al 'Arabīyah, n.d.).

'Ishmāwī, Ḥassan, al, *Qalb Ākhar li Ajl al Za'īm* (Another Heart for the Leader) (Beirut: Dār al Fatḥ, 1970).

Jammāl, 'Abd al Qādir, al, *Min Mushkilāt al Sharq al Awsaṭ* (Some Problems of the Middle East) (Cairo: Maktabat al Anjlū al Miṣrīyah, 1955).

Kaḥlānī, al Imām Muḥammad Ibn Ismā'īl, al, *Subul al Salām: Sharḥ Bulūgh al Murām min Adillat al Aḥkām* (The Ways of Peace: A Commentary on the Attainment of the Desired Support [of Qur'an and Sunnah] of [the Islamic] Rules) (Cairo: Al Maktabah al Tijārīyah al Kubrā, n.d.).

Khallāf, 'Abd al Wahhāb, *'Ilm Uṣūl al Fiqh* (The Science of *Uṣūl al Fiqh*), 8th ed. (Kuwait: al Dār al Kuwaytīyah, 1968).

Khallāf, 'Abd al Wahhāb, *Khulāṣat Tārīkh al Tashrī' al Islāmī* (The Essence of the History of Islamic Law), 9th ed. (Kuwait: Dār al Qalam, 1971).

Khallāf, 'Abd al Wahhāb, *Maṣādir al Tashrī' al Islāmī fīmā lā Naṣṣa fīh* (Sources of Islamic Legislation in Matters for Which there is no Specific Text), 3rd ed. (Kuwait: Dār al Qalam, 1972).

Khaṭṭāb, Maḥmūd Shīt, *Al Rasūl al Qā'id* (The Leader Messenger), 2nd ed. (Baghdad: Dār Maktabat al Ḥayāh wa Maktabat al Nahḍah, 1960).

Kishk, Muḥammad Jalāl, *Mafāhīm Islāmīyah: Al Qawmīyah wa al Ghazw al Fikrī* (Islamic Perspectives: Nationalism and the Cultural Invasion) (Kuwait: Maktabat al Amal, 1967).

Līlah, Muḥammad Kāmil, *Al Mujtama' al 'Arabī wa al Qawmīyah al 'Arabīyah* (Arab Society and Arab Nationalism) (Cairo: Dār al Fikr al 'Arabī, 1966).

Maḥmaṣānī, Ṣubḥī, *Al Awḍā' al Tashrī'īyah fī al Duwal al 'Arabīyah; Māḍīhā wa Ḥāḍiruhā* (Legal Systems in Arab States: Past and Present), 3rd rev. ed. (Beirut: Dār al 'Ilm li al Malāyīn, 1965).

Mālik Ibn Anas, *Al Mudawwanah al Kubrà* (The Great Compendium) (Beirut: Dār al Ṣādir, 1905).

Manṣūr, 'Alī, *Muqāranah Bāyna al Sharī'ah al Islāmīyah wa al Qawānīn al Waḍ'īyah* (A Comparative Study Between the Islamic Shariah and Secular Laws) (Beirut: Dār al Fatḥ, 1970).

Māwardī, Abū al Ḥasan ʻAlī ibn Muḥammad ibn Ḥabīb al Baṣrī al Baghdādī, al, *Al Aḥkām al Sulṭānīyah wa al Wilāyāt al Dīnīyah* (The Ordinance of Government and the Religious Offices), 2nd ed. (Cairo: Muṣṭafā al Bābī al Ḥalabī, 1966).

Mawdūdī, Abū al Aʻlā, al, *Naẓarīyat al Islām wa Hadyuh* (Islamic Theory and Guidance), translated from Urdu by Jalīl Ḥasan al Iṣlāḥi (Beirut: Dār al Fikr, 1967).

Mawdūdī, Abū al Aʻlā, al, Hasan al Banna, and Sayyid Quṭub, *Al Jihād fī Sabīl Allāh* (Jihad in the Cause of Allah) (Beirut: al Ittiḥād al ʻĀlamī li al Jamʻīyat al Ṭullābīyah, 1970).

Mawdūdī, Abū al Aʻlā, al, *Al Islām fī Muwājahat al Taḥaddiyāt al Muʻāṣirāh* (Islam in Confrontation with Contemporary Challenges), translated by Khalīl Aḥmad al Ḥāmidī (Kuwait: Dār al Qalam, 1971).

Mubārak, Muḥammad, al, *Al Fikr al Islāmī al Ḥadīth fī Muwājahat al Afkār al Gharbīyah* (Contemporary Islamic Thought in Confrontation with Western Ideas) (Beirut: Dār al Fikr, 1968).

Mundhirī, al Ḥāfiẓ ʻAbd al ʻAẓīm ibn ʻAbd al Qawī, al, *Mukhtaṣar Ṣaḥīḥ Muslim* (Summary of Muslim's [Selection of the] Authentic Sunnah), ed. Nāṣir al Dīn al Albānī (Kuwait: The Ministry of Endowments and Islamic Affairs, 1969).

Mūsà, Muḥammad Yūsuf, *Al Fiqh al Islāmī: Madkhal li Dirāsatih; Niẓām al Muʻāmalah fīhī* (Islamic Jurisprudence: An Introduction to Its Study and Its Approach to Legal Transactions), 3rd ed. (Cairo: Dār al Kutub al Ḥadīthah, 1958).

Mutawallī, ʻAbd al Ḥamīd, *Mabādi' Niẓām al Ḥukm fī al Islām: Maʻa al Muqāranah bi al Mabādi' al Dustūrīyah al Ḥadīthah* (Principles of the Political System in Islam: In Comparison with Modern Constitutional Principles) (Alexandria, Egypt: Dār al Maʻārif, 1966).

Najjār, Ḥusayn, al, *Al Sīyāsah wa al Istrātījīyah fī al Sharq al Awsaṭ* (Politics and Strategy in the Middle East) (Cairo: Maktabat al Nahḍah al Miṣrīyah, 1953).

Naysābūrī, Abū al Ḥasan ʻAlī ibn Aḥmad al Wāḥidī, al, *Asbāb al Nuzūl* (Reasons for Revelation of the Qur'an) (Cairo: Muṣṭafā al Bābī al Ḥalabī, 1959).

Qalʻajī, Jihād, *Al Islām Aqwà* (Islam is Stronger) (Beirut: Dār al Kitāb al ʻArabī, n.d.).

Qarāfī, Shihāb al Dīn Abū al 'Abbās Aḥmad ibn Idrīs, al, *Al Iḥkām fī Tamyīz al Fatāwā 'an al Aḥkām wa Taṣarrufāt al Qāḍī wa al Imām* (The Perfect Work in Distinguishing Legal Opinions from [Judicial and Executive] Decisions and Functions of the Judge and the Imam), ed. 'Abd al Fattāḥ Abū Ghuddah (Ḥalab, Syria: Maktab al Maṭba'ah al Islāmīyah, 1967).

Quṭub, Sayyid, *Al Salām al 'Ālamī wa al Islām* (World Peace and Islam) (Cairo: Dār Iḥyā' al Kutub al 'Arabīyah, 1967).

Rayyis, Muḥammad Ḍiyā' al Dīn, al, *Al Naẓarīyāt al Siyāsīyah al Islāmīyah* (Islamic Political Theories), 4th ed. (Cairo: Dār al Ma'ārif 1967).

Rāzī, al Imām Fakhr al Dīn, al, *Al Tafsīr al Kabīr* (The Great Commentary on the Qur'an) (Cairo: 'Abd al Raḥmān Muḥammad, 1938).

Riḍā, Muḥammad Rashīd, *Tafsīr al Qur'ān al Ḥakīm al Mushtahar bi Ism Tafsīr al Manār* (Commentary of the Perfect Qur'an, better known as the Manār Commentary), 4th ed. (Cairo: Dār al Manār, 1954).

Sābiq, al Sayyid, *Fiqh al Sunnah* (Understanding the Sunnah) (Kuwait: Dār al Bayān, 1968).

Sa'īdī, 'Abd al Muta'āl, al, *Al Ḥurrīyah al Dīnīyah fī al Islām* (Religious Freedom in Islam), 2nd ed. (Cairo: Dār al Fikr al 'Arabī, n.d.).

Shāfi'ī, Abū 'Abd Allah Muḥammad ibn Idrīs, al, *Al Umm* (The Mother, i.e., Basic Work of Jurisprudence) (Cairo: Dār al Sha'b, 1903).

Shaltūt, Maḥmūd, *Al Islām wa al 'Alāqāt al Duwalīyah fī al Silm wa al Ḥarb* (Islam and International Relations in Peace and War) (Cairo: Maktabat Shaykh al Jāmi' al Azhar li al Shu'ūn al 'Āmmah, 1951).

Shaybānī, Muḥammad Ibn al Ḥasan, al, *Sharḥ al Siyar al Kabīr* (Commentary on the Book of the Great *Siyar*), dictation of Muḥammad Ibn Aḥmad al Sarakhsī, ed. Ṣalāḥ al Munajjid (Cairo: Ma'had al Makhṭūṭāt bi Jāmi'at al Duwal al 'Arabīyah, 1958).

Shumayl, Muḥammad Bā, *Ghazwat Banī Qurayẓah*, vol. IV of *Min Ma'ārik al Islām al Fāṣilah* (The Battle of Banī Qurayẓah, vol. IV of The Decisive Battles of Islam) (Beirut: Dār al Fatḥ li al Ṭibā'ah wa al Nashr, 1966).

Shumayl, Muḥammad Bā, *Ghazwat Badr al Kubrā*, vol. I of *Min Ma'ārik al Islām al Fāṣilah* (The Great Battle of Badr, vol. I of The Decisive Battles of Islam), 4th ed. (Beirut: Maṭba'at Dār al Kutub, 1968).

Ṭabarī, Abū Ja'far Muḥammad ibn Jarīr, al, *Jāmi' al Bayān 'an Ta'wīl Āy al Qur'ān* (The Master of Clarity in Interpreting Verses of the Qur'an), 2nd ed. (Cairo: Muṣṭafā al Bābī al Ḥalabī, 1945).

Ṭabbārah, 'Afīf 'Abd al Fattāḥ, *Al Yahūd fī al Qur'ān: Taḥlīl 'Ilmī li Nuṣūṣ al Qur'ān fī al Yahūd 'alà Ḍaw' al Aḥdāth al Ḥāḍirah, Ma'a Qaṣaṣ Anbiyā' Allāh, Ibrāhīm wa Yūsuf wa Mūsà 'Alayhim al Salām* (The Jews and the Qur'an: Scientific Analysis of the Qur'anic Text Pertaining to the Jews in the Light of Contemporary Events; With the Stories of the Prophets, Abraham, Joseph and Moses), 2nd ed. (Beirut: Dār al 'Ilm li al Malāyīn, 1966).

Tabrīzī, Walī al Dīn Muḥammad ibn 'Abd Allah al Khaṭīb al 'Imārī, al, *Mishkāt al Maṣābīḥ* (Collections of Authentic Traditions of the Prophet), ed. Muḥammad Nāṣir al Dīn al Albānī (Damascus: Al Maktab al Islāmī, 1961).

'Uthmān, 'Abd al Karīm, *Al Niẓām al Siyāsī fī al Islām* (Political System in Islam) (Beirut: Dār al Irshād, 1968).

'Uthmān, Muḥammad Fatḥī, *Dawlat al Fikrah allatī Aqāmahā Rasūl al Islām 'Aqab al Hijrah: Tajrubah Mubakkirah fī al Dawlah al Iydyūlūjīyah fī al Tārīkh* (The Ideological State Which the Messenger of Islam Established After the Immigration: An Early Attempt in History at an Ideological State) (Kuwait: Al Dār al Kuwaytīyah, 1968).

'Uthmān, Muḥammad Fatḥī, *Al Fikr al Islāmī wa al Taṭawwur* (Islamic Thought and Change), 2nd rev. ed. (Kuwait: Al Dār al Kuwaitīyah, 1969).

Zarakhshī, al Imām Badr al Dīn Muḥammad ibn 'Abd Allah, *Al Burhān fī 'Ulūm al Qur'ān* (The Proof in the Sciences of Qur'an), ed. Muḥammad Abū al Faḍl Ibrāhīm (Cairo: Dār Iḥyā' al Kutub al 'Arabīyah, 'Īsā al Bābī al Ḥalabī, 1957).

Zarqā, Muṣṭafā Aḥmad, al, *Al Fiqh al Islāmī fī Thawbih al Jadīd*, vol. I of *Al Madkhal al Fiqhī* (Reintroduction of the Islamic Fiqh, vol. I of Introduction to [Islamic] Jurisprudence), 7th rev. ed. (Beirut: Dār al Fikr, n.d.).

Zarqānī, Muḥammad 'Abd al 'Aẓīm, al, *Manāhil al 'Irfān fī 'Ulūm al Qur'ān* (Sources of Knowledge for the Sciences of Qur'an) (Cairo: Dār Iḥyā' al Kutub al 'Arabīyah, 'Īsā al Bābī al Ḥalābī, n.d.).

Ziyadeh, Nicola (ed.), *Dirāsāt Islāmīyah* (Islamic Studies) (Beirut: Dār al Andalus, 1960).

Zuḥaylī, Wahbah, al, *Āthār al Ḥarb fī al Fiqh al Islāmī: Dirāsah Muqāranah* (The Effects of War in Islāmic Jurisprudence: A Comparative Study), 2nd ed. (Damascus: Al Maktabah al Ḥadīthah, 1965).

Zuhaylī, Wahbah, al, *Nazarīyat al Ḍarūrah al Shar'īyah Muqāranah Ma'a al Qānūn al Waḍ'ī* (The Theory of Necessity in Islamic Law in Comparison with Secular Law) (Damascus: Maktabat al Fārābī, 1969).

Works Consulted (English)

Abdul Ḥakīm, Khalīfah, *Islam and Communism*, 3rd ed. (Lahore, Pakistan: Institute of Islamic Culture, 1962).

Adams, Charles C., *Islam and Modernism in Egypt* (New York: Russell and Russell, 1933).

Aḥmad, 'Azīz, *Islamic Modernism in India and Pakistan: 1857-1964* (London: Oxford University Press, 1967).

Aḥmad, Khurshid, *Fanaticism, Intolerance and Islam*, 3rd ed. (Karachi: Islamic Publications, Ltd., 1967).

'Alī, Sayid Ameer, *The Spirit of Islam: A History of the Evolution and Ideals of Islam with a Life of the Prophet* (London: Methuen, 1922).

Anand, R.P. (ed.), *Asian States and the Development of Universal International Law* (Delhi: Vicas Publications, 1972).

Anderson, Jerome, N.D. and Coulson, Norman J., "Islamic Law in Contemporary Cultural Change" (unpublished essay written in connection with the *Enzyklopadie des Kulturwandels in 20. Jahrhundert).*

Anderson, J.N.P., *Islamic Law in the Modern World* (New York: New York University Press, 1959).

Arnold, Sir Thomas W., *The Caliphate,* with a concluding chapter by Sulbia G. Haim (New York: Barnes & Noble, 1965).

A'ẓamī, Muḥammad Muṣṭafā, *Studies in Early Hadith Literature with a Critical Edition of Some Early Texts* (Beirut: Al Maktab al Islāmī, 1968).

'Azzām, 'Abd al Raḥmān, *The Eternal Message of Muhammad,* translated from Arabic by Caesar E. Farah (New York: New American Library, 1965).

Berkes, Niyazi, *The Development of Secularism in Turkey* (Montreal: McGill University Press, 1964).

Bozeman, Adda B., *The Picture of Law in a Multicultural World,* (Princeton: Princeton University Press, 1971).

Brockelmann, Carl: *History of the Islamic Peoples,* translated by Joel Carmichael and Moshe Perlman (New York: Enpriarn Books Edition, Alien Property Custodian, 1960).

Brohi, A.K., *Islam in the Modern World,* compiled and edited under the auspices of the Islamic Research Academy of Karachi by Khurshid Aḥmad (Karachi: Chiragh-e-Rah Publications, 1968).

Chaudhri, Muḥammad Aḥsan, *Pakistan and the Great Powers* (Karachi: Council for Pakistan Studies, 1970).

Choudhry, G.W., *Pakistan's Relations with India* (Meerut, India: Meenakshi Prakashan, 1971).

Claude, Inis L., Jr., *Power and International Relations* (New York: Random House, 1962).

Coulson, N.J., *A History of Islamic Law* (Edinburgh University Press, 1964).

Daniel, Norman, *Islam and the West* (Edinburgh: Edinburgh University Press, 1960).

Davison, Roderick H., *The Modern Nations in Historical Perspective: Turkey* (Englewood Cliffs, NJ: Prentice-Hall, 1968).

Deutsch, Karl W., *Nationalism and Social Communication: An Inquiry into the Foundation of Nationalism,* 2nd ed. (Cambridge, Massachusetts: Massachusetts Institute of Technology, 1966).

Deutsch, Karl W., and others, *Political Community and the North Atlantic Area: International Organization in the Light of Historical Experience* (Princeton: Princeton University Press, 1968).

Dougherty, James E., and Pfaltzgraff, Jr., Robert L., *Contending Theories of International Relations* (Philadelphia: J.B. Lippincott, 1971).

Falk, Richard A., and Black, Cyrile E. (ed.) *The Future of the International Legal Order* (Princeton, NJ: Princeton University Press, 1969).

Fārūqī, Ismā'īl Rājī, al, "Toward a New Methodology for Qur'anic Exegesis," *Islamic Studies, I* (March 1962).

Fenwick, Charles G., *International Law,* 3rd rev. ed. (New York: Appleton-Century Crofts, 1948).

Fisher, Sidney Nettleton, *The Middle East: A History*, 2nd ed. (New York: Alfred A. Knopf, 1969).

Gabrielli, Francesco, *Muhammad and the Conquests of Islam*, translated from the Italian by Virginia Luling and Rosamund Linell (New York: World University Library, McGraw-Hill Co., 1968).

Ghunaymī, Muḥammad Ṭal'at, *The Muslim Conception of International Law and the Western Approach* (The Hague: Martinus Nijhoff, 1968).

Gibb, H.A.R., *Modern Trends in Islam* (Chicago: University of Chicago Press, 1947).

Gibb, H.A.R., *Muhammadanism: A Historic Survey*, 2nd ed. (New York: Oxford University Press, 1962).

Gibb, H.A.R., *Studies on the Civilization of Islam*, ed. Stanford J. Shaw and William R. Polk (Boston: Beacon Press, 1962).

Halpern, Manfred H., *The Politics of Social Change in the Middle East and North Africa* (Princeton, NJ: Princeton University Press, 1963).

Hamidullah, Muhammad, *The Muslim Conduct of State*, 5th rev. ed. (Lahore, Pakistan: Sh. Muhammad Ashraf, 1963).

Hamidullah, Muhammad, *The First Written Constitution in the World: An Important Document of the Time of the Holy Prophet*, 2nd rev. ed. (Lahore, Pakistan: Sh. Muhammad Ashraf, 1968).

Hourani, Albert, *"Minorities" in the Contemporary Middle East: Tradition and Innovation*, ed. Benjamin Riulin and Josephs Szyliowics (New York: Random House, 1965).

Hourani, Albert, *Arab Thought in the Liberal Age: 1798-1939* (London: Oxford University Press, 1970).

Ibn Khaldūn, Abū Zayd 'Abd al Raḥmān Ibn Muḥammad, *The Muqqaddimah* (An Introduction to History), translated from the Arabic by Franz Rosenthal, ed. N.J. Dawood, Gollingen Series (Princeton, NJ: Princeton University Press, 1967).

Kelman, Herbert C. (ed.), *International Behavior: A Social-Psychological Analysis* (New York: Holt, Rinehart, Winston, 1965).

Kelsen, Hans, *Principles of International Law*, 2nd ed. (New York: Holt, Rinehart, Winston, 1966).

Kerr, Malcom H., *Islamic Reform: The Political and Legal Theories of Muḥammad 'Abduh and Rashīd Riḍā* (Berkeley: University of California Press, 1966).

Khadduri, Majid, *War and Peace in the Law of Islam* (Baltimore: Johns Hopkins Press, 1952).

Khan, Mohammad, Ayub, *Pakistan Perspective* (Washington, DC: Pakistani Embassy, n.d.).

Khan, Muhammad Muhsin, *The Translation of the Meaning of Ṣaḥīḥ al Bukhārī* (Gujaranwala, Pakistan: Sethi Straw Board Mills Conversion Ltd., n.d.).

Kunz, Josef L., *The Changing Law of Nations: Essays on International Law* (Columbus: Ohio State University Press, 1968).

Lewis, Bernard, *The Arabs in History* (New York: Harper & Row, 1960).

Lewis, Bernard, *The Middle East and the West* (New York: Harper & Row, 1966).

Lewis, Bernard, *The Emergence of Modern Turkey*, 2nd ed. (London: Oxford University Press, 1968).

Lewis, Bernard, *Race and Color in Islam* (New York: Harper & Row, 1970).

MacDonald, Robert W., *The League of Arab States: A Study in the Dynamism of Regional Organization* (Princeton NJ: Princeton University Press, 1965).

Mitchell, Richard P., "The Setting and Rationale of Ottoman Diplomacy in the Reign of Selim III," unpublished paper.

Naff, Thomas, "Reform and the Conduct of Ottoman Diplomacy in the Reign of Selim III, 1789-1807, *Journal of the American Oriental Society, 83:6* (1963).

Nasr, Sayyed Hossein, *Islamic Studies: Essays on Law and Society, the Science and Philosophy of Sufism* (Beirut: Librairie du Liban, 1967).

Palmer, Norman D., and Perkins, Howard C., *International Relations: The World Community in Transition*, 3rd ed. (Boston: Houghton Mifflin Co., 1969).

Peretz, Don, *The Middle East Today* (New York: Holt, Rinehart & Winston, 1965).

Proctor, J.H. (ed.), *Islam and International Relations* (New York: Frederick A. Praeger, 1965).

Qadiri, Anwar Ahmad, *Islamic Jurisprudence in the Modern World: A Reflection Upon Comparative Study of the Law* (Bombay: N.M. Tripathi Pvt., Ltd.,1963).

Rafi ud Din, M., *Ideology of the Future,* 3rd ed. (Lahore, Pakistan: Sh. Muhammad Ashraf, 1970).

Rahman, Fazlur, *Islamic Methodology in History* (Karachi: Central Institute of Islamic Research, 1965).

Ramaḍān Sa'īd, *Three Major Problems Confronting the World of Islam* (Takoma Park, MD; Crescent Publications, n.d.).

Ramaḍān Sa'īd, *Islamic Law: Its Scope and Equity,* (London: P. R. MacMillan Ltd., 1961).

Razi, Murtaza, *The Frontiers of Pakistan* (Karachi: National Publishing House, 1971).

Rosenau, James N., *International Politics and Foreign Policy: A Reader in Research and Theory* (New York: Free Press, 1969).

Rosenthal, Erwin, I.J., *Islam in the Modern National State* (Cambridge, UK: Cambridge University Press, 1965).

Rosenthal, Erwin, I.J., *Political Thought in Medieval Islam* (Cambridge, UK: Cambridge University Press, 1958).

Rubenstein, Alvin Z. (ed.), *The Foreign Policy of the Soviet Union,* 2nd ed. (New York: Random House, 1966).

Safran, Nadav, *Egypt in Search of Political Community* (Cambridge, MA: Harvard University Press, 1961).

Schacht, Joseph, *The Origins of Muhammadan Jurisprudence* (Oxford: Oxford University Press, 1950).

Shaybānī, Muhammad al, *The Islamic Law of Nations,* translated from Arabic by Majid Khadduri (Baltimore: Johns Hopkins University Press, 1966).

Siddiqi, Amir Hasan, *Non-Muslims Under Muslim Rule and Muslims Under Non-Muslim Rule* (Karachi: Jamiyatul Falah Publications, n.d.).

Sills, David L. (ed.), *International Encyclopedia of the Social Sciences* (New York: MacMillan Free Press, 1968).

Smith, Donald Eugene, *Religion and Political Development* (Boston: Little, Brown & Co., 1970).

Smith, Wilfred Cantwell, *Islam in Modern History* (Princeton, NJ: Princeton University Press, 1957).

Thompson, Jack H. and Reischauer, R. D. (eds.), *Modernization of the Arab World* (New York: Van Nostrand, Inc., 1966).

Toynbee, Arnold, *Civilization on Trial* and *The World and the West* (Cleveland: World Publishing Co., 1958).

Turhan, Mumtaz, *Where Are We in Westernization?* translated by David Garwood (Istanbul: Research Centre, Robert College of Istanbul, 1965).

Watt, W. Montgomery, *Muhammad: Prophet and Statesman* (London: Oxford University Press, 1961).

Watt, W. Montgomery, *What is Islam?* (New York: Frederick A. Praeger, 1968).

Ziyadeh, Nicola A., *Syria and Lebanon* (Beirut: Lebanon Bookshop, 1968).

GENERAL INDEX

Christians, 11, 27, 29, 31, 47, 48, 109, 110, 148
civil rights, 109
Civil war, 35, 36, 52, 54, 60, 74
class struggle, 60
classical jurisprudence, 26-28, 54, 113, 119
classical jurists, 29, 49-51, 53, 113, 115, 117
classical period, 32, 76, 82
classical theory, 3, 17, 18
classical world, 82
Cold War, 154
colonies, 139, 153, 159
communal divisions, 57
communication, 26, 126, 127, 135, 141
community, 73
Companions, 7, 9, 88, 96
compulsion, 69
compulsion in religion, 12, 28
conflict of laws, 31
congregational prayer, 34
consensus, 21, 22, 72, 76, 87, 88. see also *ijmā'*
conspiracy, 113
constitution, 14, 26, 29
contemporary world, 67
contract, 20, 24
conversion, 30, 110, 111
cooperation, 129, 141
corruption, 140
Covenant of Madīnah, 48, 109, 110
criminal offences, 26
crisis, psychological, 68
Crusaders, 29
cultural challenge, 65
custom, 6, 67

D

dār al 'ahd, 19, 31
dār al ḥarb, 20, 31, 46, 51, 86
dār al Islām, 19, 20, 30, 31, 46, 51, 86
dār al ṣulḥ, 19
ḍarūrah, 69, 70
da'wah, 54
death sentence, 8
deduction, 85, 90
deductive method, 9, 87
democratic society, 59, 135
dhimmah, 28, 29, 31, 109
dhimmī, 7
dīn, 7
diplomacy, 127, 147-150
Ditch, Battle of the, 101, 103, 104
divine purposes, 5
divine sources, 17
divine will, 7, 54
doctrine, 24, 72
door of ijtihad, 14

E

early period of Islam, 7
economic system, 69
education, 3, 4, 6, 14, 28, 54, 84
  moral, 6
  of Muslim theologians, 4
  religious, 4
  secular, 4
educational system, 14, 70, 87
Egypt, 58, 153, 154
Egyptians, 98
elites, 9, 35, 36, 57
  traditional, 70
empirical observation, 4
empiricism, 85, 87, 92, 98, 142, 160
enemies of Islam, 9, 10
equality, 32, 33, 53, 54
  among nations, 30-33
ethics, Islamic. 69, see also values
Europe, 3, 33, 54, 56, 65, 135, 140, 148, 156
European ideas, 4
European occupation, 59
European powers, 4, 54, 148, 151
European rule, 58
European schools, 3
European state system, 33, 150
European thought, 57
excesses, 140
execution, see also *qawd*, 11
external relations, 5, 97, 98, 104, 136, 139, 141, 147, 160. see also foreign affairs, foreign policies,

F

faith, 68, 83
Fakhr al Dīn al Rāzī, 122
fanaticism, 12.48
Fārūqī, Ismā'īl, 90
fasting, 104
fatāwā, 13, 69
Fazlur Rahman, 87-91
fighting, 118, 123, 126, 138. see also war;
fiqh, 2, 5, 6, 7, 8, 12-15, 17, 18, 68, 71, 85,

revelation, 2, 5, 69, 71, 87
revolution, 36, 60
ribà, 65
riddah, 65. see apostasy
Risālah, al, 70, 71
ritual practice, 65
Romans, 89, 119
rule, Muslim, 51, 90
rulers, Muslim, 18, 30, 78
Russia, 152 ff.

S

Sabeans, 46
safe conduct, 10, 26
saghār, 47, 48
saghīr, 29
Ṣaḥīḥayn, 70
Sa'īdī, M., 108
Sarakhsi, al, 6, 7, 9, 10, 23, 83, 90, 138
Sayyid Quṭub, 124
Sayyid Sābiq, 80
Schacht, 72, 73
scholars, Sunni Muslim, 66
scholarship, 81
schools, European, 3
schools of Islamic jurisprudence, 2, 11, 54, 85
secular education, 4
secular institutions, 56
secular intellectuals, 69
secular society, 4
secularists, 4, 159
security, 20, 26, 83, 138. see also *amān*
self-determination, 44
self-government, 102
Shāfi'ī, Imam, 10, 12, 17, 19, 20, 22, 25, 38, 70, 71, 77, 80
Shāfi'ī school, 8, 9, 11
shahādah, 87
Shaltūt, Shaykh, 66
Sharābī, H.A., 62
Sharī'ah, 2, 5, 6, 7, 14, 31, 32, 34, 36, 37, 44, 56, 65, 70, 86
Shaybānī, Muḥammad, 17, 53, 83
Shī'ah, 73
shirk, 26
sīrah, 18, 110
siyar, 5, 6, 7, 8, 13, 14, 15, 76, 87, 92, 93, 142
siyāsah shar'īyah, 74
social change, 6
social institutions, 66, 68, 119
social interaction, 79
social justice, 28, 32, 54, 60, 63, 65
social life, Muslim, 18, 93
social practice, 26
social sciences, 4, 86, 87, 91, 92, 100
social structure, Muslim, 4, 87
social system, 18, 29, 33, 39, 61, 74, 75, 76, 77, 81, 84, 85, 86, 95, 150
  Muslim, 3, 9, 14, 56, 71, 84, 92, 124
society, 19, 45
sociology, 86
sources, 21, 24, 63, 66, 69
  textual, 64
sources of Islamic law, 7, 14, 63. see also *uṣūl al fiqh*
Southeast Asia, 47
sovereign state, 32
sovereignty, 19
Soviet Union, 56, 135, 151ff.
space-time factor, 5, 11, 35, 66, 67, 75, 79, 82, 83, 86, 95, 99, 112, 120, 125, 128, 141, 142, 159
spiritual leadership, 35
spoils, 76
state of non-belief, 12
status quo, 36
strategy, 83
Sufi teachers, 49
sultan, 33, 34
Sunnah, 2, 5, 7, 8, 9, 13, 14, 17, 18, 21, 23, 24, 26, 29, 31, 34, 45, 47, 55, 56, 63, 64, 69, 70, 71, 72, 74, 75, 77, 79, 84, 85, 92, 93, 95, 104, 109
Sunnah authenticity, 68, 93
Sunni Muslims, 73
Suyūṭī, al, 55
Sword, Verse of, 83, 90
Syria, 89
Syrians, 99
systematization, 89, 92

T

Ṭabarī, al, 122
Tabūk, 108
Ṭahṭāwī, al, 57
Ṭā'if, 108
talfīq, 3, 4, 62, 65, 70
taqlīd, 3, 4, 65
ṭawāf, 77
tawḥīd, 128, 129, 137, 156, 159
taxation, 29, 30

IIIT ENGLISH PUBLICATIONS

A. Islamization of Knowledge Series

- *The Islamic Theory of International Relations: New Directions for Islamic Methodology and Thought* (1407/1987) by 'AbdulḤamīd AbūSulaymān.
- *Islamization of Knowledge: General Principles and Work Plan*, 3rd edition (1409/1989). A German edition was published under the title *Das Einbringen des Islam in das Wissen* (1408/1988).
- *Toward Islamic Anthropology: Definitions, Dogma, and Directions* (1406/1986) by Akbar Ṣ. Aḥmad.
- *Toward Islamic English* (1406/1986) by Ismā'īl Rājī al Fārūqī. A German edition was published under the title: *Für ein Islamisches Deutsch* (1408/1988).
- *Modelling Interest-Free Economy: A Study in Microeconomics and Development* (1407/1987) by Muḥammad Anwar.
- *Islam: Source and Purpose of Knowledge*. Papers presented to the Second International Conference of Islamic Thought and the Islamization of Knowledge (1409/1988).
- *Toward Islamization of Disciplines*. Papers presented to the Third International Conference on Islamic Thought and the Islamization of Knowledge (1409/1988).
- *The Organization of the Islamic Conference: An Introduction to an Islamic Political Institution* (1408/1988) by 'Abdullāh al Aḥsan.
- *Proceedings of the Lunar Calendar Conference*. Papers presented to the Conference of the Lunar Calendar. Edited by Imād ad-Dean Ahmad (1408/1988).
- *Islamization of Attitudes and Practices in Science and Technology.* Papers presented to a special seminar on the same topic (1409/1989). Edited by M.A.K. Lodhi.
- *Where East Meets West: The West on the Agenda of the Islamic Revival* (1412/1992) by Mona Abul-Fadl.

- *Qur'anic Concept of Human Psyche.* Papers presented to a special seminar organizerd by IIIT Pakistan (1412/1992). Edited by Zafar Afaq Ansari.
- *Islam and the Economic Challenge* by M. Umer Chapra. Published jointly with the Islamic Foundation (U.K.) (1412/1992).
- *Resource Mobilization and Investment in an Islamic Economic Framework.* Papers presented to the 3rd International Islamic Economics Seminar (1412/1991). Edited by Zaidi Sattar.

B. Issues in Contemporary Islamic Thought Series

- *Islamic Thought and Culture.* Papers presented to the Islamic Studies Group of the American Academy of Religion (1402/1982). Edited by Ismā'īl Rājī al Fārūqī.
- *Trialogue of the Abrahamic Faiths*, 2nd edition (1406/1986). Papers presented to the Islamic Studies Group of the American Academy of Religion. Edited by Ismā'īl Rājī al Fārūqī.
- *Islamic Awakening: Between Rejection and Extremism* by Yūsuf al Qaraḍāwī. Published jointly with American Trust Publications. (new revised edition, 1412/1992).
- *Madīnan Society at the Time of the Prophet* (1411/1991) by Akram Ḍiyā' al 'Umarī,
    - Volume I: *Its Characteristics and Organization.*
    - Volume II: *The Jihad Against the Mushrikūn*
- *Tawḥīd: Its Implications for Thought and Life* (second edition, 1412/1992) by Ismā'īl Rājī al Fārūqī.

C. Research Monographs Series

- *Source Methodology in Islamic Jurisprudence: (Uṣūl al Fiqh Islāmī),* (third edition, 1413/1993) by Ṭāhā Jābir al 'Alwānī.
- *Islam and the Middle East: The Aesthetics of a Political Inquiry* (1411/1990) by Mona Abul-Fadl.
- *Sources of Scientific Knowledge: The Concept of Mountains in the Qur'an* (1411/1991) by Zaghloul R. El-Naggar.

D. Occasional Papers Series

- *Outlines of a Cultural Strategy* (1410/1989) by Ṭāhā Jābir al 'Alwānī. A French edition was published under the title *Pour une Stratégie Culturelle Islamique* (1411/1990), and a German edition was Published under the title *Entwurf Eines Alternativen Kulturplanes* (1413/1992).
- *Islamization of Knowledge: A Methodology* (1412/1991) by 'Imād al Dīn Khalil. A French edition was published under the title *Méthodologie Pour Islamisation du Savoir* (1412/1991).
- *The Qur'an and the Sunnah: The Time-Space Factor* (1412/1991) by Ṭāhā Jābir al 'Alwānī and 'Imād al Dīn Khalīl. A French edition was published under the title *Le Coran et La Sunna: Le Facteur Temps-Espace* (1412/1992).
- *Knowledge: An Islamic Perspective* (1412/1991) by Bakhtiar Ḥusain Siddiqui.
- *Islamization of Knowledge: A critical overview* (1413/1992) by Sayyed Vali Reza Nasr.
- *Ijtihad* (1413/1993) by Ṭāhā Jābir al Ālwānī

E. Human Development Series

- *Training Guide for Islamic Workers* by Hisham Altalib, (third revised edition 1413/1993). A Turkish and a Malay edition were published in (1412/1992).

F. Perspectives on Islamic Thought Series

- *National Security and Development Strategy* (1412/1991) by Arshad Zaman.
- *Nationalism and Internationalism in Liberalism, Marxism and Islam* (1412/1991) by Tahir Amin.

G. Islamic Methodology Series

- *Crisis in the Muslim Mind* (1414/1993) by 'AbdulḤamīd A. Abūsulaymān.

H. Academic Dissertations Series

- *Through Muslim Eyes: M. Rashīd Riḍā and the West* (1414/1992) by Emad Eldin Shaheen.

Journals

- *American Journal of Islamic Social Sciences* (AJISS). A quarterly published jointly with the Association of Muslim Social Scientists (AMSS), U.S.A.
- *Muslim World Book Review* and *Index of Islamic Literature.* A quarterly published jointly with the Islamic Foundation (U.K.).

Distributors of IIIT Publications

Belgium Secompex, Bd. Mourice Lemonnier, 152
1000 Bruxelles Tel: (32-2) 512-4473 Fax: (32-2) 512-8710

Egypt IIIT Office, 26-B Al Jazirah al Wusṭa St., Zamalek, Cairo
Tel: (202) 340-9520 Fax: (202) 340-9520

France Libraire Essalam, 135 Boulevard de Ménilmontant
75011 Paris Tel: (33-1) 4338-1956 Fax: (33-1) 4357-4431

Holland Rachad Export, Le Van Swindenstr. 108 II
1093 Ck. Amsterdon Tel: (31-20) 693-3735 Fax: (31-20) 693-882x

India Genuine Publications & Media (Pvt.) Ltd., P.O. Box 9725
Jamia Nagar, New Delhi 110 025 Tel: (91-11) 630-989 Fax: (91-11) 684-1104

Jordan IIIT Office, P.O. Box 9489, Amman
Tel: (962-6) 639-992 Fax: (962-6) 611-420

Lebanon IIIT, c/o United Arab Bureau, P.O. Box 135788, Beirut
Tel: (961-1) 807-779 Fax: c/o (212) 478-1491

Morocco Dār al Amān for Publishing and Distribution,
4 Zangat al Ma'muniyah, Rabat Tel: (212-7) 723-276 Fax: (212-7) 723-276

Saudi Arabia International House for Islamic Books,
P.O. Box 55195, Riyadh 11534
Tel: (966-1) 1-465-0818 Fax: (966-1) 1-463-3489

United Arab Emirates Reading for All Bookshop, P.O. Box 11032 Dubai
Tel: (971-4) 663-903 Fax: (971-4) 690-084

United Kingdom
- Muslim Information Services, 233 Seven Sisters Rd.
London N4 2DA Tel: (44-71) 272-5170 Fax: (44-71) 272-3214
- The Islamic Foundation, Markfield Da'wah Centre, Rutby Lane
Markfield, Leicester LE6 ORN, U.K.
Tel: (44-530) 244-944/45 Fax: (44-530) 244-946

U.S.A.
- Islamic Book Service, 10900 W. Washington St.
Indianapolis, IN 46231 U.S.A. Tel.: (317) 839-9248 Fax: (317) 839-2511
- Al Sa'dāwi/United Arab Bureau, P.O. Box 4059, Alexandria, VA 22303 USA
Tel: (703) 329-6333 Fax: (703) 329-8052

To order IIIT Publications write to the above listed distributors or contact:
IIIT Department of Publications, P.O. Box 669 Herndon, VA 22070-4705
Tel: (703) 471-1133 Fax: (703) 471-3922